"That things are not so ill with you and me as they might have been is half owing to the number who lived faithfully a hidden life, and rest in unvisited tombs."

—George Eliot, *Middlemarch*

In an anecdote about Martha Nicholson McKay, a founder of the Indianapolis Woman's Club in 1875, she was describing the newly formed club to a rabbi. "The rabbi shook his head, saying, 'Sarah's place is in her tent.' Mrs. McKay retorted, 'Oh, yes, we know. We just want her to have a window in it.'"

—Indianapolis Woman's Club Records,
1857–2007, Manuscript Collections Department,
William Henry Smith Memorial Library,
Indiana Historical Society, Indianapolis, Indiana,
www.indianahistory.org

SMART WOMEN

THE SEARCH FOR AMERICA'S HISTORIC ALL-WOMEN STUDY CLUBS

Includes directory listings of many
women's self-education groups formed at least
a hundred years ago and still meeting

Ann Dodds Costello

ISBN: 978-1-4834-3441-4 (sc)
ISBN: 978-1-4834-3443-8 (hc)
ISBN: 978-1-4834-3442-1 (e)

Library of Congress Control Number: 2015910865

Because of the dynamic nature of the Internet, any web addresses or
links contained in this book may have changed since publication and may
no longer be valid. The views expressed in this work are solely those
of the author and do not necessarily reflect the views of the publisher,
and the publisher hereby disclaims any responsibility for them.

Lulu Publishing Services rev. date: 8/28/2015

I dedicate this book to the members of those historic and utterly fascinating women's literary societies I was able to find, and to the members of the groups still hiding in plain sight throughout the United States of America.

I also dedicate this book, as a measure of my thanks to him, to my husband, Dick Costello, for his support and patience while I traveled, researched, and wrote *Smart Women*.

Foreword

Smart Women is a priceless gift for libraries, archivists, women's studies classes, and researchers seeking source materials. Ann Costello has done the spade work needed to document the results of a phenomenon that was pivotal for women's becoming involved in social actions, thereby making significant improvements in their lives and in the lives of future generations.

—Jacquelyn Masur McElhaney, author of
Pauline Periwinkle and Progressive Reform in Dallas

Contents

Introduction: A Hidden World

Four years ago, I stumbled into a hidden world. What I discovered by chance was a very special kind of women's group. I became aware of small, private study clubs or literary societies that are at least a hundred years old, require their members to present original research papers or programs, and also require their members to help with predetermined social chores—usually providing food for a tea table or luncheon on a rotating basis. With tremendous good grace, hard work, and intelligence, and in a modern world that bears little resemblance to the world they create when they convene, these women still carry on with their traditional group meetings much as their founding great-grandmothers would have done while Queen Victoria or her son sat on the British throne or when author Edith Wharton was writing about old New York society.

I had no idea that these clubs existed anywhere until a friend who lives on the other side of the country from my Los Angeles home e-mailed me four years ago and casually mentioned her all-women study club with a wonderfully old-fashioned name: Cadmean Circle. I immediately seized on the idea of visiting her group—if they would allow me to do so—and hoped possibly to find more of these clubs. Having been trained as a journalist but lacking any kind of freelance work because printed newspapers are spiraling downward, I was looking for a book project. Using my journalism skill set over the next four years, I dug into these groups and found myself in a world that few Americans know anything about.

These small study clubs, literary societies, Shakespeare clubs, and fortnightly clubs, which limit their membership to women and which have no civic component or clubhouse, and which meet in homes or church parlors to hear original papers or programs, with an occasional outside speaker, can be found—with some difficulty, as they meet and conduct business very quietly—in almost every part of America, except, alas, for mine: Southern California. The groups are independent of each other and of any larger organization, although many did belong to a state and/or national federation of women's clubs in their early days. They are private (one must be asked to join); they do not advertise their activities and, therefore, are virtually secret; and they have little or no knowledge of each other, although they are highly similar. Those I have chosen to write about have survived, against all odds, from the horse-and-buggy days of the second half of the 1800s or the early 1900s to today. The close-knit, but almost invisible, groups in this book are at least a hundred years old and still require members to research and write a paper or give an original program, usually once every year or two, and usually on a topic previously chosen for the year. They must stand and present the paper to the group. Members also socialize at their meetings—often over tea, desserts, or lunch—and many groups have several special luncheons or parties each year. They also elect officers each year, many of them rotating the key positions based on length of membership so that every member has a chance to try her hand at conducting club business. The groups' very modern members scrupulously follow club constitutions and bylaws written after the Civil War by women who wore floor-length skirts, high-neck blouses with leg-of-mutton sleeves, huge hats, and stiff corsets. With a slight nod to changing times, most groups have updated their governing documents over the years, but the basic framework remains.

The club names are a glimpse into the period of the late 1800s to the early 1900s, when thousands of these groups sprang up around the country as part of what was later called the women's club movement.[1] There are clubs named after Shakespeare, clubs with the word *fortnightly* in their name, clubs named after the day of the week on which they meet, and clubs with old-fashioned names often taken from Greek mythology. Cadmean Circle's name was so intriguing to me that it launched this book, but there are others with equally delightful names that hearken to the past, such as Cosmos, Roundabout, Coterie, Sorosis, Pierian, and Philomath.

In the clubs' earliest days, just after the Civil War, American women had few rights. They could not apply to most colleges. Their desire to self-educate led them to form these groups. Depending on what state the women lived in, if they were married they might not be allowed to own property or control their own finances. That basic right was just starting to be recognized and made a law in the United States in the middle of the 1800s, and it spread slowly from state to state. American women could not vote until 1920, and they were not supposed to leave the sphere of the home and the church. Women's literary societies, organized by women for women for the first time and not having any connection to a church, were seen by some women as an acceptable, ladylike way for them to step away from the confinement and inequality of their lives and feel that they were improving their minds, self-educating on lofty subjects, and making lifelong friends. For many young, middle- and upper-class, white (but sometimes African-American)[2] women in this country, joining a literary society was the next step after graduating from high school or a female academy. There were also study groups composed of older women springing up a hundred-plus years ago. The women in these groups were married and had children, but they still wanted to self-educate on subjects other than domestic ones and enjoy the friendship of like-minded women.

The founders of two of the first women's literary societies—Jane Cunningham Croly in New York City and Julia Ward Howe in Boston—urged American women to form groups of their own and use them to self-educate and also to do some "municipal housekeeping."[3] As they organized as groups, met, and felt a kinship with each other, women were often able to gain an understanding of the problems of their town, which might lead them to help organize, fund, and build the first public library or first art museum where they lived, or start the first symphony orchestra or first public kindergarten. Women's clubs such as those in this book helped found between 75 percent and 80 percent of the public libraries in our country.[4] This fact is missing from most local histories.

Often, women from the earliest study groups got their bearings in the clubs and then went off to form or join groups fighting for women's suffrage or Prohibition. But as time passed, the original literary societies, which began to include college-educated women as such a thing became possible, became focused only on continued or lifelong learning with a social component. The world forgot about their earlier contributions. Actually, the world forgot everything about them, and the groups were fine with that, preferring to stay private and small enough, in most cases, to meet in a member's living room or in a church parlor.

There was a parallel movement to create women's clubs among upper- and middle-class African-American women, although these groups usually emphasized civic improvements instead of being strictly literary societies.[5] As I was unable to find or connect with any surviving African-American women's literary societies that were at least a hundred years old, that were not civic-minded organizations, that didn't use outside speakers, and that were not a part of a parent organization, I've concentrated on the parallel movement among white American women. However, I do describe several African-American women's groups in the final chapter of this book, ones that come close to the subject of *Smart Women.* The chapter's name is "Additional Historic All-Women Clubs." Among the African-American clubs I include is one from which I was able to interview a stalwart and longtime member. The club is Semper Fidelis, in Birmingham, Alabama. Long ago, they donated their archives to the Birmingham Public Library, where I was able to read through them before interviewing member Dr. Danetta K. Thornton Owens. The description of Semper Fidelis and the results of my interview with Dr. Owens can be found in the final chapter.

These days, the women in historic literary societies or study clubs are almost always college graduates or holders of advanced academics degrees. They are determined to stay sharp and stay connected, usually at a point when they are leaving their child-rearing years or their employment years and heading into their later years, although there are groups with much younger members. While working on this book, I came to believe that these fortnightlies, literary societies, and study clubs may be practicing the best formula known to science for keeping a healthy mind and body: learning new things among a circle of friends, something at which women excel far better than their aging male counterparts. In almost every group I visited, I saw women in their nineties still participating in programs and enjoying the social component, which, I feel, probably helps to extend their lives and keep their mental faculties sharp.

I can also say without a doubt that the women in these historic study groups are among the most impressive and gracious women I've ever met. They are the machinery that keeps our civilization civilized, but they do what they do quietly and with good humor and social grace. In addition to working outside their clubs, they never lose sight of the fact that they can always learn more and that this can be done in a most pleasant fashion by sharing the educational chores at social gatherings with their fellow club members. This book documents the women who have been members of a study club for fifty or sixty years, as well as women in their thirties or forties who are just joining these groups.

These women run the PTA organizations, town councils, and museum boards of most of the cities and villages I visited to do my research. They also run charities and civic organizations (and, I might add, run their homes and raise their children). There have been professional women in the groups I've visited or studied, as well. I have been repeatedly struck when reading the obituaries of recently deceased club members that mention the powerful lives these little-known women lived. They were powerful and wonderful, but virtually unknown. The obituaries of several recently deceased members of the Cosmos Club in Birmingham, Alabama, moved me to tears as I read about their breadth of community service and their selfless approach to living an enlightened life.

But few readers of these obituaries would have known about the deceased women's longtime membership in a private club with an odd name like Cadmean Circle or Quarante or Sorosis if they hadn't read the death notice in the newspaper. This reminds me of a theme in George Eliot's masterpiece, *Middlemarch.* The Victorian novel's heroine, Dorothea Brooke, dies at the very end of the final chapter, having lived a very different and much quieter life than the one she had envisioned for herself or that others had envisioned for her when she was an idealistic young woman. Still, her life was an extremely happy and fulfilled one. George Eliot describes Dorothea Brooke's life this way:

Her finely-touched spirit had still its fine issues, though they were not widely visible. Her full nature ... spent itself in channels which had no great name on the earth. But the effect of her being on those around her was incalculably diffusive: for the growing good of the world is partly dependent on unhistoric acts; and that things are not so ill with you and me as they might have been, is half owing to the number who lived faithfully a hidden life, and rest in unvisited tombs.[6]

Perhaps our debt to those "living faithfully a hidden life" and lying in "unvisited tombs" is a heavy message to place in an introduction to a book meant to be something of a directory or guide, but these largely hidden, all-female literary societies, study clubs, Shakespeare clubs, and fortnightly clubs are filled with women whose combined history has much to teach us about living a healthier, more civilized life. Their achievements receive little fanfare or publicity. For the good of their study clubs, they work within a framework of personal responsibilities and good manners, as they quietly self-educate, share the fruits of their research with other members, and plan and carry out the social hour for each meeting. This is a quaint approach in our era of quickly organized "meet-ups" at the local Starbucks and of reality television, where, seemingly, people with no manners or moral compass are willing to humiliate themselves and others just to appear on air.

Literary societies and their archives are also rich national treasure troves of historical fact and a fascinating window into the subject of women's studies and women's rights in America. Looking back at the recent past, which I experienced in college in the 1960s and in the workplace in the years following, I can see that the world is much changed for the better for women. And still, historic and private literary societies, a wonderful remnant of a much more restrictive era for women, live on, still able to add much richness to their very modern members' lives.

The research and travel I did for this book have begun to bring me up to speed on the subject of women's studies, or at least the history of the American women's movement. I may have even turned myself into something of an authority on the structure, history, and traditions of this country's hundred-plus-year-old, all-female literary societies. As far as I can tell, no one has ever tried to track down these groups all over the country—as they exist today—and then write a book about them. In 1898, the founder of the first all-women literary society, journalist Jane Cunningham Croly, who founded Sorosis in NYC in 1868, published *The History of the Women's Club Movement in America.* To get the information for her book, she asked for and received reports from many of the newly formed women's clubs of all kinds all over the country—not just study groups or literary societies, which are my interest—and then put the results in one huge book. That book was published 117 years ago.

Several other fine books have been written in more recent years about the earliest clubs, not the groups as they are today. Author and university professor Katherine Scheil has recently published *She Hath Been Reading,* which details the effect of Shakespeare and Shakespeare clubs on women in America during the women's club movement (roughly, the late nineteenth century into the early twentieth century, and a bit beyond). I felt it was time that someone tracked down, visited, and documented *all* surviving literary clubs and their histories and traditions. I decided to do this with not just Shakespeare clubs, but also with small, independent literary societies that were founded at least a hundred years ago and that scrupulously follow constitutions and bylaws written then—clubs that, today, still combine a social component and original research papers or original programs in their meetings and special events.

Because the groups are private and usually do not publicize what they do, I needed to work hard to find them. Usually, I located them through a personal reference, but sometimes through a story on the Internet about their 100th or 125th anniversary, or a similar event. Then, I would begin making calls and sending e-mails to make contact with a member of the group or a librarian of the group's archives, the latter of whom might know a member of the group. When I found a cluster of groups in one area, I'd ask my contact in each club for permission to visit on a day when they were holding a regularly scheduled meeting. Often, the meetings of the groups in one geographic cluster did not mesh with my schedule, so they would very kindly move their meeting to a day or time of day that would allow me to visit, thereby making my trip as efficient as possible.

Most of the cities and towns mentioned in this book are ones that I was able to visit for the first time, so I faced quite a learning curve each time my plane landed. Once in my target area, I drove a rental car from town to town or from neighborhood to neighborhood, visiting the groups I'd uncovered. I often spent a day or two in the local historical society's or public library's archives, reading through the clubs' old ledgers of minutes and old yearbooks. Through all of this, I was learning valuable lessons in history, geography, women's studies, and human nature. Over four years, I found more and more groups, so the shape of my book changed and became more of an historical document or directory than the narrative nonfiction account I'd set out to write.

At first, the process of discovering where the groups still survived was very slow, because, as mentioned earlier, these groups generally do not publicize what they do. Their meetings are generally not open to the public. One must be invited to join or to attend. And, as I was told on the very first day of my research, groups may be wary of being described by a visiting journalist as being old-fashioned or simply out of touch. One of these groups in Birmingham, Alabama, had the unpleasant experience of (in my opinion) being unfairly and inaccurately lampooned in a "Talk of the Town" sketch called "Ladies of the Club" in *Vanity Fair* magazine in 1996. The article was written by a club member's son (now a former member's son) who is a well-known author and also a frequent contributor to the magazine. When I visited the very youthful and friendly Nineteenth Century Club, I found them to be the exact opposite of the author's description of them as elderly, conservative, and rather mean-spirited. A sketch accompanying the *Vanity Fair* article showed a row of six women with upswept and old-fashioned hairdos, their faces sagging and marked with wrinkles, with one woman napping rather than listening to the paper being delivered. With the kind of wariness that many club members felt about having someone take notes in their midst, I was, at least at the beginning of my project, walking on eggshells and writing long, explanatory e-mails or making cold phone calls. But as my research progressed and I had a track record, members of one group would recommend me to another, sometimes in another part of the country—and things began to snowball.

Then, just when I thought I was finished with my research, I fell into a gold mine. What I thought would be my golden treasure was the Syracuse / Finger Lakes area of New York State, which is rich in historic women's groups; they are scattered over the area in the region's many villages and towns, and in the city of Syracuse itself. After landing in the Syracuse airport in the fall of 2012, I first visited Seneca Falls, which is a kind of mecca for American women, as its national historical park site commemorates the first Women's Rights Convention in 1848. I then checked into a Syracuse University–adjacent hotel and used that as my base. I drove a rental car from town to town, taking five days to visit seven hundred-plus-year-old study clubs, including two vibrant and intellectually challenging groups in Syracuse. While attending meetings and interviewing members, I learned of five more historic groups in the immediate area. I quickly made contact with all of them, thinking, *What could top that?*

It turned out that something could top that. Soon after I returned to Los Angeles, I made a series of new and sometimes startling connections in many other parts of the country. These led me to a bewildering number of literary societies in a modestly sized town called Jacksonville, Illinois (population: 19,446), surely the capital of literary societies, with six historic all-women study groups, a collection of even older men's literary societies, and seven literary societies in the town's Illinois College, which promotes societies in lieu of fraternities and sororities.[7] Unbeknownst to the club members living there, Jacksonville also has the oldest surviving women's literary society in the United States and the longest-active member of any such group. The societies of Jacksonville deserve their own book, but at least I can give them a place in mine so the world will know how special the town is.

There were more discoveries in other areas. The length of my book grew and grew to include close to a hundred groups, as I felt I couldn't leave out any of my new discoveries. And yet, I know that there must be many more of these groups around America left to discover. I may need to consider writing a revised edition of *Smart Women* to include the other groups that will find me after this book is published.

As my work on this book progressed, and with e-mails introducing me to more and more historic study groups each day, I began to ask my contacts in each study club a more abbreviated list of questions. I also gave up traveling to the groups I had newly discovered, as I found that the meetings and structure for each group were virtually identical. However, this meant that I had to forgo the pleasure of meeting the members of these newly discovered groups face-to-face, and that was a shame. I would have loved to shake the hand of Gratia Coultas, the longest-active member of any group I found while researching this book. Gratia, who, I'm told, is a very active ninety-three years of age, has been a member of the Monday Conversation Club in Jacksonville, Illinois, for sixty-eight years and still presents her original papers without the aid of notes. A recent photo of her surrounded by her fellow club members shows a smiling, rosy-cheeked woman seemingly decades younger than she is.

By not visiting these other groups, I also had to forgo basking in the feeling of pride in the groups shared by the members. These busy women must work very hard to maintain their beloved clubs and to keep their bit of living history going. They must believe in the power of the history and combined synergy of their groups, and they must be very dedicated to the groups' continuing existence, especially because some people might view the clubs as an anachronism or a curiosity. Even in their early days, these groups were the object of supposedly witty ridicule proffered by husbands and journalists who found the women's efforts to self-educate amusing or threatening.

Dr. Karen Blair, an authority on women's clubs and, until recently, a professor of history and the history department chair at Central Washington University, said in her talk on the history of women's clubs that one newspaperman of the late 1800s wrote that "women have put down the broom and taken up the club."[8] Other wags saw the women's club movement as "the beginning of the end. If women could leave the house for an hour a week, maybe they would leave for 40 hours."[9] In other words, this could be the thin edge of the wedge in the coming attempt by women to worm their way into the workplace, abandoning their homes each day to go to an office. And that's exactly what happened.

Working on this book, I learned a great deal. By studying private study clubs that are based on Victorian conventions, I learned about the modern American woman, her history, her backstory, and her backbone. Researching and writing *Smart Women* for the past four years has been a labor of love and a real education—a gentle self-education in the tradition of America's historic, but virtually unknown, women's literary societies founded at least a hundred years ago. I thank all of the women who generously helped me with my research by answering long lists of questions. I couldn't have finished—in fact, I couldn't have even started—this project without them.

Author's Note: Because I feel that this book will be used mainly for research in the area of Women's Studies and not read straight through as a narrative, I have repeated important information in the narrative and the summaries and sometimes in several places within the same summary. My apologies to those of you who are more intrepid and who are reading *Smart Women* straight through.

CHAPTER 1

Birmingham, Alabama

First Stop of a Long Journey

For me and my book, it all started in Birmingham in January of 2011, through an e-mail exchange with an old college friend named Lucie Bynum, who had lived in that Southern city for her entire life. I wrote Lucie and said that I was in the early stages of researching and writing a book about American women and the groups they form to self-educate. That had been my book idea at the time. In turn, Lucie wrote back and said that she was preparing a paper for Cadmean Circle called "How Music Expresses that which Cannot Be Put into Words." Her paper fit into Cadmean Circle's yearly theme: communication.

Ann Costello: What is Cadmean Circle?

Lucie Bynum: It's a literary society—the oldest in the state. It was founded in 1888.

AC: Literary society? Your topic doesn't sound so literary …

LB: Our topics for the year vary considerably. Some are more literary than others. There are at least two other similar clubs here that friends of mine are in—not book clubs, but clubs where members present papers on various subjects and where their mothers and grandmothers or aunts or whatever were also in them.

AC: Would your group allow me to visit, and how soon could I come?

And so the book I had already started to research about American women and their yen to self-educate by becoming members of a study group morphed into a book about all-women study clubs defined by the following things:

- Members do their own research, papers, and programs.
- The group is at least a hundred years old and so is part of the women's club movement in the United States.
- The membership number is small enough for everyone to fit inside a member's living room, a church parlor, or a modestly sized meeting room.
- The group is not currently a part of a larger organization but has survived in recent years completely on its own, without outside help or guidance.

That these groups endured and weathered the technological and social changes that have occurred in the past hundred-plus years, and that they still required original research papers or programs from every member, was astonishing to me. I felt that this fact would also be astonishing to a great many others. Here was a far better book idea than my original one. My suspicion that these groups' existence would be a surprise to most people was corroborated over the next few years as I worked on the book. I met only a few people who knew that these historic clubs existed, and—to the man or to the woman—everyone was interested in finding out more about them.

I flew to Birmingham in February of 2011, about a month after my initial exchange with Lucie, and I stayed with her while using her as a tour guide and hostess. She even introduced me to members in each of the groups that interested me and fit my criteria. Without her, I would not have gotten started with Cadmean Circle or with any of the other Birmingham groups, as they are all private and do not go out of their way to publicize what they do. Having that visit under my belt, I was able to use those groups as entrée to discover still more of these groups around the country, many of which I visited, one by one—at least in the early days of my research. But, to put it in a nutshell, I owe it all to Lucie.

In most cities and towns, with the notable exception of Birmingham, I was on my own in an area that was entirely new to me, staying in a hotel, driving a rental car to points unknown, reading maps or learning to set a GPS, and making it to all of my meetings on time. The women of the groups I visited were all polite, intelligent, and charming, and they often helped me in many ways beyond answering my research questions. Some would drive me to a meeting or take me out to dinner. I reached a point where I was corresponding or had corresponded with 141 women in 67 different groups, with an additional 26 groups that were documented online and which I wrote about, but in which I was never able to find a personal contact to corroborate the club's existence. All of these correspondents and all of my research in nearly identical groups meant that I had to do some juggling and practice very good record keeping.

Once I located a contact who belonged to a certain club, I was off and running. In the beginning, I often made this first contact with the help of an archivist at a library whose press release about a club's archives had alerted me to the existence of that particular club in that particular city. I was often helped by people making suggestions during a random conversation. I'd tell someone—perhaps a clerk in a store or a dinner partner during a trip in a foreign country—about the book I was writing, and that person would suggest that I try to reach someone he or she knew who belonged to such a club in some part of the United States I hadn't yet covered. Then, after I had explained to my new contacts what I was doing and what kind of book I was writing, they all eventually followed in Lucie's footsteps and were helpful and accommodating during our exchanges online and our face-to-face meetings.

However, there were exactly three exceptions. One I overcame, and two—in Gilroy, California, and Bronxville, New York—I could not surmount, but I still achieved a good percentage. There were sixty-seven women's literary societies for which I was able to find contacts and answers to my questions.

I returned to Birmingham for a second visit, thirteen months after my first visit, to attend the meetings of two more hundred-plus-year-old study groups: the Nineteenth Century Club and Cosmos. During both trips, I was able to access large archives for these and other groups, now held for safekeeping in libraries.

There were two other vibrant and flourishing literary societies in Birmingham that interested me: the Highland Book Club and New Era. These two clubs together with Cadmean and Nineteenth

Century are called "the big four" by those in Birmingham who know about the existence of historic literary societies. But Highland has guest speakers appear at all of their meetings, and New Era was not quite a hundred years old, so I concentrated on the three Birmingham groups that met all of my criteria.

Another fine Birmingham group that I hoped would fit my criteria but that did not was Semper Fidelis Club. This club, originally founded by middle-class African-American women in Birmingham in 1900, included among its members the mother of Alma Johnson, who would marry General Colin Powell, as well as scores of school teachers and wives of prominent African-American leaders. Semper Fidelis is more of a service club or civic club and does not fit my criteria, but I found it fascinating enough to discuss in the final chapter of this book, "Additional Historic All-Women Clubs."

Birmingham offered me so much information on three all-women study clubs, all of them at least a hundred years old and doing their own papers and programs, that I chose to concentrate on them while being sure to mention those that I chose to eliminate.

Virtually all of the groups I visited had promoted some civic involvement in their earliest days and then gave it up as other groups dedicated to those causes were formed. The Highland Book Club, now using paid speakers for their meetings, is nonetheless a vibrant and sought-after organization. According to their program chairwoman for 2011 to 2012, Catherine Friend, "We are always at thirty members. There is certainly never a vacancy." The group has an illustrious past, according to Dr. Wayne Flynt, twice a Pulitzer Prize–nominated author and also a professor emeritus of the history department at Auburn University. He has had a close relationship with the Highland Book Club, providing programs for their meetings for many years. Dr. Flynt told me in a brief Internet exchange that he finds the group's history to be extraordinary.

In a written statement, Dr. Flynt reiterated a theme I heard often during my reporting and research for this book. He said that these literary societies were often involved in civic education and reform in their earliest days and that a generation of middle-class and upper-class women who had not been able to attend college set about to self-educate collectively, but in the process they "often slipped the bonds of societal constraints and soared in new directions not authorized by the society in which they lived."[1]

Dr. Flynt mentioned one Highland member in the club's very early days, Pattie Ruffner Jacob, who went on to become a state leader in the suffrage movement, and he pointed to long-ago member, Elizabeth Johnson Evans, who worked to separate children from adult male criminals in jails and who also waged a campaign against "convict lease"—the much-abused leasing of convicts by private individuals to do manual labor, with Alabama being the last state to declare the practice illegal in 1928.[2]

However sought-after the club is now, and however admirable the individual accomplishments of these two early members were, the Highland Book Club discontinued the practice of having members do their own research papers and programs, probably in the late 1960s or early 1970s,[3] so I chose to eliminate it from my book, too.

New Era—another of the so-called big four literary societies of Birmingham—is not quite a hundred years old, having been founded by Mrs. Henry Badham in 1917.

I ended up with three wonderful groups, Cadmean Circle, Cosmos, and Nineteenth Century Club, all very similar in their organization and history, but all different in interesting ways. All of the Birmingham groups—indeed, all of the groups I visited or simply researched—had remarkably similar meetings, similar rosters or yearbooks, similar traditions, and similar constitutions and bylaws. Each of their regular meetings would begin right on time with the business portion and minutes, and thereafter would come the member-led program or paper, followed by refreshments—an elaborate or simply elegant tea table or luncheon. In Birmingham, in an atmosphere permeated with what I felt was true Southern charm and warmth, I enjoyed the tea at the end of both Cadmean Circle's and the Nineteenth Century Club's meetings, which were held in gracious private homes. Also, I was treated to a very Southern luncheon at the end of the Cosmos meeting, which was held in an antebellum home open to the public as a museum of the city of Birmingham.

7

My First City, Birmingham, and My First Literary Society, Cadmean Circle, February 22, 2011

The sun was shining; the afternoon was warm. Bright yellow forsythia and daffodils were just starting to appear in sunnier spots in the hilly, affluent Birmingham, Alabama, neighborhood of Mountain Brook. It was February 22, 2011, and I was on my way to my first literary society meeting, Cadmean Circle's traditional three o'clock meeting, held every other Tuesday from October to May. This was my first historic literary society meeting ever and the first for the purposes of this book.

This was also my first trip ever to Birmingham. What I knew about the city was little – mostly having to do with the horrendous 1963 bombing of the Sixteenth Street Baptist Church, which killed four African American girls. However, 50 years later, as my plane approached the airport, the countryside around Birmingham looked peaceful and green from my window. The area had turned out to be just as pretty to drive through, with Lucie Bynum as my guide. The lush hills in which the city is nestled contain the iron, coal, and limestone that were a key reason for Birmingham's founding in 1871. Birmingham's surrounding hills are the only place in the world where useful quantities of all three of these vital ingredients for the manufacture of steel—Birmingham's signature product—are located close together. Because of its resulting reputation as the Pittsburgh of the South,[4] the city is watched over by the Roman god of the forge and fire. A massive statue of Vulcan at his forge, the largest cast iron statue in the world,[5] perches on the top of Red Mountain, overlooking the city. It was erected after being exhibited in the 1904 Louisiana Purchase Exhibition as a symbol of Birmingham's mineral riches.

On one of our drives around the older parts of the city, Lucie showed me the South Highlands area, where most of the literary societies had begun. This part of town still has beautiful examples of Southern Revival, Tudor, and Georgian homes, although there was an exodus of affluent homeowners who had lived in them when a new freeway cut through Red Mountain, taking some families "over the mountain" to newer neighborhoods like Mountain Brook, where I stayed while I was in town.

Cadmean Circle was founded by Mrs. William Hardie, who had visited her mother-in-law, Mrs. John T. Hardie, in New Orleans and had seen how much her mother enjoyed her membership in that town's Quarante Club. (Quarante is a literary club that is still meeting today. I cover it in chapter 13 of this book.) The younger Mrs. Hardie drove around Birmingham, which was only seventeen years old in 1888, in her horse-and-buggy, delivering invitations to thirty other women to join her at her home for the purpose of starting just such a club. The women met in her parlor on December 19 and organized themselves under the name Saturday Literary Club. They later changed their meeting day and changed their name to the Friday Club. Finally, they chose the name Cadmean Circle.[6] The word *Cadmean* comes from Cadmus, who was the mythological prince of Thebes, said to have introduced the Greek alphabet—ergo, the connection to literature.

On the afternoon of our Cadmean meeting in 2011, Lucie and I were welcomed at the front door of a gracious, two-story, red brick colonial by our hostess, Catherine Cabaniss, whose husband was an ambassador to the Czech Republic under President George W. Bush. The interior of the house was decorated with Catherine's own oil paintings and with Czech art and glass. Lucie and I were coatless. It was warm, although it was February, so there was no shedding of coats as we walked in the front door. I began to meet the twenty women attending the day's 3:00 p.m. meeting. We quickly gathered in the living room. There was very little chitchat as the group's members settled themselves. The roll was called, with members answering with a well-mannered "present." Because I was attending the meeting that day as a guest, the minutes were dispensed with. After roll call, I was asked to stand up and tell the group why I was visiting and what my book would cover. This was the first time I had to do this, but I would give my little talk about my book at almost every meeting I attended over the next two years of travel.

Then, the hostess for the next meeting, Frances Wheelock, invited us to visit her house on March 8. That is traditionally how each meeting is announced. Following this, the day's speaker, Lee Gewin, delivered a paper on body language called "Listen with Your Eyes" as a part of the year's concentration on communication. The suggested reference books, DVDs, and articles related to the topic were listed in the group's yearbook so that members could read in preparation for the meeting or, if they were intrigued by the paper, after the meeting. Other topics listed in the Cadmean

Circle yearbook for 2010–11 included "Too Much Communication? Too Much Information—The New Technology 101" and "Reading between the Lines of the World's Great Buildings: Architecture and Culture."

The Cadmean Circle 2010–11 yearbook contains contact information for the group's thirty-three active members and four associate members, plus a list of officers, the constitution and bylaws, a brief account of the group's history, a list of all of the upcoming programs and their topics, suggested reading, and the assigned speaker and the hostess for each meeting. Virtually every group I visited had similar yearbooks or rosters. I found the yearbooks to be so carefully designed, edited, and printed that the original yearbooks from the late 1800s to today—now largely archived at historical societies and libraries around the country—are in excellent condition and are perfect snapshots of the eras they represent.

The similarities of all of the groups I found, including their yearbooks and customs, were striking, especially as the groups today have virtually no contact with each other. I later deduced that some of these similarities must have come about because many of these groups were once members of the various federations of women's clubs and, therefore, shared information that way. But otherwise, information was shared between women friends and relatives by letter, as so many women were in study clubs in the late 1800s and early 1900s. Newspapers also carried breathless accounts, sometimes submitted by the club secretary, of the clubs' meetings and social events.

Looking through these old yearbooks, I could quickly see that in the early days, Cadmean meetings were held once a week and two papers were delivered at each meeting: a long, forty-five-minute paper and a shorter, twenty-minute paper. Now, just the longer paper is assigned, and meetings are held every two weeks, from October 5 to May 3 in 2010 and 2011. In the early days, a paid facilitator who was not a member chose the programs and assigned topics. Miss Willie Allen, a teacher who founded Birmingham's Margaret Allen School for Girls, led Cadmean as facilitator for forty years, from 1896 to 1936, the latter being the year of her death.[7] After she died, the membership took over her jobs, and this practice has continued ever since.

The tasks of delivering a forty-five-minute paper and hostessing are scrupulously rotated in Cadmean Circle so that each woman is hostess during a year when she is not delivering a paper. In other words, this group requires an original paper from each active member every other year, alternating with hostess duties every other year.

As mentioned, the program for the February meeting I attended was a presentation on body language—unspoken communication—as a part of the club's yearlong study of communication. Under the title "Listen with Your Eyes" in the yearbook, two quotations were listed: one from Mae West ("I speak two languages, Body and English") and one from an actress, Anne Parillaud ("Body language is essential for an actress. … A body talks.")[8]

Lee, our speaker, had us all participate so she could see how closely we were listening. She referred to two books that she read for her project: *Body Talk,* by Desmond Morris, and *What Every BODY Is Saying,* by Joe Navarro. She called on two volunteers and asked us to judge the truth of their statements by analyzing their posture and gestures. Lee's program lasted until 3:50, when the hostess invited us into the dining room for tea. One club member seated herself at the end of the table so that she could pour from a silver tea service. The elegant spread arrayed on the table included deviled eggs and chocolate-covered strawberries. The conversation around the table was warm and friendly, and several women introduced themselves and asked about my project. There was white wine, water, and, of course, hot tea to drink from dainty china teacups. After what could not have been more than thirty minutes of socializing, we all began to say our good-byes.

It was a welcoming group, and I felt a part of an old and honored tradition. Add to that the fact that I felt that I'd begun my journey on my book project. This had been a big day.

The days of serving powerful old-fashioned cocktails at the meetings is something I had heard and read a lot about while studying the Birmingham groups, but those days are gone. Before driving with Lucie to the meeting, she had taken me to a longtime member's home so that I could interview her, and this member also mentioned the once-traditional drink. Margaret Livingston, a beautiful and gracious woman with perfect posture and a quick mind, has been a Cadmean Circle member for sixty years. She is the longest-active member of any Cadmean membership in the group's history. She has long served on the board of the Birmingham Museum of Art and was then serving as chairwoman of that board and as a member of its members' board. Besides doing work on these and other boards, Margaret raised four children and has recently been working on a history of the museum. Luckily for me, she had saved a copy of her essay called "A Cadmean Memoir" that she delivered at a November 2004 meeting. In this memoir, she recalls her early days—the 1950s—in Cadmean.

In the memoir, Margaret remembered how dedicated she had to be to actually get to the then-weekly meetings of Cadmean, because, sixty years ago, she had four young children and many carpools to drive. She said that two papers were given at every meeting and that every member gave a presentation each year, alternating between a short paper and a longer one. She found it excruciating to be the second speaker, knowing that everyone was tired of listening. She recalled all members wearing hats and white gloves, along with their best dresses, sitting with their legs crossed demurely at the ankle. When it was a member's turn to host the meeting and the tea, that member did the planning months in advance. One member, Mrs. Arant, ordered caviar for her tea, and another, Mrs. Rudolph, always baked Charleston benne wafers. Margaret also wrote about the long-abandoned tradition of serving double old-fashioned cocktails, which she did not know how to prepare and so had to turn to a country club bartender for a lesson in preparation for her first tea."[9]

When I interviewed her at her home, Margaret recounted wonderful memories of long-abandoned Cadmean activities, including the "elaborate tableau," a kind of still-life enactment of a famous scene from literature, history, or art, with club members costumed for their parts. She recalled members from earlier days, and, really, from a different world, who had their chauffeurs set up their lecterns for them. She also mentioned the members who rode to meetings in a borrowed hearse during WWII, when cars were scarce. There were a few women considered eccentric—especially one member, an archeologist who hung her Christmas tree upside down in her three-story entry hall—but Margaret said that their creative and intellectual input was appreciated.

One paper that Margaret remembered researching and delivering was in keeping with that year's assigned subject, which, surprisingly enough, was "The Number Seven." Margaret, who graduated from Vassar and then earned a master's degree in mathematics at the University of Alabama, wrote and delivered a paper for that series called "Seven Points of Light in Seven Centuries of Art." She gave me an old yearbook from 1987 through 1988, and its cover showed a reproduction of Edvard Munch's painting *Friedrich Nietzsche.*[10] The subject for the year was "The German People, 1815–1914," and the papers delivered included "Empire of the Mind: The Germans of the 19th Century," "Goethe," "The German Song," and "Romantic Painting and the Biedermeier Style."[11]

Margaret said that she felt that all study groups were less rigorous than they used to be, the modern-day ones having lighter subject matter and fewer challenges in their approach. After all, the Cadmean constitution, as shown in the 1895 yearbook and the 2010–11 yearbook, states, "The objects and purposes of the Circle are declared to be serious attention to intellectual pursuits and a broader mental culture."[12]

Perhaps there has been some lightening of the subject matter, as a nod to changing times, but, to my eyes, recent subject matter seems as challenging as that in the late 1800s and early 1900s, when topics ranged from the study of American history to "Literature from the Standpoint of Environment" to "The Italian Renaissance."[13]

I'd also been told by several clubs' members that the current study groups are mostly composed of women in their fifties and beyond, as there are too many demands on the time of younger women who still have children at home and careers to follow. However, I found the age problem not to be a consideration in all of the groups I visited. Margaret pointed out that in Birmingham, a few professionals who were still working belonged to Cadmean Circle, among them a pediatrician, an architect, and a psychologist. It was hard for me to comprehend how those women could research and present a paper on an esoteric subject, and do the critical thinking, researching, and writing required, while simultaneously being able to clear their professional calendar in order to attend meetings every other week during the meeting season. But these women are dedicated to their group, to the women in them, and to the intellectual stimulation they get from the research that goes on within the group.

I asked Margaret what her many years as a Cadmean member had meant to her, and she replied that she "loved doing the papers." She said that the friendships were important, too. "A lot of these people I wouldn't have known without the Cadmean Circle." This was a refrain I heard repeated many times in my three years of talking to and corresponding with members of historic study clubs in all parts of the country.

I especially enjoyed reading the history of Cadmean Circle in terms of its members' impact on the community. In 1895, the group asked other literary clubs in the state to help them form the Alabama Federation of Women's Clubs, to which Cadmean no longer belongs. It was Cadmean Circle and Highland Book Club members who organized the necessary local support to enable Andrew Carnegie to help the young town of Birmingham build its first public library—a story I heard repeated by proud club members from other groups in Dallas, Texas, and Eugene, Oregon, and several other towns in other parts of the country. First, the club members applied to the Carnegie organization for funding to build a library. Second, they worked on the powers that be in city hall or in the local town council to fund an operating budget for a new library and then to fill it with books and a librarian. And all of this was accomplished long before women were given the right to vote in 1920. These literary societies had much to do with the women's newfound ability to organize in groups and work toward common goals.

Cadmean Circle members were also influential in the organization of the art museum in Birmingham, assisted by the Kresge Foundation. Many of the Cadmean Circle members of the day were on the original board of the Hillman Hospital—a hospital for the city's poor, regardless of race—in the late 1800s. A Cadmean Circle member held the shovel with three other women at the groundbreaking ceremony for a new and more modern building for Hillman Hospital in 1902. Between 1888 and 1907, it was Cadmean Circle members who served as president of the Hillman board, for seventeen of those twenty different terms.[14]

Many years after the fact, children of Cadmean members who were not themselves members can remember their mothers working on research papers or cleaning their homes until they shone in preparation for hosting one of the club's meetings. One of these children was Virginia Foster Durr, who died in 1999 at the age of ninety-six. She was a civil rights activist and a lobbyist, a friend of Eleanor Roosevelt, and the sister-in-law of Supreme Court Justice Hugo Black. In addition, she was married to Rhodes Scholar, attorney, and New Dealer Clifford Durr.[15] In a 1975 oral history interview for the Southern Oral History Program Collection of the University of North Carolina, many years after these events, Mrs. Durr recalled her mother, Anna Foster's, hard work on her Cadmean Circle papers and her preparing to be the hostess for a meeting. The Durrs had helped to bail Rosa Parks out of jail in 1955 after she was famously arrested for claiming a seat in the so-called white section of a Montgomery, Alabama, bus,[16] and yet Virginia could look with affection at the privileged world her mother moved in, as it also included a club that required hard work and attention to critical thinking and research. Virginia Foster Durr's father, Dr. Sterling Foster, was the minister at the South Highland Presbyterian Church, and the Foster home today houses the state headquarters of the Alabama Federation of Women's Clubs.

Among Mrs. Durr's memories of her mother's membership in Cadmean Circle, dating from the early 1900s, is the following:

> And the ladies in those days were dressy and everybody wore big hats and chiffons and pearls and white gloves and they would discuss literary subjects. Mother had to write papers and it was a terrible time, everybody had to stop everything and Mother would go to the library and do a tremendous research job, and she did very good papers, I understand. The ultimate of Birmingham, or at least of the Birmingham that I grew up in, was the Cadmean Circle.[17]

Members of Cadmean Circle (Birmingham) on
their 125th anniversary, October 2013
Photo credit: Bonnie H. Krebs

Cosmos Club

It was springtime again when I returned to Birmingham in March 2012—a year after my first visit to that city. I came for an efficient two-night visit in order to attend the meetings of two other historic study groups, Cosmos Club and Nineteenth Century Club. Both clubs were scheduled to meet on Wednesday, March 14—Cosmos at 11:00 a.m., ending with lunch, and Nineteenth Century at 3:00 p.m.—so I was able attend both meetings in one day.

There were masses of naturalized wisteria blooming along the roads leading to the Arlington House, the site of all of the Cosmos' meetings and the only surviving antebellum home in the Birmingham area. The stately Greek Revival building and its surrounding six acres were marked by an identifying sign in the front yard reading, "A Museum of the City of Birmingham." Built on a knoll, with a rolling front lawn and beautifully tended flower beds, the museum property is surrounded by the somewhat down-at-the heels Arlington–West End neighborhood, to the west of downtown Birmingham. The building is available to the public for meetings and events, and the group began to use it when their last meeting place was no longer viable.

Inside Arlington House, the "ladies of the club" were assembling for their annual meeting and lunch. I met them, one by one, with the help of Lucie's friend and my contact for the club, Karen Blatter, who had belonged to the club for four years. In each club I contacted and researched, it was necessary for me to have a hostess and kind of sponsor, and Karen was that key person in the Cosmos. She was invaluable in getting me into a meeting, answering my questions, and sending me clippings and other materials. I found her to be as clear-headed and no-nonsense as the other members of the club, once I met them.

The meeting and luncheon were held in the dining room, with all of the twelve attendees sitting around a long and formally set table that had been decorated for St. Patrick's Day by the meeting's hostesses. I was impressed with the kind of woman who belongs to Cosmos, and by those who had belonged to Cosmos for many years but had recently died. This was a very distinct group, in my eyes—many professional women, largely involved with teaching at the University of Alabama at Birmingham (UAB) and/or with the nursing school at UAB at the highest levels. Professors, researchers, nurses, nursing instructors, a retired endodontist, an architect, and women who have run charitable organizations with tremendous worldwide implications—these were the women of the Cosmos Club. A new member, Maggie (Margaret) Amsler, had traveled to Antarctica twenty-one times as a researcher, taking with her a team of scientists from UAB. Another new member, Dr. Gail Hill, is an associate professor in the Graduate School of Nursing at UAB and has traveled to Zambia on a grant from the Doris Duke Foundation to train nurses. Also, she worked as a nurse in India for four years as well as in several other countries.

After the meeting, Karen mailed me copies of the obituaries of three treasured members who had all died in 2011. Their deaths were a great blow, she said, to the Cosmos Club. These women—Lillian Naumann, Georgene Gainey, and Flodia Powell—lived to be ninety-seven, ninety-two, and ninety-six, respectively, and they were vital and involved into their old age. (For a description of each woman, see item 21, "Colorful or interesting members," of the snapshot summary for Cosmos.) Their life stories got me thinking—as I would many times during the course of working on this book—that belonging to these study groups must prolong a person's life. They certainly add to the quality of a woman's life on many levels.

I wrote back to Karen and said that these three obituaries had broken my heart. These amazing, quietly energetic women who greatly contributed to their communities and to the world found time to study and learn with their good friends in the Cosmos Club, and they had done so for so many years. Their loss must have felt like an actual vacuum to the group. And to have three of these women die in one year must have been a complete shock. Happily, Cosmos Club now has two new members who are also immensely capable women, so life goes on and the club is able to survive.

When she told me about these three women, Karen said to me, "It was a shame to lose them, because they are all examples of what you can do in your later years."

I'd say more than that. I'd say that these women are examples of what one can do with one's entire life, through hard work and a will to be involved.

The Cosmos meeting I attended on March 14 was their annual meeting, so there would be no paper presented. The meeting was called to order at 11:40 a.m., which was followed by a reading of a prayer I heard recited in many of the groups whose meetings I attended all over the country. The prayer was written in 1904 by a Longmont, Colorado, high school principal named Mary Stewart and was later adopted by many groups and federations of women's clubs in this country, Canada, and Great Britain. Today, the women's study clubs that still use the prayer are largely unaware that there are women in similar groups all over the country doing the same thing. Here is "The Collect for Club Women" (the pronunciation of *Collect*—a kind of prayer—is "CAH-lect"):

> Keep us, O God, from pettiness;
> let us be large in thought, in word, in deed.
>
> Let us be done with fault-finding and
> leave off self-seeking.
>
> May we put away all pretense and meet each
> other face to face—without self-pity
> and without prejudice.
>
> May we never be hasty in judgment and
> always generous.
>
> Let us take time for all things;
> make us to grow calm, serene, gentle.
>
> Teach us to put into action our better impulses,
> straightforward and unafraid.
>
> Grant that we may realize it is the little
> things that create differences,
> that in the big things of life we are at one.
>
> And may we strive to touch and to know the great,
> common human heart of us all, and
> O Lord God, let us forget not to be kind![18]

—Mary Stewart (1904)

It is the final line that I see referred to fondly and often among club members, from club to club, all over the country.

After the prayer, the Cosmos' secretary, Bonnie Armistead, read the roll and then read a letter of recommendation for a possible new member, who was then unanimously approved by the members around the table. I explained my book to the group, and then there was a second prayer—the only time I have seen two prayers at a study group meeting—followed by announcements. Next, the treasurer's report was read by my hostess, Karen. Lunch began at 11:45, with Arlington's kitchen staff serving corn chowder as a first course. While we ate a very Southern lunch of stuffed pork chops, black-eyed peas, and mashed potatoes, the group heard the lineup of officers for the coming year. Also, the group's contributions to certain charities were discussed. The meeting ended at 12:30. We all exited from the formal dining room through the Arlington House's gift shop, and Karen drove me to a parking lot where Lucie picked me up and took me back to her house to get ready for my next Birmingham meeting, of the Nineteenth Century Club.

Nineteenth Century Club

I was escorted through the doors of hostess Allison Murray's gracious home in Birmingham's Mountain Brook neighborhood by longtime Nineteenth Century Club member and past president Elberta Reid. She had also picked me up at Lucie's house and had driven me to the group's three o'clock meeting, a few hours after the end of the Cosmos meeting I had attended. Despite the stunningly insensitive and, as far as I could tell, entirely inaccurate *Vanity Fair* magazine article about them—a satiric send-up, perhaps—Nineteenth Century Club members seemed to believe that I had a different agenda. They welcomed me to their March 14 meeting, shaking my hand and introducing themselves.

Unlike the author of the piece, I heard no insensitive comments and saw no napping elderly members. In fact, this was by far the youngest group I visited, with many of the members in extremely fashionable sleeveless sheaths and high heels—beautifully turned out, smiling, alert, not napping, and on target in every conceivable way. I was told that their age range was twenty-eight to ninety.

Not only had I never seen a younger group, but also, never in my lifetime had I ever seen such a tea table as was waiting for us in the dining room when the meeting was over. When one member saw my jaw dropping at the sight of the dining room table absolutely covered with home-prepared delicacies, she leaned over and whispered to me, by way of explanation, "You are in the South." Also, the group was very large. I estimated that there were thirty-five women present, all squeezed happily into Mrs. Murray's living room or else sitting in folding chairs in a doorway.

This is a group that searches hard for new and young members so as to keep their membership at thirty active members and to help them fulfill their goal of presenting *two* twenty-minute papers every other week during meeting season. That is twenty-eight papers during the club year. Officers need not give a paper, thereby shrinking the size of the pool of paper-givers. In addition, once a member turns seventy, she is given senior status and needs not entertain the group or do research papers, so the hunt is always on for new, smart, socially adept women to take on this very particular kind of research work combined with what I call extreme hostessing. It surely can't be easy to find young women who want to take on the challenges of this historic study group in today's world of working mothers and heavily scheduled children who require multiple carpools.

Another interesting facet of the Nineteenth Century Club is its number of legacy members. One family has had four generations of women in the club. When I was given the rundown, I visualized a sort of Nineteenth Century Club family tree. My pen and brain could not keep up with the maiden names, nicknames, married names, and newly single names of the women. But I did finally work everything out with help, and I even met several of the women from this four-generation family. One, Jane McGriff, is the very talented designer and "publisher" of the club's yearbook whom I spoke to at length. Jane's mother, Alice "Acky" McGriff, and grandmother Marguerite Jones were Nineteenth Century members of long standing. They were both active members for almost sixty years. Jane's sister-in-law Leah McGriff, aunt Wita Harbert, cousin Margie Gray, and niece Mitchell Walters are currently members. I wrote myself the following

21

note after having this explained to me: "This is all very confusing, unless you grew up in Birmingham and know these women and their families and their nicknames." This collective memory goes back many years. For some women, it goes back to the earliest days of Birmingham and of the club.

The Nineteenth Century Club was founded in 1895, and the group has the distinction of having had a very fine book written about their history for their centennial celebration by Leah Rawls Atkins, who was the director of the Center for the Arts and Humanities at Auburn University and adjunct professor in Auburn's history department. She is coauthor with Dr. Wayne Flynt of the Pulitzer Prize–nominated *Alabama: The History of a Deep South State.* Her book about Nineteenth Century Club, appropriately titled *Nineteenth Century Club: Celebrating 100 Years of "Mutual Mental Improvement,"* was paid for by a grant awarded to the women of club for the project.

The book is filled with a historical overview of the group and contains photos of its early members. At first, the members are dressed in long skirts, huge hats, and leg-of-mutton sleeves, and their long hair is arranged into upswept dos or demure buns or twists. Under those long-sleeved blouses, the women undoubtedly wore stiff corsets. Then, the photos show the skirts becoming shorter, hanging looser on the body, until club members are in what we would call flapper attire. Then come the group photos of more contemporary members in dress that would be appropriate to see on the street today. The final photos in the book are of Nineteenth Century Club members posed on the porch steps or in the garden of a member's home in 1995, celebrating their centennial.

Among the ten young, single women who gathered together on July 30, 1895, to formulate their ideas for a study club, nineteen-year-old Hannah Elliott was the group's prime mover. It was Hannah, an artistic high school graduate with no plans for college, who handpicked "the group of like-minded bluestockings who were smart, fun-loving, intellectually curious."[19]

Together, the women picked the rest of the twenty charter members of the club, who were required to be unmarried. However, they chose Mrs. Lucy Hall London – a married woman - to serve as their unpaid president and guide for the next thirty-eight years. The older matron was already a member of Cadmean Circle, and many of the young women were daughters of Cadmean members, so this set up a mother–daughter relationship between leader and members that lasted for almost forty years. Leah Atkins notes in her book that Mrs. London seems to have taken a leave from the Cadmean Circle in 1895, while she was getting the Nineteenth Century Club organized. She returned to active status in the Cadmean Circle the next year.[20] There is still a close relationship between Nineteenth Century Club and Cadmean Circle today.

In 1896, the young women started to get married and had to leave the club, or they became "honorary members." After making several attempts to solve what had become a problem of keeping their membership intact, the women changed their constitution in 1904 to include married women as members. Following that decision, Hannah Elliott resigned, after ten years of membership, but she remained a popular and somewhat eccentric Birmingham figure and an acclaimed miniaturist,[21] with her work being included in the collection today at the Birmingham Museum of Art. A portrait of Hannah in 1940—forty-five years after she helped found the Nineteenth Century Club, which puts her age at sixty-four—shows a rather plump and very erect woman with wire rim spectacles, upswept hair, a black velvet ribbon around her neck, and a cigarette holder in her hand.

Hannah's father, Robert Habersham Elliott, was one of the founders of Sewanee College, which is now Sewanee University. Also, Hannah had two aunts who were schoolteachers and who doted on her—two good reasons for Hannah's seeing self-education as an imperative. She was clearly the driving force of the Nineteenth Century Club during its formation.

Hannah never married. She is said to have exclaimed that her twenty-eighth birthday was "the happiest day of [her] life," because that was the day when her mother told her that she did not have to get married. In a paper entitled "The Young Bluestocking," delivered on October 5, 1994, club member Helen London wrote, "Miss Hannah must have been an artistic Gertrude Stein with her gatherings," which led me to believe that Nineteenth Century must have been speculating about the basis of Hannah's horror at the prospect of marriage.

Even after Hannah resigned from the club, the organization remained vital. Members continued to do serious research papers into the twenty-first century. During the world wars, the women did war work and had clothing drives, as did all of the other groups I cover in this book. For many years, they supported reformist activities through their affiliation with the Alabama Federation of Women's Clubs. They also jumped on the political bandwagon on occasion, but "the club never lost its original intellectual focus."[22]

In 1971, the club left the Alabama Federation of Women's Clubs and "returned to its original purpose of being a study club," abandoning "charity work and civic work."[23] As I came to find as I traveled to visit groups across the country, this was the same pattern with virtually every group I chose to write about. They are all now independent literary societies with only an occasional charitable donation of books to a library or perhaps donations to a scholarship fund.

The Nineteenth Century meeting I attended in March 2012 began exactly at three o'clock. It was to be a business meeting, typically held at this point in the year, and featured a vote on next year's topic. Only one paper is presented at a Nineteenth Century business meeting, rather than the usual two.

Roll call was done using "Miss" or "Mrs." before the members' last names, a practice I saw in most other groups. Members were also referred to this way in the minutes. The minutes read from the last meeting had been recorded with humor and intelligence—another feature I saw in most of the groups. I was introduced after the minutes were read and was asked to explain my project, something I was to do at every meeting I attended over the next few years. After my brief remarks, a few women asked me about my project, including one question referring to the mean-spirited *Vanity Fair* article, to determine whether I was a similarly satiric writer. Once I assured the members that my book would be fairly straightforward, the meeting moved on.

Next year's slate of officers was announced, and then the Book Lady stood and spoke. This is an appointed position and a custom as old as the group, begun in the days before public libraries, chain bookstores, and Amazon.com existed. The current Book Lady announced the titles of the three books she had available to lend.

At one time, these books would have been related to the topic under discussion, but now they are for pure reading enjoyment.[24] The time limit for keeping one of Nineteenth Century's borrowed books is two weeks. The books were immediately spoken for, the Book Lady sat down, and Kay Blount stood to deliver her paper titled "Saints and Sinners in Business," focusing on the year's theme of "Saints and Sinners." The speaker compared the personal codes of ethics of two wealthy businessmen, Joseph P. Kennedy and Paul Newman, clearly indicating which she felt was the saint and which she felt was the sinner, and backing this up with carefully researched facts and clear writing.

Next year's topic of study was then chosen from a master list prepared by the program committee. The members voted several times, with low-ranking choices dropping off the new list and eventually leaving a clear winner. Choices for the coming year were as follows:

1. 1865–1914 (Before *The Guns of August*)
2. Earth, Air, Fire
3. India
4. Language
5. Rivers

The winner was "1865–1914 (*Before the Guns of August*)." This meant that in 2012–13, the group would be researching and writing study papers on assigned topics associated with the run-up to the First World War.

The meeting was adjourned. Several members introduced themselves to me, including Edith Quarles, who said that she graduated from Duke University—my college—in 1959 and had been a member of Nineteenth Century for forty-five years. We all headed to the dining room, where the heavily laden tea table awaited us. I was told that every baked good, every sandwich, and even the floral centerpiece had been made by the hostess, Allison, or by a member of her family. In addition to a silver tea service, the table was covered with platters full of beaten biscuits, molasses cookies, tiny pimento sandwiches, strawberries, tea-size shrimp salad sandwiches, raspberry squares, and more. Allison told me, with a look of pleased relief, that this was her last time to hostess, as she was turning seventy before the next cycle of papers and hostessing.

Before Elberta and I left, I met several of the younger club members and asked about their careers. These women mentioned a member who was a landscape artist, one who was an attorney, and one who was a law professor. Then our discussion turned to an extraordinary member who died in 2011 at the age of ninety-seven, after being a member of Nineteenth Century Club for fifty-five years—Bibby Smith. Her name was Elizabeth Taylor before she married Herbert Smith, and that alone piqued my interest. I admit to having Googled Bibby while writing this section. The Nineteenth Century Club members described her as a kind of Renaissance woman, and the information I found about her online said that she had been a high school principal and then, during WWII, rose in the ranks to become a lieutenant colonel in the Women's Army Corps (WAC). She served on the board of the Birmingham Museum of Art and, well into her extreme old age, still travelled to New York City and Santa Fe for the opera every season. She was also an accomplished amateur painter. I was told that Bibby would often participate when there was a Nineteenth Century field trip to another city. Here was another example of incredible women who, into their nineties, work at keeping their minds and bodies active by belonging to and participating in a beloved study group.

The three Birmingham groups I chose to study might have had an extra patina of Southern hospitality, but they shared virtually every aspect of their history, structure, traditions, and future hopes with the other groups I visited around the country, although most of them were unaware that other groups like theirs existed.

But, most important, all of these groups—whether in the Deep South, in the Pacific Northwest, in the Rocky Mountains, in the Southwest, in the Midwest, in central New York State, or elsewhere in this country—seemed to share an important feature. They all contributed greatly to the lives of the women who were members, especially adding a life-enhancing social and intellectual component to the inevitable aging process.

Snapshot Summary of The Cadmean Circle

1.   **Official name of the club:** The Cadmean Circle.[25] Cadmus was the mythological prince of Thebes who is said to have introduced the Greek alphabet.

2.   **Date founded:** December 19, 1888,[26][27] making it the oldest surviving women's literary club in Birmingham and, very probably, the oldest in Alabama.[28]

3.   **Founded by:** Mrs. William W. Hardie, who held the first meeting in her parlor.[29] It is said that Mrs. Hardie wanted to have a club in Birmingham that was similar to the Quarante Club in New Orleans, which included the brightest and most cultured women in the city[30] and had been founded in 1886.[31] (I cover Quarante in chapter 13 of this book.) Mrs. Hardie had visited her mother-in-law, Mrs. John T. Hardie, in New Orleans and was impressed by the older woman's club.[32] Thirty women joined the younger Mrs. Hardie at her home on December 19, 1888, calling themselves the Saturday Literary Club. They later changed the club name to the Friday Club, before eventually settling on Cadmean Circle.[33]

4.   **Size of club as stated in bylaws:** "No more than 36 Active members, and not more than five Honorary members."[34]

5.   **Size of club today:** Thirty-five active members (thirty-six in the fall of 2013),[35] five associate members (who are on extended leave), and one honorary member.[36]

6.   **Meeting schedule:** The meetings begin on the first Tuesday in October and end in early May. Generally, the club meets every two weeks, on Tuesdays, at 3:00 p.m. The norm is thirteen to fourteen meetings per year.[37] Usually, there are no meetings in December,[38] but there are years when there is an early December meeting. Scheduling is always dependent on when Thanksgiving and spring break fall.[39]

7.   **Where they meet:** In members' homes, with occasional exceptions.

8.   **Election of new members:** New members are nominated when a vacancy occurs. A two-thirds vote is required to be elected to membership.[40]

9. **Object of the club as stated in bylaws:** "The object and purposes of the Circle are declared to be serious attention to intellectual pursuits and a broader mental culture."[41]

10. **Dues:** $20 a year per member.[42]

11. **Club colors, flower, and motto:** Possible club colors and flowers are no longer referred to in the Cadmean yearbooks or histories. The original motto, "To Serve the Present Age," has fallen out of use. However, the group is admonished in every yearbook to remember article 12 of their bylaws: "Members of the Circle shall maintain the spirit of fellowship which pertains to all honorable organizations."[43]

12. **Paper or program assignment schedule:** Each member presents one original research paper every other year, alternating with hostessing duties every other year. One paper is presented at each meeting, although two were given in earlier years.[44]

13. **Length of papers or programs:** Thirty to forty-five minutes.

14. **Location of the club's archives, yearbooks, minutes, and scrapbooks:** Main branch, Birmingham Public Library, Department of Archives and Manuscripts, on the lower level of the 1927 neoclassic library building that overlooks Linn Park in the heart of downtown Birmingham.

15. **Civic achievements of the group or its members:**
    - Cadmean Circle was instrumental in the founding of the Alabama Federation of Women's Clubs on April 17, 1895, in the South Highland Presbyterian Church, Birmingham.[45]
    - Several Cadmean members were vital to the formation of the city's art museum.[46]
    - Club members were among the founders of Hillman Hospital, a charity hospital and the forerunner of the current University of Alabama at Birmingham Hospital. Before the hospital was given to Jefferson County in 1907, Cadmean Circle members chaired its board of managers for seventeen of twenty years.[47]

16. **Special events:**
    - A picnic may be the main feature of the last meeting in early May, although this is more the exception than the rule.[48]
    - In 2013, Cadmean Circle celebrated its 125th anniversary. To mark the occasion, members made a "major donation to the Jefferson County Library Cooperative, to help them keep going."[49] Also, a small committee gathered historical information about the group for a commemorative brochure.[50]

17. **Refreshment highlights:** At the end of each meeting, the members are invited to enjoy an enticing tea table. One member is chosen to pour tea from a silver service. There might also be white wine along with nonalcoholic beverages. In past times, double old-fashioned cocktails were offered.[51] The choice of dishes is left to the hostess, but she may have trays of small sandwiches, savories, cookies, and/or fruit.

18. **Special traditions:**
    - Cadmean members always arrive at each meeting on time, and they insist that members always say yes when asked to write a paper or perform any job for the club.
    - The correct response to roll call is "present," and members refer to each other as "Mrs.," "Miss," "Ms.," or "Dr." when the roll is called and when speaking to or about each other during the meeting.[52]
    - The time for delivering papers is generally forty-five minutes or less.[53]

19. **Example of overall yearly theme or topic:** In 2010–11, it was "Communication."[54]

20. **Example of individual paper or assignment based on that topic:** "Read My Lips: The Blunder Heard Round the World. The Best and Worst Political Communicators." There is a reading list suggested by the program committee for each topic.[55]

21. **Particularly colorful or interesting members, present or past:**

- Many of the founding mothers and early members of Cadmean Circle would have been old enough during the Civil War to remember the war. A look at a list of early members shows Mrs. David Roberts, whose maiden name was Belle Sumter Yates. She joined Cadmean in 1902. A footnote in the list, compiled by Cadmean members, reveals that she was born on the night of April 12, 1861, during the bombardment of Fort Sumter, while her father, Colonel Yates, was engaged in the fighting. She was christened Belle Sumter in honor of the event, and the family name was passed down to her daughter and great-granddaughter.[56]

- In the club's early days, a paid facilitator, who was not a member, chose the programs and assigned topics. Miss Willie Allen, a teacher who founded Birmingham's Margaret Allen School for Girls, led Cadmean as facilitator for forty years, from 1896 to 1936, the latter being the year of her death. After she died, the membership took over her job. One of the boarders at the Margaret Allen School remembered many years later that she and the other boarding-school girls would help Miss Allen get ready for her appearance at the Cadmean Circle each Friday afternoon. When Miss Allen returned from the meeting, the girls would listen to her summary of the program over dinner in the school dining hall.[57]

- Anna "Nannie" McLester, who was a member of Cadmean Circle for fifty-six years and was last listed on their rolls in 1944, was also the president of the Birmingham YWCA for twenty-five years, the president of the Alabama Federation of Women's Clubs, the president of the Women of Birmingham's First Presbyterian Church, and a board member of the Boys' Industrial School and also of Hillman Hospital. She is also the great-grandmother of Mary

Dunn French's husband, James. Mary is a current Cadmean associate member.[58]

- Margaret Livingston has been a Cadmean Circle member for sixty years—the longest-active membership of any Cadmean member in the group's history—and is currently serving as chairwoman emeritus on the board of the Birmingham Museum of Art (BMA). She is also a member of BMA's members' board. Besides doing work on these and other boards, Margaret raised four children and has recently been working on a history of the museum. She granted me an interview when I was in Birmingham for the Cadmean Circle meeting, and I found her to be helpful, charming, and in possession of a razor-sharp intellect.
- A certain Mrs. Randolph, a member in the 1950s, is said to have hung her Christmas tree upside down, to have been an archeologist, and to have brought surprise guests to meetings, much to the dismay of the hostess of the day.[59]

22. **Example of legacy members:** There have been several chains of family membership in Cadmean, but one legacy chain began with one of the "intellectual leaders" (to quote longtime member Margaret Livingston) of Cadmean, Mrs. Douglas (Letitia) Arant. Her daughter, Adele Stockham, is said to have been a valued and fascinating member until her death in April 2013. Mrs. Arant's granddaughter Adele Culp is still an active member.[60]

Snapshot Summary of The Cosmos Club

1. **Official name of the club:** The Cosmos Club.[61]
2. **Date founded:** February 1908.[62]
3. **Name of founders:** Mrs. J. B. Simpson, at her home on Avenue F in the Ensley neighborhood of Birmingham (then an independent city).[63] The charter members were all married women. Aside from Mrs. Simpson, the seventeen

charter members were Mmes. J. W. Minor, H. E. Agerton, J. B. Simpson, H. C. Kegley, W. H. Wynne, D. B. Bird, P. A. Eubank, C. G. Goldsmith, W. O. Garrett, A. Poss, J. Moog, W. H. Vibber, C. C. Johnson, J. S. Colyar, D. A. Cox, M. V. Averyt, and O. C. Cowan.[64]

4. **Size of club as stated in bylaws:** Twenty-five active members, any number of associate members, and any number of honorary members.[65]

5. **Size of club today:** Nineteen active members and four honorary members.[66] Their newest member is a PhD who is an associate professor in the University of Alabama at Birmingham's School of Nursing. Many Cosmos members teach at UAB or have professional degrees.[67]

6. **Election of new members:** This is done by way of an uncomplicated procedure. Prospective members are voted on, and a two-thirds vote "shall elect."[68]

7. **Where they meet:** Since 2002, the club has met in Birmingham's only surviving antebellum home, Arlington House, in the neighborhood—once an independent town[69]—where the club was founded, Ensley.[70] [71] Before meeting at Arlington House, the group met at the Women's Club House, which was later put up for sale.[72]

8. **Meeting schedule:** Second Wednesday of each month, September through May, at 11:00 a.m., including a December meeting. Lunch, prepared by Arlington House staff, always follows a brief meeting and a half-hour program.[73]

9. **Object of the club:** "Mutual helpfulness in intellectual matters, a united effort to stimulate an interest in literature, to keep abreast with the current thought of the day, and to strengthen individual effort by organization."[74]

10. **Dues:** $20 per year per active member; $10 for associate members. Luncheon charges for each active member are an additional $125 (for nine lunches), whether or not a member misses a meeting.[75]

11. **Club colors, flower, and motto:** Their colors are pink and white, and—obviously—their flower is the cosmos.[76] The motto is no longer referred to, but an original objective of "mutual helpfulness in intellectual matters"[77] is referred to.

12. **Paper or program assignment schedule:** A sign-up list is passed at meetings so that members may volunteer for hostessing and for programs of their own choosing. Hostessing involves providing a centerpiece and take-home goodies, and there are two hostesses for each of the nine meetings.[78]

13. **The length of papers:** Thirty minutes.[79]

14. **Location of the club's archives:** Main branch of the Birmingham Public Library in its archives section.[80]

15. **Civic achievements of the group or its members:**
    - A longtime charitable association with the Poarch Band of Creek Indians in Atmore, Alabama, via member Eloie Bradshaw. She headed the Cosmos Club's committee of Indian affairs for ten or eleven years and worked with—and often lived with—the Creek Indians as an Episcopal church volunteer from 1954 to 1974.[81]
    - A note in the group's centennial history reads, "Almost every member has at some time served as president of some parent–teacher association."[82]
    - A new member runs training sessions for nurses in Zambia.[83]

16. **Special events:** There is a guest speaker at the opening meeting in September, and a Christmas-themed meeting in mid-December. In December 2011, the meeting featured seasonal music played on the hammered dulcimer, performed by the husband of member Kathy Angus. Dr. Robert Angus is a professor at University of Alabama at Birmingham, as are many of the members of this group.[84]

17. **Refreshment highlights:** Lunch, which follows the programs, is prepared by the catering staff of the Arlington House.[85]

18. **Special traditions:** The club chairwoman reads "The Collect for Club Women" (a traditional prayer used by many historic study groups) after the call to order, and there is another prayer before lunch.[86]

19. **Example of overall yearly theme or topic:** They do not have an overall topic for the year. Members may speak on whatever topic they choose.[87]
20. **Example of a paper or program:** A biography of Louisa May Alcott.[88]
21. **Colorful or interesting members, present or past:**
    - When Lillian Naumann died in 2011 at the age of ninety-seven, she had been a member of Cosmos for almost seventy years, having joined in 1943. She had been a professor in the biology department of the University of Alabama from 1958 to 1983, had won awards for her teaching, and had so many volunteer jobs and headed so many committees, including being the president of a school PTA, that her volunteer involvements took up 5.5 inches in the newspaper's obituary column. However, what struck me with the greatest force was the final paragraph of her obituary, which detailed her Dickensian childhood. She was orphaned at the age of ten, first by the great flu epidemic in 1918, which killed her father when she was four years old, and second in 1924, when her mother died from a stroke. Lillian prospered, she claimed, with the help of relatives and a court-appointed guardian, and she rose in life through academic hard work, always believing, "There are many good people in the world."[89]
    - Club member Karen Blatter described longtime Cosmos member Georgene Gainey as "an actor and seasoned performer to the end." Gainey's obituary in the *Birmingham News* said that she was still rehearsing lines for a production put on by a troupe of senior thespians called the Seasoned Performers on the day she died at the age of ninety-two. She and her husband had performed as a team for fifty years, hosting radio and television programs and appearing in commercials. She often appeared in local community theater productions and also taught speech arts at the Altamont School until her retirement

in 1980. That was over thirty years ago. During her so-called retirement, Georgene threw herself into theater work, her Cosmos work, and church work, and she even became certified to teach water aerobics so she could lead a class at the YMCA.[90]

- Flo (Flodia) Powell, who died on October 1, 2011, at the age of ninety-six, had been one of nine children born to a family in a tiny Alabama town. She taught elementary school in Tennessee, Pennsylvania, and New Jersey, and she became an elementary school principal in New Jersey. Thereafter, she retired from a remedial reading teaching position she had held for ten years after her husband's death in 1977. She moved back to Birmingham, where she had an active retirement for the next thirty-four years. In those years, she was a devoted Cosmos member as well as a hardworking church volunteer, parent, and grandparent.[91] Her daughter, Kathy Powell Roebuck, who is a retired dentist, was the president of Cosmos when I visited the club. Kathy sat on my right during the meeting I attended.
- Eloie Jeter Bradshaw, who died in 1985 at the age of eighty-nine,[92] lived with the impoverished Creek Indians in Escambia County, Alabama, for six years, while volunteering through her Episcopal church. Her church work with the Indians began in 1954 and continued for twenty years.[93]

22. **Legacy members or longest-active members:** The president in 2011–12, Kathy Roebuck, is the daughter of longtime member Flodia Powell, who died in 2011 after having been a member for thirty-four years.[94] Another longtime member, Lillian Naumann, also died in 2011; she was a Cosmos member for sixty-eight years.[95]

Snapshot Summary of the Nineteenth Century Club

1. **Official name of the club:** Nineteenth Century Club.
2. **Date founded:** July 30, 1895.
3. **Name of founder:** Hannah Elliott. When she was nineteen years old, she invited ten young, unmarried friends from the South Highlands area of Birmingham to her house at 2036 Thirteenth Avenue South. They discussed forming a literary club. These women invited ten more, bringing their numbers up to twenty charter members plus a sponsor/president, Lucy Hall London, who was seen as a wise older woman. She was married and was a member of Cadmean Circle. Despite the seeming conflict of interest (Nineteenth Century originally limited itself to unmarried women), Lucy Hall London led the group as its president for thirty-eight years, until her death in 1933.[96] Longtime club member Elberta Reid told me that many of the first members of Nineteenth Century Club had mothers who were Cadmean members. With Mrs. London as the leader, the two groups developed a close association that continues to this day. Each group invited the other when it celebrated its hundredth anniversary.[97]
4. **Size of club as stated in bylaws:** Thirty active members.[98] In 1904, the club voted to accept married, as well as single, women.[99]
5. **Size of club today with breakdown of membership:** Thirty active members plus eighteen senior members. The latter, having turned seventy, no longer give papers or hostess meetings.[100]
6. **Meeting schedule:** Every two weeks, from early October to early May. There is no December meeting. Meetings are on Wednesdays at 3:00 p.m. The last meeting of the year is a picnic at noon.[101]
7. **Where they meet:** In members' homes.[102]
8. **Election of new members:** New members are proposed if an active member dies or turns seventy.[103]
9. **Object of the club as stated in bylaws:** "Mutual mental improvement."[104]

10. **Dues:** $10 per year. The only group expenditure is for books for the Book Lady.[105]

11. **Club motto, colors, and flower:** Mutual mental improvement; grass-green and white; no flower.[106]

12. **Paper or program assignment schedule:** Twenty-eight papers are given each year, with two twenty-minute papers presented at each of the club's meetings, except for the business meeting in mid-March, where only one is read. The club takes great pride in the fact that it has no guest speakers. Only members deliver papers.[107] However, the president and secretary are excused from this requirement.[108]

13. **Length of papers or programs:** Two twenty-minute papers are given at virtually every meeting (see above, item 12).

14. **Location of archives:** Archives section, main branch of the Birmingham Public Library.

15. **Civic achievements of the group or its members:** As with all of the groups mentioned in this book, the Nineteenth Century Club's members have been involved in every civic project and PTA board imaginable. In its early days, the group actively supported many civic causes and charities. However, as with most of the groups, they now concentrate on being a study club.[109]

16. **Special events:**
    - A picnic at the last meeting in early May, featuring a competitive game, usually designed to reflect the topic of the year. The woman assigned to design and run the game does this in lieu of doing a research paper that year.[110]
    - Every few years, the club offers it members a field trip that ties in with the yearly topic. Club member Jane McGriff gave me two examples: (1) When studying roads, they visited New Orleans and its River Road area. (2) When studying the Constitution, they visited Philadelphia and its historic sites.[111]

17. **Refreshment highlights:** What I experienced when I visited this group in March 2012 was an absolutely spectacular tea table groaning under the weight of artfully constructed and tasty tea sandwiches, beaten biscuits, and cookies, all

homemade by the hostess and her family members. As one club member said to me as I gawked at the splendor of the spread on hostess Alison Comer Murray's table after the meeting, "You are in the South."

18. **Special traditions:**
    - The club's Book Lady serves as a kind of librarian, bringing a basket of books to each meeting and circulating them among interested members.[112]
    - Another tradition that is observed in many groups, including this one, is that members are addressed or referred to by their surnames during most of the meeting. Their first names are not used until teatime.[113]
    - A third tradition is the club members' emphasis on and pride in legacy members.

19. **Example of overall yearly theme or topic:** "Saints and Sinners" in 2011–12.[114]

20. **Example of individual paper or program assignment:** At the November 2, 2011, meeting, the two papers were "In Literature: *Atlas Shrugged, Paradise Lost,* and Oscar Went Wilde" and "In High Tech and on the Internet: Unfriending the Enemy / Surfing for Saints."[115]

21. **Example of an extremely colorful member, present or past:**
    - Elizabeth "Bibby" Smith, who died in 2011 at the age of ninety-seven and rarely missed a Nineteenth Century field trip. She had served in the WAC in WWII and was the first woman to reach the rank of lieutenant. When she retired, she was a lieutenant colonel.[116] Bibby was an accomplished amateur artist and a board member of the Birmingham Museum of Art. Her maiden name was Elizabeth Taylor.[117]
    - When club founder Hannah Elliott (1876–1956) died, her obituaries, now housed in the club archives in the Birmingham library, painted a picture of an eccentric but influential artist whose works were exhibited in "most of the leading galleries and museums in this country and Europe."[118] Her obituary also gave her credit for the "dream of a museum of art in

Birmingham."[119] Among this rather regal character's forebears were six Episcopal bishops. Her grandfather, Bishop Stephen Elliott, was a "significant founder" of Sewanee[120]—an Episcopal college now called the University of the South.[121] [122] However, what sticks in my mind is Hannah's assertion that the happiest day of her life was her twenty-eighth birthday, when her mother told her that she did not have to marry. Hannah left Nineteenth Century—her creation—after the club voted to accept married women.[123]

22. **Legacy members and longest-active members:**
  - The most vital family legacy chain I've found in any group so far is in Nineteenth Century. There are four generations of one family represented in Nineteenth Century, including five current members. They are all related to Marguerite Jones, who was a member from 1929 to 1988 and had two daughters, Alice "Acky" Jones McGriff (who died in 2010) and Wita Jones Harbert, the latter of whom is still a member as I work on this section of the book in late March 2013. Their daughters Jane McGriff and Margie Gray are also members, as well as a granddaughter-in-law, Leah McGriff, and a great granddaughter-in-law, Mitchell Walters.[124]
  - The longest-active members—who are now senior members as per the club's rules, but who still attend meetings—are Joan Edmonds, who joined in 1959 (fifty-six years ago), Jean Miller, who joined in 1968 (forty-seven years ago), Edith Quarles (1970, forty-five years ago), and Franny Seibels (1972, forty-three years ago).[125]

CHAPTER 2

Dallas, Texas

A Cluster of Three Historic Clubs

I made my first visit to Dallas shortly after visiting Birmingham for the first time. This was ironic, as this city, like Birmingham, was also the scene of horrific events in 1963—fifty years before my visits. For Dallas, the event was the assassination of US President John Fitzgerald Kennedy. However, like my Birmingham visits, my Dallas visits showed me a friendly and welcoming town that had long since shed its shame about the traumatic events of 1963 and had moved forward. What I saw and experienced—aside from the tremendous welcome and help I received from the women in the groups I was studying—was a traffic-choked, quickly growing, contemporary city on the flat north Texas plains. This was a far cry from the Dallas I'd grown up in, in the 1950s and early 1960s. As a girl, I knew nothing about the three historic women's study clubs that I would discover and visit fifty years later in my old hometown. These clubs are Dallas Shakespeare Club, the Standard Club, and Pierian Club.

I actually made three research visits to Dallas to get what I wanted. On May 23, 2011, my first visit, I was able to pore through the archives of the Dallas Shakespeare Club. I'd located these records after seeing an online press release, which led me eventually to the industrial park home of the Dallas Historical Society on the far north end of town. While I was inside the storage facility of the historical society, doing my research and taking notes, the society's researcher and volunteer coordinator, Susan Richards, told me that they also kept the archives for another historic women's group that was at least a hundred years old and still doing its own programs or papers—the Pierian Club. She was nice enough to contact someone at the club to explain my project and see if the members would be interested in communicating with me. That was the beginning of my connection to Pierian and to club member Marie Chiles, whom Susan had contacted. I would come back to Dallas in November of the same year and visit regularly scheduled meetings of Pierian and the Shakespeare Club, as well as an informal minimeeting of a third group, the Standard Club, that met my requirements.

On a third trip, in February 2012, I attended a second Shakespeare Club meeting and a regularly scheduled meeting of the Standard Club—its 126th anniversary meeting.

During the first Dallas trip in May 2011, I drove downtown to the main branch of the public library. While there, I also did research on another women's group, the Dallas Literary Society, whose helpful contact, Kathy Elkins, invited me to a year-end luncheon at a member's nearby lakeside home. Unfortunately, the group was founded in 1954 and was not old enough to be included in my book. In fact, it was not really a study club in which members gave papers or programs. It was, instead, a book review club with paid book reviewers, a kind of women's club for which Dallas was well-known for many years. In fact, Dallas was the home of at least two massively influential women reviewers who are no longer alive but whose names are still attached to many thriving "classes"—organized women's clubs that schedule speakers on a variety of subjects or do book reviews. The most famous of these women are Emance Rejebian (1906–1989) and Mary K. Craig (1842–1941). Clearly, self-education has held a longtime appeal for Dallas women.

Meeting the Women of Dallas's Three Historic Study Clubs
Dallas Shakespeare Club, May 23, 2011, November 4, 2011, and February 24, 2012

Scrambling to find my way and to arrive on time at the address I'd been given for my first Dallas Shakespeare Club meeting, I parked in front of a classic two-story home in the upscale University Park section of Dallas and was greeted at the front door by the club president, Susan "Suki" Jarzemsky, and by the home's owner, Jenifer Flynn, who was the meeting's hostess. I quickly took a seat among forty tastefully dressed women who were already seated in the home's den, waiting for the meeting to begin. It was just past 2:30 on a balmy Friday, November 4, 2011, and this was the meeting of the oldest literary society in Dallas, having been founded in January 1886. One other surviving literary society in Dallas, the Standard Club, was founded one month after Dallas Shakespeare Club.

First, Suki called the meeting to order and gave a brief rundown of member news. Roll was then called and answered by "here" or "present" or with a quotation from the year's chosen Shakespeare play, *Othello.* One woman used a quotation from *Othello,* "Was someone as beautiful as you meant to be a whore?", and was rewarded with the sound of conspiratorial laughter from her colleagues. I knew that using a quotation from the author being studied to answer roll call was common in the early days of similar literary societies.

Attendance at meetings is important. Members of Dallas Shakespeare Club must religiously attend the thirteen bimonthly meetings, held between late September and mid-April, as did their Victorian-era predecessors. If they miss three of these meetings without an excuse during a half-year term, then they will, in the words of their constitution, "forfeit their membership."[1]

The brief business portion of this meeting, which would culminate with the reading of act 3 of *Othello* by a cast of members, was moved along swiftly and efficiently by Suki, who spoke in a jolly, upbeat voice. A teacher in various Dallas schools and outreach programs over the years, she had already been a tremendous help to me. In May, she had efficiently and graciously pulled together seven club members to meet with me and to cover basic information about the group. At the end of that meeting, the women gave me leads to another historic literary society in Dallas—the Standard Club—and, even better, the name of a personal contact in that group. It was during that same trip to Dallas that I paid a call to the downtown main branch of the Dallas Public Library, where the Shakespeare Club's 1986 gift to Dallas—a Shakespeare First Folio, commemorating the club's hundredth anniversary—is ensconced in its own elegant and dimly lit room, which was decorated and furnished with the help of the club.

Today, a Shakespeare First Folio is worth several million dollars. The most recent sale of a different First Folio was for $3.87 million, and some copies are valued at $15 million. This extraordinary gift

45

was spearheaded by Mrs. A. Earl Cullum Jr., the mother of a current member, Margaret Anne Cullum, who attended my first informal meeting in May and who was the actor or reader with the part of Casio in the presentation of act 3 of *Othello* at the November meeting.

As with all of the clubs in this book, Dallas Shakespeare is private and one must be asked to join. The members will readily tell you that it helps if you have a mother, sister, grandmother, mother-in-law, or aunt who was a member. After Googling a few of the club's members, I would add that it might also help to have graduated from Hockaday, the prestigious all-girls' school in far north Dallas, although this appears to be merely an asset, not an guarantee of or requirement for membership. After all, this is how these groups form: from interest groups and shared affiliations within communities. The founding members in 1886 were said to be either Presbyterian or Episcopalian,[2] and I would guess that today's members are mostly from families who worshipped at mainline Protestant churches.

When Dallas Shakespeare was founded, the club found itself in the midst of a great women's movement in this country, a movement to self-educate and to form groups to make group self-education possible. Members' efforts to read all there was on a particular subject, as assigned by a committee or by one of the group's officers, was made even more difficult by the fact that when most of these groups started, there were no public libraries. For this reason, members of many of these groups, Dallas Shakespeare included, helped found the first public libraries in their young towns with the help of Andrew Carnegie, who reached out to the women's literary clubs to get the ball rolling. I found this to be the case in Dallas, Birmingham, Eugene, and other towns I visited or researched long-distance.

One of this group's strengths and a reason for its survival is the seriousness with which its members take their club's history and stated objectives. Their constitution says of the club, "Its objects shall be a thorough and earnest study of Shakespeare, the drama, and general literature."[3]

The following sonnet written by member Anne Coke, printed here with her permission, is one of seven clever odes to the group that she composed in an English or Shakespearean rhyme scheme during the club's 2006–07 season, when the group studied the Bard of Avon's sonnets. It neatly illustrates the point about group loyalty:

> It is said that if a member killed her spouse
> In a fit of pique or anger or in sport,
> The Shakespeare Club would boldly brand him "louse"
> Attend the trial in droves to lend support.
> "She did *not* do it," loudly chants our chorus:
> "No member of *our* club would smite him dead:
> Your accusations, well, they frankly bore us:
> We know it was an accident instead."
> What is it generates such staunch devotion
> Or overlooking faults some piddling, some enormous?
> It is the Shakespeare Club which sets in motion
> A fond, supportive group whose love will form us.
> As yet no murder's been committed,
> But if there were, we'd get our girl acquitted.
>
> —Anne Schoellkopf Coke

The members of Shakespeare Club take great pride in current and past members and in the group's history. During my first exploratory meeting in May with a few members of the group, several of them had piped up with historical tidbits. One told me that May Exall, the first president, was a student at Vassar during Custer's Last Stand in 1876. She served as president for the first fifty years of the club, from 1886 to 1936. Her great-granddaughter-in-law Marion Exall sat on my left at the May meeting and had served the group as president in 2001–02.

I was also told that the Dallas Shakespeare Club's tremendously bright, active, and then 99-year-old member (now 103 years old), Margaret McDermott, who was married to Eugene McDermott, one of the founders of Texas Instruments, was once the society editor of the *Dallas Morning News* and worked as a journalist in occupied Japan and Germany after the end of WWII. I later discovered that she is about to have a new bridge over the Trinity River, designed by Santiago Calatrava, named after her—the Margaret McDermott Bridge, to be completed by the year 2017.[4] Margaret, sometimes through the foundation named for her and her husband, Eugene, has given a vast number of works of art to the Dallas Museum of

Art. Many of them are iconic masterpieces that I enjoyed seeing on a recent visit.

The women in the minimeeting also told me that the Dallas Shakespeare Club is mentioned as "the club to be in" in the pages of the novel *A Woman of Independent Means*—a story set mostly in Dallas during the early 1900s that follows its heroine (played by Sally Field in a television miniseries) into the 1960s.

The list of professional and civic accomplishments among Dallas Shakespeare Club's members is a long one, and, as in every one of the other literary societies, fortnightly clubs, and Shakespeare clubs I visited, the members are the absolute bedrock of local organizations. But no one here makes a big splash. They contribute quietly and help hold the community and civilization together.

I met many of these women during the November meeting, including a few whom I will describe in the coming pages. As the meeting carried forward, I was charmed and stimulated by each woman's part in the afternoon. Even the recording secretary, "Schatzie" (Natalie) Lee, an art historian and author, showed a combination of wit, wisdom, and dramatic zest when she read her minutes from the group's prior meeting.

At one point, Schatzie cleverly cited the action during the reading of an act of *Othello* by reporting, "Mrs. Mackintosh's trumpeting sounds announced her own appearance." (Prudence Mackintosh, a noted writer and an adjunct professor at the University of Texas, was playing both a herald and a second senator in that earlier reading.) At the end of her amusing and definitive minutes, Schatzie even noted the pattern on the china on which the final teatime treats had been served.

Schatzie Lee is an example of one reason that some of these historic groups have survived. I have come to believe that the sheer force of key members' personality, intelligence, wit, and charm holds their group together and makes the groups desirable to join—that and a certain social cachet. I saw it all around me at the November meeting. Who wouldn't want to sit with these bright, funny, happy, well-connected women and learn something at the same time?

In all of the groups I found, the road to membership is carefully laid out in the constitution and bylaws. For Dallas Shakespeare Club, a membership committee receives letters of recommendation for candidates for active and honorary membership.[5] There are rather elaborate rules for voting on the prospective members, which is done at one meeting in February.

During the roll call at the November meeting, Suki used "Miss" or "Mrs." before each member's last name. At the end of that (and all) meetings, when tea was served, members used each other's first names. It is one of the entrenched traditions of the group and of many other groups just like it across the country. Another Dallas Shakespeare Club tradition, handwriting all invitations and correspondence in purple ink, has finally been replaced with printed postcards and Internet communications. Purple seems to have been chosen because the club's original colors were purple and gold, although that is my theory, based on my study of the club's archives, and not a fact that any member could confirm.

After roll call at the November meeting, member Harriet Stoneham, one of the fall directors, introduced the action to come in act 3 of *Othello* and explained what to expect. Suki later told me that there are three fall directors and three spring directors. The play chosen for the year is given a dramatic reading, act by act, in the fall term, and then members and, sometimes, a guest speaker deliver original papers on the chosen play in the spring term. "The fall directors direct the play and take turns introducing the acts and handling the play each meeting," Suki said. "The spring ones arrange for and introduce the speakers." Providing other pointers at the November meeting, Harriet also talked about the concept of a MacGuffin, a favorite Hitchcock device, and said that Desdemona's lost handkerchief would be the MacGuffin—an object that drives the plot.

Once the play reading began, Margret Cullum stood with the other readers with a sign hung around her neck identifying her as Casio. All of the readers, identified as a character by wearing similar signs, stood to read their parts, faced the audience of their peers while reading, and then sat when they were finished. Jane Hancock was in modified military dress for her role as Othello. She was sporting what I was later told was one of her son's military uniform dress jackets, which he wore while serving in Afghanistan. She was also wearing tall leather boots and trousers. There was a clown or jester in the lineup, wearing a colorful foolscap, and there was a bit of a ringer in the person of Gloria Hocking, who is both an actress and a Shakespeare Club member. Ms. Hocking was reading the part of Iago. Desdemona was read by Marion Exall, whose great-grandmother-in-law was the founding president of Dallas Shakespeare Club.

The reading went smoothly, with some of the women's delivery marked by soft, north Texas accents. In between acts, Harriet stood to explain what would happen at one point, saying that the handkerchief would be used as proof against Desdemona, showing her infidelity to Othello. After explaining that Othello will ask Desdemona to swear that she has been faithful, Harriet said, "The pledge is the climax of the play. Othello is turned from hero to villain with this pledge."

Some of the members were following the action by looking at their personal copies of the play. All were watching and listening intently. I saw no one sleeping. At 3:15, our hostess, Jenifer Flynn, silently slipped out of the den through its sliding doors and went into her dining room, where a catering staff was setting up the tea delicacies on her dining room table.

Back in the den, where the play was being read, "Emilia"—member Lou Sabo—finally picked up Desdemona's dropped handkerchief. Every eye was on her, as all of us in the audience knew that Iago would be using the handkerchief to impeach Desdemona's good name with her husband, Othello. We all clapped when the act reading came to an end, after which most of the women hopped up and headed to the dining room for chatter and tea.

Busy interviewing those around me, I missed the actual tea pouring, but I was later told that Jenifer, our hostess, had served tea from a silver service that had belonged to her mother-in-law, who was a past president of the Dallas Shakespeare Club and who had used the tea service when she hosted meetings. Glancing into the dining room from my spot in the front hall, where I found myself surrounded by members who introduced themselves to me, I could see trays of tiny sandwiches, nuts, and savories, plus the tea set for hot tea and glasses for cold drinks.

Before I was introduced to Margaret McDermott, who had been sitting in front of me during the meeting, Suki reminded me that this longest-active member joined the club in 1962 and would be 100 years old on February 18, 2012. In fact, Margaret turned 100—and then 101, 102, and 103—while I was researching and writing this book. She was feted on her 100th birthday by the Dallas Shakespeare Club and by different groups to which she had contributed over the years as one of Dallas's best-known philanthropists. While writing this book, I've checked on the progress of the bridge across the Trinity River to be named after Margaret. I found that its completion date, originally set at 2013, had been moved to 2017, with much discussion and dissension about its cost and design. As this book was in its final editing process in the summer of 2015, the futuristic steel forms that would eventually form an entire bridge were finally being erected.

As the play-reading ended, members whirled around Margaret, who sat on the couch with a younger woman, Sallie Loop, who told me that she herself was a fourth-generation Shakespeare Club member. Sallie's grandmother Sallie Bell had invited Margaret to join the group when Margaret was heading the board of the Dallas Museum of Fine Arts in the early sixties. Margaret told me that she had been wary of extra entanglements, but she had joined anyway, remaining a devoted member for more than fifty years.

I found Margaret welcoming and happy to talk to me. She was smartly dressed in a suit jacket and slacks. Rather than answering my questions, she kept asking *me* questions. I tried to dodge and weave around these. She then invited me to come to lunch at her house with Suki the next time I was in Dallas. She said that she was very happy in her own home—not in a retirement village—and was content to be a homebody now, after years of traveling, especially with her husband, who died in 1973. Then, with a sparkle in her eye, she said, "Let's snoop around!" I declined, but Margaret and Sallie headed off to explore other rooms on the lower level of the house.

Among the members who introduced themselves to me was author Prudence Mackintosh, whose humorous books and magazine articles about raising her sons in Dallas and about her long-running book group were sent to me by my mother in Dallas when I was raising my sons in suburban Chappaqua, New York, and attending my own long-running book group. Prudence and the other women swirling around me during the social hour were beautiful, slim, and well-groomed. Seemingly, these club members had all found the fountain of youth. There were only a few gray or white heads in the room, and I found myself wondering if these lively, intelligent women who were (I believe) at least in their fifties had discovered that the best tonic as one ages is studying, researching, writing, and, of course, getting together on a regular basis with good friends.

Most of the members had left the November meeting by 4:00 p.m. I stood in the front hall with Suki and Jenifer. Suki made sure that I understood that I would be welcome at the group's March 9 meeting, when member Anne Coke would deliver an original paper entitled "Iago: Deceit, Revenge, or Jealousy?" as a part of the spring series of member-driven lectures. As mentioned before, these papers always refer to and discuss the play read in the first half of the year, which is called the "fall term."

Instead, I had to schedule a visit to Dallas in late February and would be hearing a paper delivered by a guest speaker, Raphael Perry, director of the organization called Shakespeare Dallas, on "Racial Perceptions in the Portrayal of *Othello.*" Shakespeare Dallas, which has no affiliation with Dallas Shakespeare Club, has been presenting the Bard's plays, inexpensively and in open-air amphitheaters, in Dallas since 1971. I didn't mind hearing a guest speaker, but I didn't want to do it more than once. I thought it might show me what the nonmember-led meetings were like.

Before I walked out the door after the November meeting, I asked about the caterer for the meeting and was told that two club members, Mimi McKnight and Byrd Teague, were partners in the catering company helping with today's tea table. I was also told that Mimi was a friend of the author Alexander McCall Smith and that he had dedicated *The Ladies' Number One Detective Agency* to her and her husband, the latter of whom had served on the Southern Methodist University (SMU) faculty with Smith in the late 1980s. Smith also used the couple's names as characters' names in another book, *The Right Attitude to Rain.*

As fascinating as this generation of club members was, I had already found the previous generations of club members to be equally so. Finding out about them had been made easy by the archivist at the Dallas Historical Society and by the members of the club, who had already done a great job writing their own history and preserving their files and yearbooks over the years.

Nearly every group I encountered when I was writing this book had small, carefully printed yearbooks dating back to their founding, and many groups had printed histories of their group, researched and written by club members who were interested, and often trained, in historic research. In fact, I found that several of the groups I met with had historians as members who had published books on historic subjects. For some reason, the study clubs called fortnightlies often seemed to be in college or university towns. These clubs had many members who were married to faculty members, who were themselves on the faculty, or who had retired from teaching. Perhaps their academic connections made for a clear understanding of the value of keeping and preserving archives and the need for accurate histories of the groups.

My search for the history of the Dallas Shakespeare group began with a set of histories done by club members over the years, housed in the Dallas Historical Society. In a report done by committee members in 1956, I found a fairly concise history, thanks largely to the fact that the club's every move in the early days was reported in the local newspapers. I felt this might be because of the social status of its members and perhaps the scarcity of news sources in a day before home radios, television, and Internet—even before most homes had telephones. Those days—referred to by some as a more gentle time, "after plumbing, but before taxes"[6]—were the true heyday of women's study clubs.

In January 1886, Mamie Trezevant, described as a "young matron from St. Louis,"[7] was hoping to start a group to educate herself and other women in Dallas, which was then a railroad town of about thirty-five thousand people. She is remembered today as the founding mother of the Dallas Shakespeare Club and as the first wife of J. T. Trezevant, a prominent Dallas insurance man, a former colonel in the Confederate army, and the founder of many social institutions, among them the Dallas Golf and Country Club. Mamie and her friend Miss Miriam Morgan drove around Dallas in Mamie's dogcart, delivering invitations to a mysterious meeting at the town's most prestigious hotel, the now defunct Grand Windsor.[8] What kind of dog was pulling the dogcart has been lost to time, but I can imagine the two women in their floor-length coats and dresses, with huge hats pinned on top of artfully arranged hairdos, driving along unpaved, possibly muddy, roads, carrying their mysterious but beautifully penned invitations, full of plans for a more enlightened future.

In the 1880s, East Coast businesses were sending executives to head up their Dallas divisions. The result of this was that the city soon gained a reputation for being more Yankee in its sensibilities than other Texas towns. The women who were married to the men who headed divisions of East Coast businesses were said to be well-educated, well-traveled, and interested in keeping sharp.[9] It was these women whom Mamie Trezevant hoped to interest in a literary society like the ones she had seen in other cities that were a result of the women's club movement of that era.

The meeting at the Windsor Hotel went well. Mamie Trezevant told the young women who had gathered there about her idea of forming a weekly study club focused on "a thorough and earnest study of Shakespeare, the drama, and general literature"[10]—the first of its kind in Dallas and one of the first in Texas. On January 28, the group met again and elected Miss May Dickson as their president. She had graduated from Vassar six years earlier and was well-known as a woman with a brain and organizational ability.[11] May Dickson married in 1887 and became one of Dallas's most influential movers and shakers as Mrs. Henry Exall. She was the president and the only program planner for the Shakespeare Club for its first fifty years, until her death. That work is now done by sixteen officers and directors. She also helped to found the Dallas Federation of Women's Clubs, the Dallas Public Library—with the assistance of Andrew Carnegie and his nationwide public library building scheme—and the Dallas Museum of Fine Arts.[12] There have been Exalls in the group since its formation.

For its first seventy years, the club met every Friday from October to April. It wasn't until 1956 that they began meeting every other Friday afternoon.[13] They have studied a wide range of subjects over the years—not just Shakespeare, as they do today. In the group's constitution, the object is stated as "a thorough and earnest study of Shakespeare, the drama, and general literature."[14]

In the wartime years of 1942–43, the club studied an astonishing array of subjects, dramatic and otherwise: *Antony and Cleopatra* by William Shakespeare, *Caesar and Cleopatra* by George Bernard

Shaw, *All for Love* by John Dryden (a treatment of the Antony and Cleopatra story), *Shakespeare in America,* a landmark book by Esther Cloudman Dunn, and *War and Peace* by Leo Tolstoy— perhaps to gain an understanding of their own wartime years. In addition to these works of literature, they also covered the topics "Recent News Developments," "Ruling Political Organizations," "Geography of the Battlefront," "Modern Chinese Literature," "Brief News from India," and more.[15]

Music—usually, members' singing or playing the piano or violin— was also once a part of many special meetings and club celebrations, but this is no longer the case. I found that musical interludes were common in the earliest days of many of the clubs I studied. In this club's early years, its members often staged elaborate celebrations, e.g., Shakespearean revels with costumes, to which the public might be invited, and equally elaborate *tableaux vivants,* a nineteenth-century concept in which famous scenes are posed by actors in costume, completely frozen in place and silent, much like a living snapshot. There were also competitions to see which woman knew the most Shakespeare quotations and the like. And for over eighty years, there was a Texas Independence Day celebration.

Texas Independence Day is an annual legal holiday in Texas. It commemorates the adoption of the Texas Declaration of Independence on March 2, 1836, on which date settlers in Texas officially broke free from Mexico and created the Republic of Texas. In 1959, the club stopped observing the day with a traditional luncheon and a Texas-based program.[16] A few other traditions have also disappeared in these more sophisticated times. This is a common trend among these historic clubs.

There are many more demands on a woman's time today; therefore, this club, and many others, has pared down its yearly schedule and simplified its procedures. But still, each year there are twelve or thirteen meetings of Dallas Shakespeare, with one being an opening luncheon and business meeting in late September, the latter being a meeting that includes voting on new members. Meetings then come every two weeks. As mentioned earlier, the chosen Shakespeare play is read in the fall term and is followed by papers or programs about the play in the spring term. Since the club's founding, there has always been a special luncheon in January.

This meeting now combines celebrations for the club's birthday and Shakespeare's birthday. The final meeting in April is another luncheon and business meeting called the president's luncheon, which takes place at the president's house. The other luncheons are typically held at a local country club or in Arlington Hall in Lee Park. Arlington Hall is a replica of General Robert E. Lee's Virginia home. A statue of Lee, dressed in his Confederate uniform and astride his trusty horse, Traveller, stands in the park, which is nestled in one of Dallas's prettiest areas, the banks of Turtle Creek, not far from the meeting place for my November visit. The Shakespeare Club has used the park and Arlington Hall for its celebrations, large and small, since its earliest days.

The Dallas Morning News carried the following account of the Shakespeare Club's celebration of the three hundredth anniversary of Shakespeare's death, on April 30, 1916, with the headline, "Homage to Bard Done by Revelers."[17]

> Several thousand persons, witnessing the festival commemorating the tricentenary [*sic*] of the death of William Shakespeare at Oak Lawn Park [now called Lee Park] yesterday afternoon, were carried back to the days when great Fletcher [Author's Note: Elizabethan actor, Lawrence Fletcher[18]] trod in buskin. Beautiful scenes were presented in the Dallas Shakespeare Club Festival. There were several hundred revelers, costumed as shepherds, fairies, jesters, rogues, nymphs, harvesters, dancers, pages, and heralds accompanied by appropriate music from the Elizabethan period, as they trooped and bowed across the woodland stages.[19]

Aside from the women of the Shakespeare Club, the celebration included children and young people from several private schools, and one dancing group. They presented tableaux or scenes from plays and danced to period music around a maypole. The weather was pronounced "perfect," as was everything else having to do with the spectacle. The newspaper congratulated the women of the Dallas Shakespeare Club, "under whose auspices the performance was given."[20]

Club programs might also be made up of a combination of *tableaux vivants* from history, musical interludes with club members playing the piano or violin or singing, and the staging of scenes from Shakespeare's plays. For one of the club's Texas Independence Day celebrations, on March 2, 1917, the *Dallas Morning News* was effusive and long-winded in its descriptions, citing the "love portraits from Texas history" and "pictures from Shakespeare"[21] in flowery language. Rather than being comical, this was the acceptable voice for society editors of the day. The "love portraits" were *tableaux vivants* featuring club members posed inside a gold frame, costumed as different heroes from Texas history, beside their wives or girlfriends. They were glorified as paragons of domesticity and virtue when sometimes the opposite was true.

> The first number on the program entitled "Texas Dawn" was posed by Mrs. Alex Slaughter, who wore brown draperies. The background for the picture was a field of Texas bluebonnets. The closing number of the first part of "Texas Fulfillment" was posed by Mrs. Alfred H. Belo, who wore white draperies and a diadem about her brow.

> Other numbers in the program were "LaSalle and His Indian Sweetheart," posed by Mrs. J. C. Harley and Miss Marie Everman; "William B. Travis and His Girl Wife," posed by Mrs. J. P. Haven and Mrs. Alex Camp; "James Bowie and Maria Vermendi," Mrs. Dero Seay and Miss Mary Aldridge; "David Crockett and His Quaker Maid," Mrs. J. C. Robertson and Mrs. B. C. Epperson; [and] "Sam Houston and Margaret Moffett Lea," Mrs. Robert Ralston and Mrs. H. C. Bramley.

> In Part Two, the following living pictures were shown: "Antony and Cleopatra," Mrs. Alex Coke and Mrs. W. W. Caruth; "The Merry Wives of Windsor," Mrs. E. Callier and Mrs. J. S. Kendall; [and] "Paulina and Hermione from *A Winter's Tale*," Miss Marie Irvine and Mrs. J. W. Rogers.[22]

The description of the Shakespearean scenes continues for another ten lines, followed by a paragraph describing the members who played the piano and the violin between scenes. Of course, refreshments followed the program, and they were described in the article. Today, meetings and luncheons are much simpler and well below the radar of the press and nonmembers, and that is the way the club likes it. There are no *tableaux vivants* and no musical interludes—just readings of plays, research papers by members, or lectures by outside authorities on the plays, which are done in businesslike meetings held every other week in season, plus the same three luncheons every year. The club calendar for 2011–12 shows regular readings, act by act, of *Othello* in the fall term, followed by papers or programs about *Othello* in the spring term, plus three luncheons. As mentioned, the member's paper I was sorry to have missed was Anne Coke's, entitled "Iago: Deceit, Revenge, or Jealousy?"[23]

Of the occasional non-Shakespearean topics I heard and read about, my favorite was one delivered by club member Paula Mosle in the 1980s entitled "The O," discussing sexuality. Paula, a graduate of prestigious Rice University in Houston, requested that she be allowed to cover the subject, as it was one she had always found fascinating. The members who spoke to me about this were proud of this very intellectual member who, they said, "brought them into modern times." Then, they added that it was the seemingly unstoppable Margaret McDermott who first wore a pants suit to a Shakespeare Club meeting, in the 1980s, thereby ending the need for dresses every other Friday—another lurch into the modern world and a big change from tradition.

Another modernization has been in the area of charity. Outreach today is nothing like the civic warfare of the club's earlier days, when they and similar groups all over the country got together to convince their town and Andrew Carnegie's organization to build and fund the first public library in their area. Or they might join together to bring about the building of the town's first art museum or the founding of a local federation of women's clubs.

This type of civic housekeeping is no longer performed by any of the independent historic study clubs I encountered. Today, the Shakespeare Club quietly manages its Sally Dickson Scholarship Fund, begun in 1927 and named after the first president's mother.[24] It was originally used for individual scholarships for deserving students. Recipients from past years include John Lundsford, a former art museum director and curator, and Randy Moore, who was said to be Dallas's finest actor[25] and who recently played Falstaff in a production of *Henry IV,* much to the delight of local theater critics.[26]

Today, managed and dispersed by the Communities Foundation of Texas and constrained by more modern tax codes and laws that require the fund to go to 501(c)(3) organizations, Sally Dickson Awards no longer go to individuals. Instead, they go to charitable groups. Members told me that there were six recipient groups in 2010–11: Dallas Historical Society; Dallas Institute for Humanities; Emily Ann Theatre and Gardens (a summer high school Shakespeare program in Wimberley, Texas, a town which suffered from severe flooding while this book was being edited, late May of 2015); Friends of the Dallas Public Library; Shakespeare Dallas; and William B. Travis TAG Academy.

Members repeatedly told me that they were proud of their group and all it stands for, especially because it has stood the test of time. Citing it as an ever-friendly refuge, one member wrote in 1954 (sixty-one years ago, but relevant today):

> Through the changing world of carriages and coachmen on quiet streets to that of a modern city with its crowded thoroughfares, automobile parking problems ... the Dallas Shakespeare Club meetings, in the homes of its members, with the challenge of writing-it-yourself papers, and the ever fresh appeal of Shakespeare, is a refuge, indeed, from the chaotic world of today.[27]

At the mid-May minimeeting, various members told me why they think their group has survived:

- "The group is fun."
- "You're expected to participate."
- "We like the people in it."
- "The group is very supportive. You could read the phone book instead of a paper, and we wouldn't bat an eye."
- "You'll have fifty-four people at your funeral."
- "It's a sweet club and a supportive club."
- "I wouldn't miss a meeting."

- "When you're at a meeting, it's like you've left the rest of the world."
- "The members are all individuals. We often don't know each other before we join, but we get to know each other well after we do."

Add to this the discipline of research, writing, and critical thinking, and you might start to understand how Shakespeare Club has survived and flourished since 1886.

The Pierian Club, November 2, 2011

The wind was blowing with such force that I was virtually swept across the street from the parking structure where I'd left my rental car. I was back in north Dallas, about to enter one tower of a newish high-rise apartment complex called The Heights at Park Lane, located conveniently near a chic and gargantuan mall, North Park Center. North Texas can be hit by sudden and violent storms, combining a powerful rush of cold air, hail, and rain—a weather system we used to call "northers" when I was a girl growing up in Dallas—but this was just wind. The bright, blue sky was dotted with benign white clouds, and the temperature was mild for this November meeting of the Pierian Club, which was then 123 years old.

Pierian member Marie Chiles, who was my contact for the club, met me at the elevator a few minutes before one o'clock, introduced herself to me, and took me immediately into a bright and very contemporary meeting room on the fifth floor, the Aqua Lounge, which looked out onto a rooftop swimming pool. Already seated in rows of folding chairs and waiting for me were the women of Pierian, nicely dressed in suits or tailored pants outfits and ready for Marie's introduction of me, to be followed by my explanation of my book project.

I plunged right in, explaining to the thirty-five women assembled before me what my book was about and why I thought the subject of historic women's study groups was important. I said that I'd be interested in talking to them after the meeting and that I hoped they would introduce themselves to me. I had been asked to make this introduction at every meeting I attended, so I was getting a bit better at it. I actually found that things went better if I didn't worry about my introduction ahead of time. My natural enthusiasm for the subject would always take over, and the words would come. I finished, thanked the group for allowing me to attend, found an available seat next to Marie, and sat down. The nuts and bolts of the meeting began.

Throughout the meeting, the glass doors in the Aqua Lounge rattled, howled, and sometimes banged open with violent force. The persistent noise from the wind supplied an uncivilized soundtrack for the very civilized meeting going on inside.

The Pierian Club was founded in 1888 as the Chautauqua Literary and Scientific Circle, and for twenty-five years it followed the extension course given by the *Chautauqua Magazine*.[28] The club then disassociated itself from the Chautauqua movement and its highly organized and standardized approach to adult education. The women set off on their own, having already taken their present name from a classical allusion—the Pierian Spring, said to be in ancient Greece, which inspired those who drank from it.[29] The following verses by Alexander Pope appear in the Pierian Club yearbook, in a section called "Our Pierian Heritage":

> A little learning is a dangerous thing;
> Drink deep or taste not the Pierian Spring;
> Thin shallow draughts intoxicate the brain,
> And drinking largely sobers us again.[30]

It seems to be typical of many of these early literary clubs that their members elevated a strong leader and stuck with her. In this case, Pierian Club's founder, Susan Downs Ardrey,[31] wife of Alexander C. Ardrey, a Dallas alderman who had fought in the Civil War on the Confederate side,[32] served as the club's first president until she died, eleven years after the club's founding in 1888. To get the club organized, Susan Downs Ardrey had gathered nine women to pursue the Chautauqua course of study, and together they studied the history of various foreign countries, literature, art, music, economics, and politics.[33] In keeping with the "strong woman" pattern established by Mrs. Ardrey, a second leader took over after the founder's death. This was a woman cleverly named Katie Muse, who served as Pierian's president for twenty-six years.[34]

The group has one of the best mottos I heard while researching this book, "I rest, I rust," which sums up the reason why women chose to do the hard work of belonging to these literary societies. Pierian has also held onto its official colors (white and green) and flower (Cape jasmine).[35] Many of the surviving groups I found had forgotten these rather antiquated bits of their club history.

At the wind-punctuated November 2011 meeting that I attended, the current president, Carolyn Miller, explained that the membership needed to vote on a new member. Carolyn then read off the prospective member's accomplishments and volunteer activities, which were extensive and impressive. Paper ballots were passed out, marked, and returned to be counted. The club's recording secretary, Jane Bates, beautifully dressed and perfectly groomed, then made her way to the front of the room to read the minutes from the previous meeting. At the end, she read, "The meeting was adjourned, and tea was served," and then gave the directions to the next meeting.

Carolyn Rogers, program chair, came to the front of the room and talked a bit about the safari vest she was wearing, which she had been required to buy and wear during a recent trip to South Sudan, the world's youngest nation, having gained its independence in 2011. "No purses," their guide had stressed to the women in the group. She showed us South Sudan on a map and then introduced Barbara Taylor, the day's speaker, who would be covering health in Africa as part of the year's concentration on Africa.

The year's first program had been held at the Ibex Ethiopian Restaurant, and the program, which was given by Mrs. Rogers that day, was entitled "Now Voyager." The title, printed in the group's yearbook, caught my eye as being clever and possibly referring to a film gem—the 1942 Bette Davis movie by the same name, based on a novel by Olive Higgins Prouty, which took its title from two poems by Walt Whitman found in different editions of Whitman's ongoing *Leaves of Grass* poetry collection: "Now Finale to the Shore" and "The Untold Want." In the first, Whitman wrote the following:

Now finale to the shore!
Now land and life, finale, and farewell!
Now Voyager depart! (Much more for thee is yet in store)[36]

As with all of the programs listed in the Pierian yearbook, the bare facts of each meeting—the date, the hostesses, the location of the meeting, the subject to be covered, and the member who would deliver her program or paper on the subject—all are followed by a relevant quotation. For the "Now Voyager" program, Mrs. Rogers had chosen a quotation from a website called Feint and Margin, which describes itself as being "a weekly, online, Pan-African publication featuring writings and thoughts from Ordinary Africans who have Extraordinary minds. We represent the True Voice of the African Citizen."[37]

Here is an insightful and completely original (to my very American mind) quotation from Feint and Margin's October 2010 piece by African writer Kate Nkansa, entitled "It's Time for Africans to Tour Africa": "I often listen to Africans speaking and boasting about how many European countries they have been to. They, however, fail to mention one African country they have visited. ... Westerners know more about our beautiful continent than Africans."[38]

To my mind, this was a wonderfully thought-provoking quotation to start a listing of the year's programs. I mentally gave Pierian's program committee high marks. In fact, I thought that every quotation under every listing of programs in the Pierian yearbook for 2011–12 was just as intriguing.

At the November 2011 meeting, the speaker, Barbara Taylor, covered "Health in Africa" and did a good job explaining the progress of the fight against HIV and AIDS, other sexually transmitted diseases, malaria, tuberculosis, and childhood and maternal diseases. She discussed the efforts to combat these diseases in Kenya, Zimbabwe, Ethiopia, and Tanzania. At first, she read from her carefully written report, and then she delivered it without having to refer to her text. She talked knowledgeably and comfortably about new hospitals, efforts to establish clean water supplies, and efforts to provide birth control to women who want it. She also touched on the role of Doctors Without Borders and on mission teams and other groups that travel to Africa to help. Throughout her report, Barbara Taylor was competing with the banging of the doors in the wind, but she did not seem to let it bother her.

At the end of Barbara's program, Carolyn Rogers stood again and quickly put in context the medical assistance that Africans receive from Western countries, saying, "There is a downside to all of this medical assistance, although there is no right or wrong, no clear answer. We save the kids, and they become reproductive adolescents who become adults with no jobs. We have made these people unsatisfied. Also, there is never enough water."

The meeting was adjourned. The members moved to a tea table, which had been set up at the front of the meeting room. My contact, Marie Chiles, brought me a slice of tiramisu and a cold drink. I talked to several members who introduced themselves and talked with me about what Pierian has meant to them in intellectual terms. One member, Claire Cunningham, had joined in the 1960s and remembered "doing Lewis and Clark two years before the two hundredth anniversary of their expedition, so we were way ahead of the curve." She was chairwoman that year—2002—and was so inspired that she mapped out a car trip along the Lewis and Clark National Historic Trail with her husband, daughter, and two granddaughters, which they completed successfully and happily, going from historic site to historic site, "by the seat of [their] pants."

There is also a forty-member offshoot of the Pierian Club, and I found that members of the two clubs I had already visited actually knew the offshoot group better than they knew the parent club. The group is the Junior Pierians, and they are strictly a book review group and are too new to be covered in detail in this book of hundred-year-old groups. Marie Chiles explained to me in our first telephone interview that the junior group is made up of younger women (currently required to be at least thirty-eight years old, but not older than forty-seven) and said that when it was founded for the daughters of Pierian members in 1924, it was meant to be a "feed-in group" to supply members to the parent club. However, that no longer happens. When Junior Pierian members reach the age of forty-eight, they must leave the club. Marie told me that she is wary of the aging of the senior Pierians and wishes that the junior group would make the transition, as intended by its founders.

The president of the Junior Pierians in 2011, Ledee Sachs, told me that the group members read contemporary literature. She also said that the summer reading chairperson has the toughest job, compiling a list of forty fiction and forty nonfiction books published in the last twelve months. Members sign up to read and report on these books, with two twenty-minute reports presented at meetings every other week during the school year, and one forty-minute book review presented four times a year. Junior Pierians' meetings are held from 12:30 p.m. to 2:00 p.m., because, as Ledee told me, "We are all mothers." All of them need to be ready for carpooling and other after-school activities.[39]

The Standard Club, November 3, 2011, and February 28, 2012

All of the seven meetings of the Standard Club each year start with a luncheon at 12:00 noon. The Standard Club's 126th anniversary luncheon meeting, which I attended, was held on a gray but mild February day in the traditional, pink brick home of the club's past president Sue John, in the Highland Park section of Dallas. Sue was also a member of an informal group of Standard members who had gathered to be interviewed in November 2011. She greeted me with a hug as I walked through her door. Her home's decor was both lovely and welcoming, with a stunning collection of porcelain displayed throughout the downstairs rooms. I was immediately urged by that year's president, Gayle Allison, to put my purse on a chair in the "red room"—a small library to the left of the front door—in order to save myself a seat at one of the tables that were set up for lunch service in several of the downstairs rooms.

As with every group I visited, Standard Club's members had arrived well in advance of the meeting time and were ready to start. Lunch service came first and began very close to the 12:00 noon starting time for the meeting. I managed to eat and take notes as I talked to the nine other women at my table about legacies and family connections to the group. Our lunch was Mexican: enchiladas, slaw, black beans, and flan for dessert. Service was quick—instantaneous, really—to get the meal over and done with so that the actual meeting could begin. The caterer was Standard Club's usual, Spice of Life Catering, listed on page three of the group's yearbook. I got the impression that the caterers knew how to be quick and efficient for this particular group.

We finished our meal and adjourned to the living room, which was highlighted by huge bay windows looking out over an extensive back garden. There were about thirty women, who quickly seated themselves in rows of chairs and were then poised and ready for the meeting to begin.

Because it was the club's 126th anniversary, President Gayle Allison introduced Sue Lebowitz, the entertainment cochair, whose job it was to take us back in time to the club's founding. She read newspaper articles from 1886 and 1890, as no minutes from that period have survived. Sue explained that in those early times, the club secretary would take the minutes to the society editor of the *Dallas Morning News,* and then the newspaper would print an account of the meeting. Sue told us that one columnist from those days wrote, "The Standard Club balances Senior Scholarship with elegant entertaining."

Members were then reminded that checks for the club's scholarship fund for art students at SMU were due at the meeting. After that, the slate for the coming year was announced and approved. An honorary member (an active member who becomes honorary has fewer responsibilities—a custom in virtually every group I found) was proposed, and this motion passed. President Allison pointed out, "That leaves a space for an active member, so send me your letters of proposal." This was of interest to me, as it meant that the club was at capacity, with all active membership slots filled. This was not always the case with the groups I found as I researched this book. Many groups in other cities and towns were hard-pressed to find women, especially younger women, who wanted to do the work involved and who also had the time.

Member Mary Lynn Ryder introduced the speaker for the day, Susan Hawkins, by providing a biographical sketch. As I traveled around the country, I saw this practiced in several other groups: having one member give a bio of the speaker before the woman being introduced delivered the program for the day. Mary Lynn gave Susan's background in very broad strokes and then explained that the paper Susan would present about Freya Stark was entitled "Passionate Nomad," which is also the title of a biography of Stark by Jane Fletcher Geniesse. The overall theme of study that year was "Remarkable Women—Extraordinary Lives, Extraordinary Careers," which included programs on Maria Callas (the famous—and eventually infamous—opera singer who performed several times in Dallas in the 1950s) and Émilie du Châtelet (French author, mathematician, and physicist who lived in the 1700s and was a translator of Sir Isaac Newton's most important work).

To begin her report, Susan asked how many in the group had heard of Freya Stark. Only a few hands went up. Susan said she also read Stark's book *The Southern Gates of Arabia* in preparation for her paper on this extraordinary British explorer and travel writer, and she gave a succinct summary of the author's dramatic life and career, which ended with Stark's death at a hundred years old in 1993. Stark worked almost to the end of her life, publishing her final work in her early nineties. Susan's paper summing up her life took about thirty minutes to deliver.

I was then called on to stand and talk about my book. There was a pleased response, especially to the title. The meeting was finished by 2:00. I drove myself to Dallas/Ft. Worth Airport for my flight back home to Los Angeles.

Before this regularly scheduled meeting, I had also attended an informal minimeeting on November 3, 2011, of a few Standard Club members at the Highland Park home of President Gayle Allison, arranged by the club's extremely knowledgeable historian, Jackie McElhaney, who was my principal contact for the group. Jackie and Gayle were longtime friends and former college roommates at nearby SMU an unbelievable fifty years ago. This informal meeting was attended by eight members who were past presidents or who were otherwise extremely well-versed in the club's history and traditions. One woman who attended, Mary Frances DeLoache, was at that time the club's longest-active member, having joined in 1966 and having served as president in 1973–74.

Much of the information in this group's snapshot summary at the end of this chapter comes from this informal minimeeting, where I was able to get a feeling for the group, learn of its links to Dallas history, and gain a better idea of the group's operation and traditions.

I was also able to fit in a morning of research on the group at the wonderful DeGolyer Library at SMU the day before that meeting. There, I received invaluable help from Pamalla Anderson, head of public services for DeGolyer and also author of a commemorative booklet about Standard for its 125th anniversary. This library is by far the most elegant and well-run research facility of any I visited anywhere in the country—archival to the max. The Standard Club is lucky to have its archives stored there. Pamalla had all twenty boxes of club archives waiting for me when I made it to the rather grand and dust-free library at 8:30 in the morning. Neiman Marcus department store magnate Stanley Marcus gave the money to establish the Stanley Marcus Room, where I sat to do my research. His portrait hung on a wall, over my shoulder, as I worked. Modernist tapestries also decorated the walls, which were dark wood, polished and glowing in a kind of rarified light, or so it seemed to me. I had also done work on this book in some very dingy—almost prison-like—library archives and storage facilities, so this was a treat.

The Standard Club held its 125th anniversary tea at the DeGolyer Library, where members could look at select archives, old yearbooks, photos, and artifacts. Clearly, the Standard Club has a close relationship with the library and the university.

Flying home from Dallas after the 126th anniversary meeting of the club that day in November 2012, I felt that I'd really covered the three Dallas groups in depth and would probably never be able to top the kind of information I'd been able to find there. Although I never spent more time with any other groups while doing my research, I found myself, as my book project grew and grew, surprised at every turn by the number of historic clubs waiting to be discovered around the country, by their acceptance of me, and by their willingness to share information about their clubs and traditions.

Standard Club (Dallas), circa 1900, photo reprinted by permission
of DeGolyer Library, Southern Methodist University

Standard Club (Dallas), February 20, 2011, 125th anniversary
reception, photo reprinted by permission of DeGolyer Library, SMU

Snapshot Summary of the Dallas Shakespeare Club

1. **Official name of the club:** Dallas Shakespeare Club.
2. **Date founded:** January 28, 1886, making it the oldest literary club in Dallas.
3. **Founder's name and charter members:** Mamie Trezevant, founder, was the first wife of a prominent Dallas insurance man, John Timothee Trezevant, who had been a colonel in the Confederate army and who was a founder and president of the Dallas Country Club.[40] Mamie drove around Dallas in a dogcart in January 1886, accompanied by her friend and soon-to-be charter member Miss Miriam Morgan, delivering invitations to a mysterious meeting, which turned out to be the first organized meeting of the club. The women met in the parlor of the now-defunct Grand Windsor Hotel. There were forty-three charter members, all said to be either Episcopalian or Presbyterian.[41] Miss May Dickson was immediately elected as the group's president and, as Mrs. Henry Exall, remained the president for fifty years. Honoring her contributions to Dallas and to the club, the Shakespeare Club refers to her in its yearbooks and histories as "founder president."[42]
4. **Size of club as stated in bylaws (size limit):** Membership is limited to fifty-five active members and as many honorary members "as the club may elect."[43]
5. **Size of club today, including all categories of membership:** The 2012–13 yearbook lists fifty-five active members and five honorary members.
6. **Meeting schedule:** Recently, the group has started to kick off the year with a luncheon and business meeting on a Friday in late September. Every other Friday at 2:30 p.m., from October to March, they hold twelve meetings covering the reading and discussion of one of Shakespeare's plays. There is only one meeting in December. Luncheon meetings may start at a variety of times. A directors' luncheon, which is also a celebration of the club's and Shakespeare's birthday, is held in January. The president's luncheon and a business

meeting is usually held in April at the president's house. Originally, the group met once a week, on Friday afternoons.

7. **Where they meet:** The club usually meets in members' homes, but the luncheons may be held elsewhere—in a country club or Arlington Hall at Lee Park, for instance. The first meeting of this group I attended was in the University Park neighborhood in the lovely home of a club member whose mother-in-law had also been a member. The second meeting I attended was held in a meeting room of the Nasher Sculpture Center in downtown Dallas's arts district.

8. **Election of new members:** Candidates must have the nomination of one sponsoring member and two seconds. Openings are filled in the spring term, or if they come late in the year, are carried over to the following year. Names of prospective members are read at the first meeting in February and then read again and voted on at the next meeting. This is done by written ballot, with each member voting for all of the nominees of her choice—as many votes as there are vacancies. Those nominees with the most votes are elected.[44]

9. **Object of the club as stated in its constitution:** "Its objects shall be a thorough and earnest study of Shakespeare, the drama, and general literature."[45]

10. **Dues:** Yearly dues are $75.[46] New members also pay a one-time initiation fee of $25.[47]

11. **Club motto:** None found.

12. **Club flower:** None found, although in the early days purple violets and golden chrysanthemums or yellow daffodils and jonquils were often used in luncheon centerpieces, but that was probably to emphasize the club's colors, which are now largely ignored.

13. **Club colors:** Probably purple and gold, but this is my personal theory and not a fact. Until recently, tradition dictated that the corresponding secretary write reminders on purple cards to all members every two weeks. The archives contain purple-bound programs with gold crests, and purple and gold flowers were used for the earliest decorations on tables, so I feel that these were probably the club's original colors.

14. **Paper or program assignment or rotation schedule and hostessing rotation schedule:** The president chooses six directors. The directors choose the play to be studied and, working from a master list of past assignments, assign the papers or speakers. Hostesses are selected by the arrangements chairwoman. The directors host the January luncheon, which celebrates both Shakespeare's birthday and the club's birthday.

15. **Location of the club's archives:** Dallas Historical Society, 12005 Forestgate Dr., Dallas, TX 75243

16. **Civic achievements of the group or its members:**
    - As with many of the groups I studied, Dallas Shakespeare Club's early members helped facilitate Andrew Carnegie's contribution to the city – the building of its first public library. To begin with, the Dallas Shakespeare Club and its intrepid leader, Vassar-educated May Exall, were instrumental in forming the local Federation of Women's Clubs in 1899, which then worked to form a library association, with May Exall at its helm.[48] (The Shakespeare Club no longer belongs to any federation, nor do any of the strictly independent groups I studied.) The library association drummed up citywide support for joining with Mr. Carnegie to fund and maintain a public library.[49] The association authorized Mrs. Exall as their president to write to Andrew Carnegie. She did, thereafter securing $50,000 to build the first library in Dallas.[50] In 1922–23, May Exall and the Shakespeare Club founded the Dallas Woman's Club.[51] Mrs. Exall is also listed as a founder of the Dallas Art Association, the forebear of the current Dallas Museum of Art. According to an article in the Dallas County Heritage Society's *Heritage News,* Mrs. Exall "was basically a shy, private person, and it was largely through her involvement in the Shakespeare Club that she was able to develop the confidence which enabled her to expand her organizational abilities into wider arenas."[52]

- After the death of Mrs. Exall and with the formation of civic improvement and special interest groups, the club ceased to involve itself in public matters and instead concentrated on being a study club. But in 1986, club members, led by Mrs. A. Earl Cullum Jr., mother of current club member Margaret Anne Cullum, donated a valuable Shakespeare First Folio to the Dallas Public Library and installed it in a beautifully decorated space—a former seventh-floor cloakroom—in the library's main branch in downtown Dallas. This spectacularly generous gift to the people of Dallas commemorates the Dallas Shakespeare Club's hundredth anniversary.

- Longtime club member Margaret McDermott and the foundation named after her and her late husband, Eugene, who was a founder of Texas Instruments, have given tremendous gifts to the City of Dallas and to its art museum, on whose board Margaret serves. In item 21 ("Colorful or interesting members"), find further discussion of this lively 103-year-old whom I met at the meeting I attended in November 2011 and who took my breath away with her conversational gambits and adventurous nature. "Let's snoop," she suggested to me as she eyed the layout of the gracious home where the meeting was held.

17. **Special events of the year:** Recently, one member, Margaret McDermott, has given a special opening luncheon in September. A directors' luncheon, which combines a celebration of the birthday of Dallas Shakespeare Club and a celebration of Shakespeare's birthday, is planned for January. A president's luncheon, which includes a business meeting, is held in April. The outgoing president hosts the event. In earlier days, the club celebrated Shakespeare's birthday in April and Texas History Day in March, the latter to commemorate Texas' declaration of independence from Mexico on March 2, 1836.

18. **Refreshments:** Although a section called "Customs" in the club's yearbook says that refreshments are offered at

a hostess's discretion,[53] I attended two meetings and saw a beautiful tea table and plentiful offerings at the end of one meeting and a catered, sit-down tea at another meeting that was held in a museum's meeting room.

19. **Special traditions:**
   - First names are not used until teatime, which is at the end of the meeting. (This custom is seen in other groups.)
   - Members often answer roll call with a quotation from the Shakespeare play being studied. (This custom is seen in other groups, as well.)
   - I was also told that members always say yes when asked to perform any task. (This was also the case in many of the groups I studied.)
   - Another custom I saw being observed - and of which I found some variation in a small number of the groups I uncovered - is that each new member is asked to serve as recording secretary after completing at least one term of membership.

20. **Example of a yearly theme:** One of Shakespeare's plays is read in the fall term and discussed in the spring term. The chosen play was *Othello* when I visited the group in 2011 and 2012.

21. **Example of an individual paper or program based on that topic:** During the first term, club members provide the programming by presenting readings of the chosen play, with occasional commentary by the member who is acting as director. During the second term, a combination of club members and outside speakers deliver papers or programs based on the first term's play. I was able to experience both. I enjoyed a well-rehearsed dramatic reading of act 3 of *Othello* at a meeting in November 2011, where members chosen to read the parts stood dressed in bits of costume before their fellow club members, with signs hanging from their necks saying which character's part they were reading. At a January meeting of what the group calls their second term, which starts in January, I heard a guest speaker, Raphael Perry, director of the Shakespeare Dallas organization,

deliver a paper titled "Racial Perceptions in the Portrayal of Othello." Had I come to the next meeting, I would have heard member Anne Coke deliver her paper called "Iago: Deceit, Revenge, or Jealousy?"

22. **Colorful or interesting member, present or past:** No question about it: this has to be Margaret McDermott, whom I interviewed at the first meeting I attended in November 2011. She turned a hundred shortly after my interview, on February 18, 2012. She has been a Dallas icon for many decades. In fact, at this point, a bridge named after her, partially designed by famed Spanish architect Santiago Calatrava, is being built across the Trinity River, with a projected completion date of 2017, although the project has been fraught with budgetary problems. Margaret's husband, Eugene McDermott, who died in 1973, was one of the founders of Texas Instruments. Mrs. McDermott has been a vital philanthropic force at the Dallas Museum of Art and elsewhere in Dallas via a foundation bearing her and her husband's names.

23. **Legacy members and longest-active member:** The current longest-active member is the same Margaret McDermott who joined in 1962. As for legacy families, the first club president, May Dixon Exall, served in that office for fifty years and started a family tradition of Shakespeare Club membership. The Exall family has ten members who are past or present members,[54] including Marion Exall—Mrs. Henry Exall, Jr., an Exall by marriage. Marion was the group's president in 2001–02. She read the part of Desdemona in the club's presentation of *Othello* when I visited a meeting in 2011. Shakespeare Club members proudly admit that they have a special fondness for aunts, cousins, sisters, and daughters when choosing new members, so there are many family connections.

Snapshot Summary of The Pierian Club

1. **Official name of the club:** The Pierian Club.
2. **Date founded:** The club was founded in August 1888, as the Chautauqua Literary and Scientific Circle. In 1891, the club changed its name to Pierian Circle. It became Pierian Club in 1899. Until then, the club followed the Chautauqua Association's formal course of study.[55] After the members changed the club name, they were on their own.
3. **Founder's name:** Mrs. Alexander C. Ardrey, who served as the club's president until she died, eleven years after founding the club. Mrs. Ardrey asked nine women to join her for the first meeting, making ten charter members.[56]
4. **Size of club as stated in bylaws:** Membership is limited to fifty active members, twenty associate members, and any number of honorary members.[57]
5. **Size of club today:** In 2012, there were forty-six active members, three new members about to join, eight associate members, and three honorary members.[58] All of the honorary members had joined the club in the early 1960s. Associates must pay dues, but they may not vote or hold office. They must attend at least three regular meetings a year and can only be an associate for two years (if they don't apply for an extension). Honorary members may not vote or hold office. They are excused from paying annual dues and may become honorary after forty years of membership or after having "tendered long and faithful service to the Club" or having "done the Club some special favor."[59] Neither honorary nor associate members need to contribute research papers.[60]
6. **Meeting schedule:** The first and third Wednesday of each month, usually at 1:30, October through April, with the president's luncheon to be held on the first Wednesday in May at noon. There is only one meeting in December—a holiday guest tea. In 2011–12, this added up to thirteen meetings.[61]
7. **Where they meet:** In members' homes or in a public space at a member's apartment building, condo, or retirement community.[62]

8. **Election of new members:** One member writes a letter of recommendation, and two members cosign it. Voting follows at a subsequent meeting and is done by written ballot. The forty members of a group called the Junior Pierians, which was founded in 1924 as a "feed-in" to the Pierian Club, must have joined the Junior Pierians before reaching the age of thirty-seven and must leave when they reach the age of forty-seven, supposedly moving on to Pierian membership. However, that has not been happening in recent years, which has slowed the input of younger members to the Pierian Club, whose average age is creeping upward.[63] Junior Pierians read and review recently published books and hear two members give a twenty-minute book review at most meetings. One member presents a forty-minute book review four times a year.[64] In contrast, the Pierian Club studies a broad range of subjects.

9. **Object of the club as stated in bylaws:** "Its object shall be mutual help and encouragement, and the stimulation of individual effort."[65]

10. **Dues:** $40 annually, the high rate owing to the expense of a valet parker for many meetings. In addition, a new member must pay an initiation fee of $15.[66]

11. **Club motto:** "I rest, I rust"[67]—a wonderful motto, in my opinion. **Club flower:** Cape jasmine. **Club colors:** White and green.[68]

12. **Paper or program rotation schedule:** To quote member Marie Chiles, "There is no schedule. It is up to the program chair to invite people to give a program."[69]

13. **Length of papers or programs:** Marie Chiles wrote me that the club is considering changing to one meeting a month and to two twenty-minute papers at each meeting. Currently, papers are longer than that.[70] When I visited the Pierians, the paper—really, quite a long program about the quality of health care in Africa—was easily thirty to forty-five minutes long.

14. **Location of the club's archives:** Dallas Historical Society, 12005 Forestgate Drive, Dallas, TX 75243

15. **Civic achievements of the group:** The club's official history claims that members were instrumental in starting the first circulating library in Dallas (see "Colorful or interesting member," below) and also mentions their involvement in founding many civic groups in the club's early days, which were also the early days of Dallas. Pierians joined with other groups to form the Dallas Federation of Women's Clubs in 1897. They are no longer members of this or any larger organization.[71]

16. **Special events of the year:** A reassembly luncheon in early October, a holiday guest tea in early December, a spring guest luncheon in late March, and the (outgoing) president's luncheon in early May.[72]

17. **Refreshments:** At the end of each meeting, tea, cold drinks, cookies, and desserts are served, unless there is a special event, for which the food may be more elaborate and may be a complete luncheon.[73]

18. **Special traditions:** Every year since 1925, Pierians have contributed to a scholarship fund for SMU's Dedman College, the liberal arts school. Called the Florence Shuttles Pierian Scholarship Fund, it was named in honor of the club's third president, Mrs. R. H. Shuttles. The club also traditionally donates books to SMU's library.[74]

19. **Example of a yearly theme of study:** The program committee picks the yearly theme. In 2011–12, it was "Africa: Modest Brushstrokes Covering Large Canvases of Life on the Darkest of Continents."[75]

20. **Example of a paper or program based on that topic:** On December 7, 2011, the group enjoyed "Death on the Nile," about Cleopatra and the Ptolemaic dynasty.[76] Marie Chiles reports that the club's first paper for the 2012–13 season was an "outstanding one—'The Birth of the Blues.'"[77] The program I heard at the November 2011 meeting was "Health in Africa." Member Barbara Taylor was knowledgeable enough about her subject to put down her written report and speak extemporaneously about health issues in several African nations.

21. **Colorful or interesting member, present or past:** Grace Simpson Allen, wife of prominent early Dallas physician Richard Wisdom Allen, opened her home one day a week to the public so that they could access the club's four hundred volumes, thereby creating what the group claims was "the first circulating library in Dallas."[78] Club members acted as librarians. That house, built by Dr. and Mrs. Allen in the late 1800s, is still standing today at 2630 Fairmount Street and is the city's prime example of Queen Anne domestic architecture of the era.[79]

22. **Legacy members or longest-active members:** Three honorary members on the club's rolls joined in the early 1960s: Patsy Butler, Mary Echerd, and Mary Williams. In 1968, when the club celebrated its eightieth anniversary, there were ten distinct family legacies represented among Pierian members.[80] Currently, there are five families with legacy members.[81]

Snapshot Summary of The Standard Club of Dallas

1. **Official name of the club:** The Standard Club of Dallas.
2. **Date founded:** February 23, 1886,[82] almost one month after the founding of the Dallas Shakespeare Club, making it the second oldest literary club in Dallas.
3. **Founders' names:** Sophia Cowart (Mrs. Robert E.), in whose home the group met, Mattie Davenport (Mrs. M. H.), Belle Gay Smith (Mrs. Sydney), and Elizabeth Wallace (Mrs. Theodore). The club members elected Elizabeth Wallace as their first president.[83] Most of the thirty women who came to the first meeting lived in a once-fashionable area of Dallas, then called The Cedars, south of downtown Dallas.[84]
4. **Size of club as stated in bylaws (size limit):** Active members are limited to forty. There is no limit to the number of associates or to the number of honorary members. After five years of service, an active may become an associate after submitting a request in writing. Honorary membership may be granted by a vote of the membership after a member

has ten years of active membership. Associate and honorary members may not vote or hold office, and they need not fulfill any of the active duties.[85]

5. **Size of club today:** Forty active members, three associate members, and three honorary members.[86]

6. **Meeting schedule:** Meetings are luncheons and are held at noon on the last Tuesday of the month, from September through April, with no meeting in December. Luncheon is followed by a business meeting and program. There are seven meetings per year.[87] At the first luncheon meeting, the first vice president gives an overview of the study to be undertaken in the year to come. At the final meeting, the club historian gives a review of the club year, and officers are installed.[88]

7. **Where the club meets:** In members' homes, except on special occasions.

8. **Election of new members:** Candidates must be recommended by an active member and seconded by two more active members. An active may recommend or second only one candidate per year. A letter of proposal is read to the club in February, and the prospective member is voted on at the March meeting, by "written, preferential ballot."[89]

9. **Object of the club as stated in bylaws:** "The object of the Club shall be to promote the knowledge and study of Standard Authors and to stimulate individual effort."[90]

10. **Dues:** In 2011–12, annual dues, including the cost of lunches, for active members were $110; associate members, $20; and honorary members, $18 (a luncheon fee), if attending meetings. New members pay a one-time fee set by the executive board.[91]

11. **Club motto:** "He most lives who thinks most, feels the noblest, acts the best," which is a quotation from the poem "Festus" by Philip James Bailey. **Club flower:** The daisy. **Club colors:** White and yellow.

12. **Paper or program assignment schedule and hostessing schedule:** Members are asked to hostess or deliver a paper, but never both in the same year. The first VP chooses the

programs or paper topics; the second VP, the meeting venues and catering.

13. **Length of papers or programs:** Twenty to thirty minutes.

14. **Location of the club's archives:** The club's archives are professionally catalogued and archived in acid-free containers in Southern Methodist University's DeGolyer Library's Special Collections. They are part of the library's "Archives of Women of the Southwest" and are watched over by Pamalla Anderson, head of public services for DeGolyer. Ms. Anderson is the author of "Standard Club 125th Anniversary: Happiness Is Being a Clubwoman," published by the DeGolyer Library in 2011. She was a tremendous help to me when I was using the DeGolyer for research. She had the many boxes of Standard Club archives organized and waiting for me when I arrived at the impressive Stanley Marcus Room of that library as it opened for the day in November 2011.

15. **Civic achievements of the group or its members:** This section contains an embarrassment of riches, largely because the Standard Club not only has a long list of notable members, but it also has had, for several years, the very good fortune to have author and historian Jackie McElhaney tackling the job of organizing Standard's archives as the club's historian. Jackie and forty-year member Margot Gill assembled a beautifully printed and well-researched history of the club for its 125th anniversary in 2011—"From the Beginning: The Standard Club, Dallas Texas, 1886–2011." The following summary is mostly gleaned from this keepsake booklet.

Early members were as involved as Shakespeare Club members in the establishment of a public library and a public art museum in Dallas, as well as free public kindergartens. Looking over their membership rolls from 1886, I saw many women with last names that are today the names of the streets and highways of Dallas, and an astonishing nine women who were either wives or mothers of Dallas or Highland Park mayors. Minerva Miller was the wife of a lieutenant governor of Texas, and Belle Gay Smith was married to a secretary of state of Texas. Olivia Dealey was the wife of the publisher of the *Dallas Morning News.* She founded the Public School Art League in Dallas in the early 1900s. The founder of the prestigious Hockaday private school for girls, Ela Hockaday, was a Standard Club member in the mid-1950s. Mary K. Craig was an honorary member from 1887 to 1921. She began what is known in Dallas as the Mary K. Craig Class, which originally had members speak on a particular educational topic, but which today is a very popular speakers' series. Another club member, Mary Hay, was first dean of women at SMU after a successful business career. Her husband was mayor of Dallas. Club member Vera Hartt Martin helped organize the Dallas Symphony League in her home in 1947, was the group's first president, and was the president of several other civic organizations. Mrs. Gross R. Scruggs brought the garden club movement to Dallas from the East Coast and established the Dallas Garden Club and the Marianne Scruggs Garden Club. She served as president of the National Council of Garden Clubs and of Texas Garden Clubs, Inc. She was also the coauthor of a book, *Gardening in the Southwest.*[92] In the 1920s, Erin Bain Jones was the first woman to earn a law degree at SMU. She later earned two master's degrees and a doctorate. She traveled to the North and South Poles, where she studied such contemporary issues as the environment and pollution.[93] In addition, she was cofounder of many of the early civic groups that formed the basis of the library, art museum, opera, and theater organizations in Dallas today.

16. **Special events of the year:** The club's luncheon meeting in February is a birthday celebration of the club. I attended their 126th birthday meeting in 2012. Their luncheon meeting in April always includes a review of the club year and the installation of new officers, presented by the entertainment committee. There was an anniversary tea at the DeGolyer Library at SMU to celebrate the club's 125th birthday in 2011, and the 100th anniversary party was held at the Dallas Woman's Club, with members dressed in costumes of the 1880s.

17. **Refreshments:** Catered luncheons are served punctually and efficiently at the stroke of noon, usually by Spice of Life Caterers. At the February 2012 meeting, which I attended at member Sue John's artfully decorated home, the menu was Mexican, and the thirty or so women who attended ate at tables set up in several downstairs rooms. I was seated at a table with nine other women in a cozy red library. While taking notes, I still managed to clean my plate, including the traditional flan for dessert.

18. **Special traditions:**
    - The club's regular meetings are luncheon meetings, which absolutely start on time.
    - The members always celebrate their club's birthday at their February meeting.
    - A scholarship, the Standard Club Award at SMU, is awarded every May to an undergraduate art student, "as a motivational boost."[94]

19. **Example of a yearly theme of study:** In 2011–12, it was "Remarkable Women—Extraordinary Lives, Extraordinary Careers."

20. **Examples of individual papers based on that topic:** "Maria Callas," "Émilie du Châtelet," "Irène Némirovsky," "Freya Stark," and "Rosamond Bernier." I heard a paper on Freya Stark delivered at the meeting I attended.

21. **Particularly colorful or interesting member, present or past:** Several of these women were mentioned above, in "Civic achievements." Among my favorite historical tidbits is this: club member Margaret Greer, who joined the club in 1916 and died in 1953, helped finance the "discovery well" of legendary oil wildcatter Dad Joiner in 1930, in the East Texas Oil Field, which became the largest oil field in the United States at the time.[95]

22. **Legacy members and longest-active member:** The history of Standard Club, assembled by Jackie McElhaney and Margot Gill, includes notes on many members. It shows a large number of legacy links to past members. One chain was started by Alice Skillman, who joined Standard in 1917 and whose daughter, Margaret Holt, became a member in

1938, followed by Alice's granddaughter Margot Gill in 1972. Forty-three years later, Margot is still a member, working with Jackie McElhaney on the history of the club and serving as the club's president in 1981–82.[96] Current member Day Watson, who joined Standard in 1992 and was its president in 2002–03, is related to members who were her aunt, her great-aunt-in-law, her mother-in-law, and her grandmother-in-law—so, another three-generation legacy family.[97] Mary Frances DeLoache has been a member since 1966—forty-nine years—and was proposed by Jeanne Simpson, who has been a member for fifty-one years, making her currently the longest-active member.[98] Jeanne is also a link in a three-generation chain of Standard members.[99]

CHAPTER 3

Denver, Boulder, and Golden, Colorado

A Cluster of Four Historic Literary Societies

I made two trips to visit historic women's study clubs in the Denver area from my home in Los Angeles, first visiting Boulder and its Fortnightly Club during one very long day on April 21, 2011. I flew into Denver International Airport very early in the morning, caught a commuter bus to Boulder, and flew home late that night after doing research and attending a meeting. I also visited three groups in Denver and Golden, March 18–22, 2012, using a downtown Denver hotel as my base for this second visit and driving a rental car to get where I needed to go. These hundred-plus-year-old groups were Denver Fortnightly, the Denver Monday Literary Club, and Golden Fortnightly. I also did research on all of the clubs' archives in the library of the University of Colorado (for Boulder Fortnightly), in the main branch of the Denver Public Library (for Monday Literary Club and Denver Fortnightly), and in an historical society in Denver called History Colorado (for Golden Fortnightly).

I'd made the first trip very early on in the life of this book after finding an article about Boulder Fortnightly online and successfully contacting member Kathy Raybin and arranging a visit to one of their meetings. Kathy was a tremendous help to me over a period of several years as I worked on the book. She was one of the people who helped me when I was despairing of making any connections and then of getting answers to my questions. In the article I'd found, she was mentioned as being club president at the time of publication. I was able to track her down via the Internet's white pages listings. At that point, I had not found the other three surviving women's study clubs. When I eventually did find them, I was, after considerable effort, able to work out the details of combining my visits to a meeting of each of the groups into one doable trip.

Also a tremendous help to me in my research was Denver Monday Club longtime member Helen Christy, who met with me privately before I attended one of their meetings. Helen also did considerable research to answer some of my questions about her club that I'd been unable to answer through my research. Golden Fortnightly club member and president at the time of my Golden visit, Frani Bickart, was also a tremendous help, during what was a difficult time in her life. She became something of a correspondent. Mollie Eaton, who was president of Denver Fortnightly while I was researching her group, was also extremely helpful and forthcoming.

I attended meetings of all four groups and found them to be very similar, although none had more than the most basic contact with the others, if they knew about them at all. All followed the same meeting format: business at first, then introductions of guests, then introduction of the speaker or program. After that, a club member would speak on her subject or deliver her paper, and then the meeting would be adjourned so the members could enjoy a beautiful tea and a short period of socializing. However, one of these groups, Golden Fortnightly, had dessert at the beginning of the meeting, which made sense, as their 1:00 meetings come right after lunchtime.

Surely, one of the most incredible stories I found in my three years of researching and writing this book was about the primary founder of Boulder Fortnightly—University of Colorado Professor Mary Rippon. You will see a brief account of Mary's life in the following snapshot summary of the group, in items 3, 15, and 21. In short, although she was a woman, Miss Rippon was able to succeed in the academic world by hiding and juggling her private life to an extent that few could imagine or manage. She produced and supported a child from a secret marriage to someone with whom a romantic relationship would never have been considered proper. She did what she had to do to survive, and she lived two parallel lives for half of her long life. She found support and friendship during this challenging part of her life in the group of intelligent women that made up Boulder Fortnightly.

My trips to visit groups in Denver, Boulder, and Golden marked the first time I had ever spent time in any of these towns. I found the city of Denver easy to navigate on foot and by car, and the capital area where I was staying turned out to be the perfect choice. I walked to the capital building, which sits one mile above sea level, and stood on its steps to admire the legally protected view of the Rocky Mountains.[1] From my hotel, I could also easily walk to the main branch of the Denver library and to all of the museums I'd earmarked for a visit. I did encounter some aggressive panhandlers whenever I was on foot in the area, but no one gave me any real trouble.

Golden is a charming and tiny mining town, home of the Colorado School of Mines and the Coors beer brewery. A babbling brook, Clear Creek, the source of Coors' water, actually runs through the center of the miniature and quaintly old-fashioned downtown. Boulder is larger, bustling, rather hip, and beautifully set next to the Flatiron Mountains. I spent most of my time in Boulder on or near the busy University of Colorado campus, with a quick trip to a beautiful home in the outskirts of the city for the meeting of Boulder Fortnightly. My Boulder hostess and great help, Kathy Raybin, had even fed me lunch and driven me by the town's historic and beautifully maintained Colorado Chautauqua Park and cottages after I'd expressed an interest in Chautauqua, an adult education movement started in the nineteenth century.

The groups in these three towns, which were within a short drive of each other, knew little or nothing of each other, although Boulder Fortnightly had recently made contact with Denver Fortnightly. After I'd visited and shared my information with the four groups, there was some further communication and an exchange of invitations between at least two of the clubs. My impression was that three of the groups, Boulder Fortnightly, Denver Fortnightly, and Denver's Monday Literary Club, were healthy and moving forward, but Golden Fortnightly was struggling a bit to survive, looking for younger members to augment its dwindling numbers. This was the story I found throughout my research and travels: the stronger groups survived through a combination of intelligence, determination, outreach to new members, social cachet, and a love of the group's historical importance. Most important of these is the fact that it takes constant attention to the business of finding younger new members for these historic all-women literary societies to stay alive. Those groups that did not have the ability, or perhaps the allure, to attract younger members were, once I found them, either just calling it quits or wondering how they would survive. The refrain in those groups was always the same: "Young women are all working now or are just too busy to do this."

Snapshot Summary of Boulder Fortnightly

1. **Official name of the club:** The Fortnightly Club of Boulder, but its original name was the Ladies Literary Club.[2]
2. **Date founded:** November 5, 1884.[3]
3. **Founder:** Mary Rippon and ten other women, split between "town and gown" (townspeople and university wives or faculty members), met in Mary's rented room at the corner of 14th Street and Front Street (now Walnut Street).[4] In 1878, six years earlier, Miss Rippon, at the age of twenty-seven, had become the first female professor in Colorado, teaching romance languages and German at the new University of Colorado in Boulder, serving as its unofficial dean of women, and even helping to plant trees around the only university structure, Old Main.[5] A single woman in a Victorian era, she had a rock-solid reputation and a keen intellect. However, as you will see in item 21, she had a secret life.
4. **Size of club as stated in the bylaws—i.e., size limit:** Originally, the limit was thirty-five women, equally representative of "town and gown," as Boulder is a university town. However, in 2012, the club voted to increase its membership limit to thirty-eight active members.[6] Members told me that as Boulder has grown over the years, "town" is now more heavily represented, although there are still many academics among the honorary members. Eleven of the fifteen honorary members have university connections, whereas only six or seven active members have college-related jobs.[7]
5. **Size of club today:** Thirty-five active members, thirteen honorary members, and space for three new members.[8]
6. **Meeting schedule—months, day, time:** Every other Thursday at 2:00 p.m., from early October to mid-May, when the club members hold their final picnic. There is only one meeting in December.
7. **Where they meet:** In members' homes.
8. **Election of new members:** A candidate must be recommended by a sponsor, who writes a letter about her and her qualifications. These letters are kept in order and are

used to fill a place when one opens up after a member dies or resigns. The prospective member must be voted on.[9] She must have attended two meetings of her choosing if she is to become a member. There is also a yearly guest day, when prospects may visit.[10]

9. **Object of the club as stated in bylaws:** Club member Kathy Raybin, who was so helpful to me, wrote answers to some of my questions, including this one about the object of the club. She said, "The Fortnightly Club's intent of providing an outlet for women to explore and expand their intellect has remained the same throughout its history."[11]

10. **Dues:** $15, but soon to be raised to $20, which, according to the president, will "enable the club to have a larger yearly donation to an organization in the area."[12]

11. **Club motto:** None is known. **Club flower:** White carnation. **Club colors:** Green and white.[13]

12. **Paper or program and hostessing rotation or assignment schedule:** Former President Nancy Sievers wrote to me and said, "One alternates yearly in being hostess and giving a paper. A sign-up list with the dates of the next year's meetings is passed out at the last meetings of the year for members to sign up for their assignments for the following year. A list is also available as to who needs to sign up for a paper or hostess, although most of us know what we did the previous year. This is mainly for those who may have taken a year's leave of absence."[14]

13. **Length of papers:** At each meeting, the reading of the paper is preceded by a member's reading a biography of the woman who will be delivering the paper. These bios last for about five minutes. Then, the member who's just been introduced delivers her original research paper, which is usually about twenty pages long and takes about forty-five minutes to read.

14. **Location of the club's archives:** The archives are stored in Norlin Library's lower level, University of Colorado, Boulder.

15. **Civic achievement of the group or its members:** Mary Rippon not only worked as a professor at the university and founded Fortnightly of Boulder, but she also founded the local Women's League, which later became the YWCA.

She also spoke in support of women's rights, especially the right to vote.[15] In addition, to quote a member-written history: "Fortnightly Club members have served the Boulder community by serving with different feminist, church, educational, and artistic projects throughout their lifetimes. It is primarily a literary club, but it has made contributions to local charities and organizations throughout its history—scholarships, hospitals, etc."[16]

16. **Special events:** A guests' meeting in April (which I attended in 2011), a Christmas meeting in December, and a final picnic in mid-May, during which officers for the coming year are installed.

17. **Refreshments:** At the end of each meeting, members gather around a full tea table set with finger foods and a silver tea service. This is presided over by one member who pours the tea. As with most of the groups I visited, this is the time for happy and spirited social interaction.

18. **Special traditions:**
    - There are three special events of the year: guest day, a Christmas meeting, and the final picnic.
    - Members become president for a one-year term in the order of when they joined, moving up after serving for a year as first vice president.
    - Meetings begin absolutely on the dot at 2:00 p.m.
    - On guest day, the meeting begins with each member who has brought a guest introducing herself, followed by her guest's introducing herself and telling the group something about herself. The historian then reads a history of the club. After this, another member delivers a biography of the member who is about to read her research paper. When I attended guest day in 2011, the large living room belonging to our hostess, member Barbara Hill, was filled with what I estimated to be sixty women, members and guests. We could clearly see the snow-topped mountains that surround Boulder through the room's windows.
    - Prospective members must attend two meetings before joining.[17]

19. **Example of a yearly theme of study:** In 1999–2000, the overall topic was "Visions and Visionaries."[18] The theme of study was always determined a year in advance, so that members could come up with their own ideas for paper topics. These ideas were delivered in July, during the summer break, so that they might be included in the upcoming yearbook. However, having a yearly theme has just recently become a thing of the past. Past President Kathy Raybin said that yearly themes have been eliminated, because, "Many of us had areas of interest which we wanted to do research on and which may not have fit into [an overall] theme."[19]

20. **Example of an individual paper:** "Some Funny Things Happened on the Way to the Millennium."[20]

21. **Particularly colorful member:** That would have to be Mary Rippon, who founded the club and who was the first woman professor in Colorado when the university campus in Boulder consisted of a barren landscape, livestock pens, and one building, the still-standing Old Main. Because female teachers in those days were not allowed to be married, Miss Rippon had a secret life, a secret husband (a twenty-five-year-old student at the university) and child, while living the life of a dedicated spinster academic with a spotless reputation. After an elderly grandson stepped forward in 1976 to donate her photos to the university library and later offered her journals, her real story was revealed.[21] This led to the publication of a book in 1999 called *Separate Lives,* by Silvia Pettem. By all accounts, she was a brilliant woman and had been well educated in Europe.[22] She taught at the university for thirty-one years and saw its faculty grow from three professors to over three hundred. Simultaneously, the student body grew from fifteen to more than three thousand.[23] Boulder Fortnightly remained a lifeline for Mary for many years. Despite her grueling workload and teaching schedule, she held a variety of positions in Fortnightly. She was still a member in 1934, when she was eighty-four years old. She died a year after that. The women of Fortnightly were among the mourners who came to her funeral, which was held in her home.[24] Today, there is an outdoor theater on campus

bearing her name, which I visited when I was in Boulder for the day.

22. **Legacy members and longest-active member:** Peggy Archibald, who joined in 1966, is currently the longest-active member.[25] There is one current member who is the daughter-in-law of another member, and this represents the only legacy chain in the group.[26]

Snapshot Summary of the Denver Fortnightly Club

1. **Official name of the club:** Denver Fortnightly Club.[27]
2. **Date founded:** April 13, 1881, probably making it the oldest still-active women's literary society in Colorado. There is some question as to whether the Monday Literary Club of Denver is actually older, but bragging rights have always gone to Denver Fortnightly. (See the snapshot summary of Monday Literary Club.)
3. **Founders:** Eleven Denver women, from the area around Cherry Creek, met at the home of Mrs. Charles Denison, 1400 Champa Street, and became the club's charter members. It was Mrs. Denison's idea to start the club after her mother, who lived in Chicago, visited her and described the Fortnightly Club of Chicago. This inspired Mrs. Denison to call six women, who each asked a friend to join.[28] Sadly, it was Mrs. Denison who, a year after the formation of the club, suffered a great loss. The beautifully handwritten minutes for April 26, 1882, which I found in the original ledger for the group, relate, "On account of the death of Mrs. Denison's little girl, the meeting was postponed until one week from today."[29]
4. **Size of club as stated in bylaws (size limit):** Forty-five actives. No limit on sustaining and nonresident members.[30]
5. **Size of club today:** Forty-two active members, four sustaining members, seven nonresident members, and one inactive member. In February 2013, the group was recruiting for three new members to bring their number of actives up to forty-five.[31]

6. **Meeting schedule:** There are executive board meetings in early November, mid-January, and early March, at 2:00 p.m. Membership meetings are held at 2:30 p.m., with guests invited for 3:00 p.m., at which point the guests are introduced to the group. The first meeting is the president's opening luncheon on the first Tuesday in October, and the final meeting is the annual meeting and spring luncheon on the second Tuesday in April, with the current president acting as hostess, assisted by cohostesses. A summer picnic is held anytime and anywhere the incoming president wishes and is organized by her. There is usually a speaker on Colorado history at these picnics.[32]

7. **Where they meet:**
   - Usually, they meet in members' homes, but they might also meet at Arapahoe Tennis Club, Denver Country Club, Byers-Evans Historic House, or Women's Press Club.[33] Sites for the summer picnic vary widely from mountain ranches to botanic gardens.[34]
   - For the Louisa Ward Arps Essay Contest meeting in April, the group has most recently met in the lower-level children's room of the historic Tattered Cover Book Store, across the street from the participating high school. The building is an art moderne landmark and is on the National Register of Historic Places. It was built in 1953 as the Bonfils Memorial Theatre. Formerly, this essay contest ceremony took place in the boathouse at Washington Park.[35]

8. **Election of new members:** A new member must have two letters of recommendation and must have attended three meetings as a guest. Her election is by ballot, with a two-thirds vote needed.[36] A new member receives a copy of the bylaws and is introduced to the club by her original sponsor.[37] "Members may propose or second only one candidate annually for membership."[38]

9. **Object of the club as stated in bylaws:** "The object of the Denver Fortnightly Club shall be the union of congenial minds for study and discussion and the furtherance of good

in such practical ways as may from time to time be approved by the club."[39]

10. **Dues:** $35 for active and sustaining members; $20 for nonresidents.[40]

11. **Club motto:** "To truth, add other truth."[41] **Club flower:** Either the Maréchal Niel rose, a noisette double yellow rose[42] described in the club's archives, or the Harrison yellow rose,[43] a favorite of the pioneers, described in a member's paper as the club's flower. **Club colors:** The only color noted is yellow.[44]

12. **Paper assignment schedule and hostessing assignment schedule:** The incoming president acts as the program chairwoman. She passes a list on which members sign up for a date when they'd like to give the program of their choice. Hostesses and chairs of the day volunteer in the same fashion.[45]

13. **Length of papers:** No more than forty minutes. Each paper is preceded by the chairperson for the day reading a biography of the woman about to deliver a paper.[46]

14. **Location of the club's archives:** Denver Public Library, central branch, Western History Collection.

15. **Civic achievements of the group or of an individual member:** Early members included two of Colorado's most renowned suffragettes, Mrs. John (Ione) Hanna and Dr. Alida Avery.[47] A charter member, Mrs. John Hanna helped establish public kindergartens in Denver. A number of the club's early members joined a committee to work on establishing a public library, which was finally built in 1889.[48] The president at the time of my research, Mollie Eaton, pointed out that today's members are all tremendously involved in community efforts, such as the Colorado Symphony, charities, and endeavors too numerous to list, but she said that they are all very private people and probably do not want these achievements announced to the world.[49]

16. **Special events during the year:** The president's opening luncheon in early October; the presentation of the winning essays in the Louisa Ward Arps Essay Contest (an essay contest for East Denver High School Seniors) in late

March—the meeting I attended; and the annual meeting and spring luncheon in mid-April, with the president as hostess. The archives are full of beautifully designed invitations for the luncheons up to the present day. Another special event is a summer picnic. The archives reflect that summer picnics were often organized at a member's ranch or home in the mountains. These picnics were, and still are, organized by the incoming president. In 2012, the picnic was held at Mt. Evans Ranch, near the scenic spot pictured on the cover of the group's yearbook. The ranch is the home of a member's grandmother, a former Fortnightly member.[50] Today, the picnic may be held in a variety of places. The choice is at the president's discretion.

17. **Refreshments:** Often, there is a spectacular tea table with a silver service at either end of a lace-covered table, with two members pouring hot beverages into fine china teacups, and a floral centerpiece—perhaps the club's yellow roses. This teatime takes place at the end of the meetings. Sometimes, this is catered, but homemade treats are more traditional for this group. Recently, mother–daughter duos have shared the hostess duties at the tea party.[51] At the spring luncheon, the president may share the hostessing duties with several other women. Wine, fresh lemonade, and a "gourmet feast" are served.[52]

18. **Special traditions:**
    - A "chairman of the day" introduces the essayist at each meeting and conducts the discussion about her paper.[53]
    - "A member becomes president in the chronological order of her election to membership, assuring that each member eventually assumes that responsibility."[54]
    - The order of business laid out by the founding mothers is still used.[55] It consists of the call to order, reports from the secretary and treasurer, miscellaneous business, a discussion of the paper presented at the preceding meeting, the president's announcement of the next meeting, the reading of the assigned paper and subsequent discussion, and adjournment.[56]

- The year's best papers, selected by an anonymous committee appointed by the president, are added to the club's archives at the central branch of the public library in downtown Denver.
- As with virtually every club I studied, Denver Fortnightly is proud of its legacy members and long family traditions of membership.
- The cover of the club's yearbook is an early sketch of nearby Mt. Evans, plus a tree branch, and the letters *DFC*. The cover remains the same from year to year, with the printed contents being updated. The remarkable woman who drew the etching of Mt. Evans was Helen Henderson Chain, whose artwork was the subject of a show at the Denver Library's central branch's Western History Department Art Gallery in 2014. See item 21 for a brief summary of Ms. Chain's life and contributions. She is one of the women I encountered while researching this book who deserves to have an entire book devoted to her life.
- The club has a traveling tea set, complete with china.[57]

19. **Example of an overall yearly theme of study:** There is no overall theme. Mollie Eaton wrote that it is "up to the author to select the theme of her chosen essay with hopes that it will be chosen for filing in the historic treasure chest,"[58] a reference to the file of especially good papers chosen by an anonymous committee of members to be stored in the group's archives at the central library downtown.

20. **Example of a paper:** A paper with an intriguing title is "Chasing the Mermaid's Tear," presented by Cindy Foster on February 21, 2012. It is a paper about pearls. This year, member Elizabeth ("Biddie") Houston presented a paper titled "Dumb Heroes," about animals in the US military. Another recent paper dealt with the Guggenheim Museum in New York and its anniversary, which was marked by an exhibition of the works of Wassily Kandinsky.[59]

21. **Particularly colorful or interesting member, present or past:**

- American sportswoman Penny Tweedy (Penny Chenery) who bred and raced Secretariat, the racehorse that won the Triple Crown in 1973 and the subject of a feature film released in 2010, still attends meetings and has been a member since 1962.

- Louisa Ward Arps (1901–1986) received her BA from the University of Colorado and her master's degree in library science from Columbia University. She worked as a librarian at East Denver High School, which is the school whose seniors have participated in the group's yearly Louisa Ward Arps Essay Contest since 1987. She also worked as a librarian in South Denver High School and was later on the staff of the Denver Public Library and the Colorado Historical Society. She was the archivist at the local Episcopal cathedral and was involved in the early days of the city's public television station, Channel Six. She was an activist for many causes. Joining Fortnightly in 1960, Arps was a member for twenty-six years and was its president in 1979–80.[60] She published six books on local history between 1940 and 1980. She was also an avid mountain climber, as was her husband, Elwyn, who was the first person to photograph and hike all fifty-plus Colorado peaks 14,000 feet high or higher. A 12,383-foot peak near the ghost town of Hancock, Colorado, on the Continental Divide in western Colorado, was named after Louise in 1987. It is called Mt. Arps. Louise died of a burst aneurysm at the age of eighty-five in 1986, a day after taking a hike in Rocky Mountain National Park—something almost unbelievable for a woman her age—in the cold and snowy month of January.[61]

- Helen Henderson Chain (1849–1892), said to be "Colorado's first resident woman artist,"[62] was a club member during Fortnightly's earliest days. This remarkable woman created the etching of Mt. Evans that graces the cover of the club's yearbook. In a unique practice of tradition, club members today reuse this cover from year to year, replacing only the contents of the yearbook. I've seen a photo of Ms. Chain dressed in one of the long, heavy dresses women would have worn in the late 1800s. She might even be trussed up with a corset and other uncomfortable underpinnings. Sporting a huge hat, she is happily holding a hiking staff and posing on a mountain trail with a friend. She is said to have been an "enthusiastic mountaineer" who climbed "all of Colorado's highest peaks."[63] She also explored Mesa Verde soon after its discovery. In a 2014 *Denver Post* article by Tom Noel about a recent exhibition of Chain's work, the journalist noted that Chain had painted in New Mexico long before the Taos school of painters did. Noel wrote that Chain was the first woman to show her paintings at the National Academy of Design in New York City. In addition to her artistic abilities and daring, Chain felt deeply that the Chinese in Denver were mistreated, and she watched in horror the anti-Chinese riots of 1880. As a result, she set up a school for Chinese immigrants in her husband's bookstore, to teach them to read and write English.[64]

Aside from being the first Anglo woman to climb (and paint) certain peaks, Chain was a noted teacher of aspiring artists and often took them into the backcountry to paint. In addition, she was a lover of the art and culture of the Far East. On a trip to Japan with her husband in 1892, she wrote and illustrated a Japanese-inspired scroll of art and commentary, which she then mailed to Fortnightly before boarding a steamship bound ultimately for India. This scroll was later read in her memory and then cut into pages and displayed at the bookstore owned by her husband, after the couple's tragic death on this steamship, the *Bokhara,* which sank in a typhoon in the South China Sea between Shanghai and Hong Kong.[65]

22. **Legacy members and longest-active member:**

- Current member Jill Cowperthwaite is a fourth-generation member, a chain that began in 1884 with Mrs. E. F. Hallack, who married Jill's great-grandmother's brother. Jill's great-grandmother Mrs. Charles Hallack joined in 1896, and other family members joined in 1915, 1917, 1941, 1941, and 1992 (1992 is when Jill joined).[66]

- Current members Gretchen Bering and Ceci Wells both have family members who belonged to Fortnightly. Gretchen's great-grandmother was Ella Strong, who came to Denver from Chicago and married Dr. Charles Dennison. It was Ella whose idea it was to found Denver Fortnightly and to model it after Chicago Fortnightly (see "Founders," above). Gretchen reports that her Fortnightly legacy includes six family members of four generations.[67]

- Currently, the longest-active member is Lynette Emery, who joined the Denver Fortnightly Club in 1961. After Lynette comes Penny Tweedy, originally Penny Chenery, who joined in 1962. She is the sportswoman who bred and raced Secretariat, the 1973 winner of the Triple Crown, mentioned in item 21, above.[68] According to Mollie Eaton, Penny Tweedy still attends meetings at the age of ninety-one, although her name is not listed on the 2011–12 roster. Penny's daughter, Kate Tweedy, and daughter-in-law, Susan Tweedy, are also members. After Penny Tweedy comes Alice Bakemeir, who joined in 1966 and who is the author of several books about Denver's older neighborhoods.[69]

Snapshot Summary of The Monday Literary Club of Denver

1. **Official name of the club:** The Monday Literary Club of Denver.

2. **Date founded:** Officially, the date of the club's founding is October 1881. However, this is muddled by the preexistence of the group's forerunner, the Pleasant Hours Club, itself an outgrowth of a women's group of the Central Presbyterian Church.[70] This prior group began to organize itself with a constitution and bylaws at a meeting held in October 1881.[71] The club's first formal meeting was on November 7, 1881,[72] but still as the Pleasant Hours Club. The members added three new members to the original list at this meeting (see "Founders' names," below).[73] They changed their name to the Monday Literary Club on February 1, 1889.[74]

3. **Founders' names:** Mrs. Cornelius (Ermina) Ferris (president), Mary Bolles (vice president), Mrs. J. E. Hood (secretary and treasurer), Mrs. J. R. Howard, Mrs. W. McClintock, Lenora Bosworth, a mysterious Mrs. McPersh (who was never mentioned again[75]), and Mrs. S. M. Gaylord.[76] At the November meeting, they added a Mrs. Chiles, a Mrs. Richard, and a Mrs. Vickers to the club's membership roll.[77]

4. **Size of club as limited by bylaws:** Thirty active members. No limit to the number of honorary members.[78]

5. **Actual size of club today:** Thirty active members and seven honorary members.[79]

6. **Meeting schedule:** Thirteen meetings, one every two weeks, on the first and third Mondays, from the first week of October to the middle of April, at 1:00 p.m. There is only one meeting in (early) December.

7. **Where they meet:** Members' homes.

8. **Election of new members:** A prospective member is asked to attend a meeting to meet the members and see if she would like to join this kind of group. She needs a sponsor and two seconders, who, if she does want to join, send proposal letters to the president. These letters are read during the next

business meeting and then a second time, at the meeting after that. When a vote is taken, it is by secret or private ballot. Three or more noes keep the prospective member from joining.

9. **Object of the club:** According to the club's constitution, the object of the club is "mutual improvement, sociability, and the cultivation of whatsoever is noble, beautiful, just, and true." In the 1899–1900 yearbook, the object is said to be "to bring together women interested in intellectual culture."[80]

10. **Dues:** $10 per year.

11. **Club motto:** "Progress is the law of being." **Club flower:** The carnation. **Club colors:** None.[81]

12. **Paper or program assignment schedule:** Each member, except for top officers, gives a paper every other year, rotating with hostessing duties every other year.

13. **Length of papers or programs:** Forty-five minutes.

14. **Location of the club's archives:** Western history and genealogy department, Denver Public Library's main branch, downtown Denver.

15. **Civic achievement of the group or its members:**
    - Forty-year member Helen Christy told me that her "generation did a lot of volunteer work, serving on boards, such as Friends of the Denver Public Library, and of the Denver Art Museum." Members also volunteered time to other civic groups.
    - Eileen Ewing Archibold, 1899–1992, was a Republican elector for Colorado in 1940, a member of the Republican National Committee of Colorado from 1944 to 1948, and a delegate to the Republican National Convention in 1952.[82] She is said to have been a childhood friend of Mamie Eisenhower's, and she was a longtime Monday Club member until her death.
    - Current member and lawyer Chris Citron Moore, who graduated from Yale and from New York University School of Law, is a historic preservation and environmental activist and a community organizer who helped create the Colorado Center for Literature

and Art. She continues to fight the good fight for many causes. She was deeply involved in saving Denver's Mayan Theater in the 1980s.[83]

- Current member Jeanne Robb is serving her third term on the Denver city council.[84]
- Caroline Maddox, who has been a Monday Club member for sixteen years, has a long history of board membership and development work for Denver nonprofits.[85]
- Over the years, many Monday Literary Club members have served on the Denver Public Library friends' board.[86]
- Helen Ring Robinson (1878–1923) was the second woman elected to a state senate[87] and the first woman elected state senator in Colorado (1913–16).[88]
- "The early members were wives of men who shaped the future of Denver."[89]

16. **Special events of the year:** Usually, there are no special events, but there was an elaborate party given to commemorate the group's 100th anniversary in 1981. Some members remember it in detail. There was also a 125th anniversary party at Helen Christy's home in 2006. Helen recalls that members wore costumes if they wanted to—from any era of the club's history that they chose. Helen said that "everyone pitched in with a different detail" and that, in her downsized home, tables were set up in many rooms, including the master bathroom. Of the latter, she said, "It was everyone's favorite room. It was the most fun."[90]

17. **Refreshments:** An elaborate tea table, usually anchored by a silver tea service plus a coffee service, is enjoyed at the end of the meeting.

18. **Special traditions:**
   - One of the program co-chairwomen gives a bio of the speaker before her paper presentation.
   - Meetings start promptly at 1:00 p.m. After the presentation of the paper, the group breaks at about 2:00 p.m. for socializing around a beautifully loaded tea table, which I experienced firsthand when I

visited. The timing of the meeting's finale depends on the length of the paper presentation that day.

19. **Example of a yearly theme:** There is no theme. Women speak on what interests them.[91] However, in 1976, in honor of the country's bicentennial, all papers had an American history theme.[92]

20. **Example of a paper:** Some papers I heard described were about apes and their sign language, the life of honeybees, and the concept of zero. Forty-year member Helen Christy has researched and delivered twenty papers. Two that piqued my interest were "The Shakers" (given in 1976) and "The Wild Horse Inmate Program, or WHIP" (given in 2012).[93]

21. **Particularly colorful or interesting member, present or past:** Recently deceased member Frances Fulenwider Hepp was the subject of a book, *In Love and War: An American Girl and a German Diplomat,* published by member Helen Christy and her husband, Gary. Frances was born in 1913 in Denver and grew up there, becoming a Powers model. In 1937, she married a German journalist, Ernst Hepp, who was not a Nazi but who found himself working in the Nazi regime as a press advisor during WWII. He was able to convince Nazi Germany's Foreign Minister Joachim von Ribbentrop to let him and his wife and two children move to Sweden and to safety, but he was forced to return to Germany at one point. After the war and a twenty-year stay in South America, the family moved to Denver, where Frances joined the Mondays in 1972 and was a member until her death at the age of ninety in March 2004.[94]

22. **Legacy members and longest-active members:**
   - Joanne Abbott joined the Monday Club in 1963 (fifty-two years ago), Cynthia Nagel in 1968, and Nancy Doyle in 1970. They are all honorary members. The longest-involved active member is Barbara Benedict, who joined in 1970, forty-five years ago. She told me that her most recent paper was "T. E. Lawrence: Mythic Hero or Mirage?" Active member Helen Christy, whom I interviewed at length and who was my first contact in the group, joined in 1972. Sarah

Hite joined in 1978. It seems remarkable for such a small group—thirty active members—to have three still-participating members who have been members for forty-five, forty-three, and thirty-seven years, respectively.

- As for legacy members, I met Katie Wilkins and her mother, Sarah Hite, at the March 19, 2012, meeting. Sarah's mother, Mabel Hoper, was also a member of Monday Club. I also met two of the three generations of Abbott women: Joanne Abbott, currently the longest-active member of the Mondays, is the mother of Carol Abbott. Carol is the granddaughter of the late Elizabeth (also called Elsie) Lilly, a Smith College graduate and longtime Monday Club member.[95]

Snapshot Summary of Golden Fortnightly Club

1. **Official name of the club:** Golden Fortnightly Club.[96]
2. **Date founded:** The club organized on October 14, 1886, as the Addison Chautauqua Circle, following the rigorous and demanding Chautauqua curriculum and studying for diplomas. They were a Chautauqua club for seven years.[97] Then, they reorganized for three years as a Macaulay club, studying the writings of Thomas Macaulay, British essayist, historian, reviewer, and secretary at war in the mid-1800s.[98] The group finally became Golden Fortnightly in the fall of 1893.[99]
3. **Names of founders:** Mrs. C. C. Welch plus ten more charter members, which include Mrs. A. H. DeFrance, Mrs. J. H. Wells, Mrs. J. W. Barnes, Mrs. Nellie Moody, Mrs. D. C. Crawford, and Mrs. W. A. Dier.[100]
4. **Size of club as limited by bylaws or constitution:** Twenty-five active members. Associate members, a category bestowed on longtime members who request this status, seem to be unlimited in number.[101]
5. **Size of club today:** Fifteen active members and six associates, and one member on a leave of absence. The

club members were actively recruiting new members in the fall of 2012 when I visited them and had hopes that at least two more would join at that time.[102]

6. **Meeting schedule:** The club usually meets on the second and fourth Tuesday of the month, from 1:00 p.m. to 3:00 p.m., from the fourth Tuesday in September through the second Tuesday in May, except for the fourth Tuesday in November and the fourth Tuesday in December,[103] on which dates meetings are not held. This makes for fourteen to fifteen meetings a year.

7. **Where they meet:** Members' homes, except for special occasions.

8. **Election of new members:** Prospective members must visit two nonconsecutive meetings as a guest and then be proposed by one member and cosponsored by another member. Voting on members is done by written ballot.[104]

9. **Object of the club as stated in bylaws:** "To promote the intellectual and cultural growth of its members."[105]

10. **Dues:** $15, recently increased from $10.[106]

11. **Club motto:** "The secret of success is constancy of purpose" —Benjamin Disraeli.[107] **Club flower:** Carnation. **Club colors:** Silver and gold. (I think that this is very appropriate for a club based in a town that is home to the Colorado School of Mines.)

12. **Paper or program assignment schedule:** A sign-up list is passed at several meetings in the spring so that the members may sign up to hostess or present a program or a book review during the following academic year.

13. **Length of papers or programs:** About an hour.

14. **Location of the club's archives and/or scrapbooks:** The club historian keeps the scrapbooks for the past twenty-five years, but the rest of the scrapbooks and archives are stored in the facilities of History Colorado in Denver, whose headquarters and museum I visited to do research on the group.[108]

15. **Civic achievements of the group or its members:**
    • In 1907, the group donated money for the first panel of a plaster cast of a six-foot-tall marble

frieze, by renowned Icelandic/Danish sculptor Bertel Thorvaldsen (1770–1844), of Alexander the Great's entrance into Babylon. The original hangs in the Christiansborg Palace in Copenhagen. The Fortnightly panel and twenty others in the series, donated by various graduating high school senior classes in the original Golden High School building, now hang in the cafeteria of the new Golden High School.[109]

- As with virtually every group I studied, Golden Fortnightly rolled bandages for the troops during WWI and sewed for the Red Cross in WWII. They also contributed over the years to a variety of local projects and charities, including sponsoring a Campfire Girl group and the early Golden Library.[110] Current member Frani Bickart chaired the Jefferson Symphony's board of directors for two years, and Genie deLuise, at whose house the meeting I attended was held, was on the city council. Member Carol Dickinson was executive director of Foothills Art Center for ten years,[111] and she and her husband have endowed a sculpture garden there.[112]

16. **Special events of the year:**
    - The club begins and ends the year with a salad luncheon, splitting the food assignments among the members. Members with last names starting with a letter in the first half of the alphabet bring salads to the first luncheon. Members with last names starting with a letter in the second half of the alphabet bring salads to the second luncheon.
    - The final luncheon is also the annual meeting.
    - Every other year, the club members host a guest day—a luncheon or tea with an outside speaker.[113]

17. **Refreshments:** This group serves tea and/or coffee and other beverages with desserts at the *start* of most meetings. The meeting time is 1:00 p.m., and perhaps the idea is that the women will have a light lunch before heading to

Fortnightly, where they may enjoy some dessert. In the club's earlier days, refreshments were served after the meeting.[114]

18. **Special traditions:**
    - For every paper, the secretary or presenter writes a summary. The chair of the program committee keeps these summaries on file and presents a written year-end report to all the members. Members may check these to see if a subject has been covered.
    - In every yearbook, there are two to four quotations on the reverse side of the title page. The club president deems these quotations inspirational.
    - The order of each meeting has remained the same since the club's beginning: call to order, reading of minutes, roll call, reports of committees, correspondence, unfinished business, new business, announcements, literary program, and adjournment.[115]

19. **Example of overall yearly theme of study:** Unlike in earlier days, when each year had a study theme that was literary or historical in nature, there is currently no overall theme. Instead, the group does book reviews or presentations on a variety of subjects, which are the individual members' personal choice.

20. **Example of a paper on this theme:** Member Ann Camy gave a presentation called the "History of Golden Fortnightly Club" at the Golden History Center in October 2011. Ann's paper placed the club's history in the context of the history of Golden, the state of Colorado, and the United States as well. On the day I visited, member Julie Ann Terry gave a talk on cheeses. She had samples for us to try, plus other foods to accompany the cheeses. A look at the club's yearly schedule from 2011 to 2012 shows six programs or presentations on a variety of subjects, all in the first part of year, and eight book reviews, done between January 24 and the final salad luncheon on May 8.

21. **Particularly colorful or interesting member, present or past:** Currently on leave after a serious accident, member Ann Camy once ran a pub in England. She also taught creative writing at Red Rocks Community College and taught

high school English. She writes cowboy poetry and was the treasurer of the Colorado Poetry Society. She is the author of young adult books and was a tour leader for bus tours to various destinations in the USA. Her mother was a longtime member of Fortnightly. Her father worked in public relations for Coors and was also the mayor of Golden at one time.[116]

22. **Legacy members and longest-active members:**

- Lois Goad was eighty-six when I visited and was an associate member. She has been a member since 1958—an astonishing fifty-seven years.[117]
- Dorothy Carpenter, who died soon after I visited the group,[118] joined in 1963—fifty-two years of membership. The club's 1986 scrapbook has a stunning photo of Dorothy dressed in a turn-of-the-century gown for the group's hundredth birthday. She was still beautiful in a 2009 photo.
- Genie deLuise, who hosted the meeting especially scheduled for my convenience, had been a member for thirty-nine years when I visited. She hugged me hard when I stepped through her front door, welcomed me with great gusto and warmth, and was a consummate hostess.
- I met Harriet Lubahn at the meeting I attended. She joined in 1961—fifty-four years ago—but she did take a twenty-year break to work as a school librarian before rejoining the group. Sadly, Harriet died in September, a few months after my visit to the Golden group.[119]
- I also met May Williams, who has been an active member for forty-four years.[120]
- As for legacy members, both Clare Taylor's mother and Ann Camy's mother were members of Golden Fortnightly. But at least one member assured me that daughters of members do not get an automatic "in."[121]
- Mrs. William A. Dier was one of the group's charter members. Her daughter, Katherine Dier Lowther, "was a member of Fortnightly until her death in 1971."[122]

CHAPTER 4

Eugene, Oregon

Cold, Wet Eugene, Oregon, Where I Found Three Warm and Welcoming Women's Study Groups

I certainly never saw worse weather during my book research and travel than I did in Eugene, Oregon. I was in town during April 1–5, 2012, to visit a cluster of three historic women's study clubs and access their archives. I arrived by plane on a Sunday that was both April Fool's Day and Palm Sunday. Looking back, I see that this oddity of the calendar may have been a portent of the combination of bad luck (bad weather) and high moral purpose (the goals of self-educating and socially involved groups of women) that I'd find in Eugene.

Before landing at the town's airport, I had looked out my airplane window at the soggy, green countryside and had seen sheep standing with their lambs in flooded fields. I worried that the poor lambs had been born in the standing water. Once the plane landed at 1:00 p.m., I found that the temperature on the ground was a bone-chilling forty-one degrees. Also, it was raining. At home in Los Angeles, it was seventy-five degrees and sunny. I stood with the other passengers in the rain by the side of our small Horizon Air / Alaska Air prop jet, waiting for our carry-on bags to be freed from the luggage bay under the plane.

Having collected my bag, I picked up a rental car and drove into town, where I checked into my hotel. For my four nights in Eugene, I stayed in the completely unique, appropriately aged (a hundred-plus years old, just like my women's groups), stone Excelsior Inn, which began life in 1910 as a sorority house for the nearby University of Oregon and which currently identifies its rooms by naming each after a famous composer. I was in Schubert, one of the inn's two smallest rooms. Once unpacked, I called the women who would be my hostesses and guides while I was in town. They told me that this had been an especially cold and miserable spring, with a freak snowstorm having ravished the newly leafed-out trees just the week before, causing them considerable damage. The streets and sidewalks were littered with broken branches, which I saw as I made my way around town. The local rivers, the Willamette and the McKenzie, were both very high. However bad the weather seemed to me, university students seemed to take it all in stride. As they streamed by on the sidewalk in front of the hotel or across the adjacent campus, I noticed that a good number wore high, jaunty rubber boots. Some wore short shorts despite the frigid temperature. During my four days in town, I spent considerable time on the campus, either in its Knight Library, going through club archives, or walking there from my hotel. I would say that the school's mascot, the Oregon duck, was appropriately chosen to suit the local weather conditions. It even sleeted one afternoon while I was doing research in the library, with the sleet hitting the windows like buckshot. The weather is so typically horrible in Eugene that weather reporters on television get very excited about anticipated sunny spells, calling them "sun breaks," which made me smile.

All of this horrific weather was in complete contrast to the warm welcome I received from the three groups and from one friend of a friend, Susan Verner, who picked me up shortly after I arrived. She gave me a succinct tour of the area and invited me to dinner at her house, which her husband obligingly prepared while she walked me around her neighborhood and gave me the lowdown on Eugene's politics, life, and lore.

However, Susan knew nothing of the three historic women's study clubs that I'd found through some digging and some pestering of sources. The next day, two of these groups, Eugene Shakespeare and the Monday Book Club, managed to work together to pick me up and move me from one meeting to the next, having already changed their meeting times by an hour each so that I could attend the two meetings in one day. In addition, members of Eugene Shakespeare took me out to dinner after their meeting in the very fine restaurant on the ground floor of the Excelsior. On top of that, I stupidly left my raincoat at the home where the Eugene Monday Book Club was meeting, and that began a chain of very hospitable events in which club members arranged that my coat be taken to the symphony performance that night, passed off to another club member, and then given to me the next day when I met with Fortnightly and Monday club member Anne Carter and was taken to her house to go through her Monday Club archives. Being in Eugene without a raincoat was a frightening prospect. I was very thankful for the women's generosity and resourcefulness in getting my coat back to me, especially as the homes where I met the two groups involved in the rescue operation were far from my hotel and far from each other.

The incident of the raincoat was, as far as I was concerned, a perfect example of the kind of intelligent, thoughtful, and socially and culturally involved approach to life that motivates the women in this country's historic study clubs. They share the tasks at hand and work together in a very civilized manner.

My first meeting on Monday had been with the sixteen-member Monday Book Club. One of these members, Sally Weston, picked me up at my hotel and gave me a bit of a guided tour as we made our way to the home of member Liz Hall. I enjoyed a sit-down luncheon there, produced by our hostess, followed by a brilliantly done, highly detailed book review of *Terrorists in Love: The Real Lives of Islamic Radicals,* delivered by member Shirley Clark. The group takes turns giving book reviews or reports, telling the entire story of the book, which is usually nonfiction, although members have reviewed plays and poetry.

After that meeting, I was picked up by the president of Eugene Shakespeare, Flo Avergne, and driven to that club's meeting. There, I heard an absolutely first-rate historical background of and reading of *Henry V,* acts four and five. Member Sigrid Lambros gave the historical background and then directed the reading performed by several of the fifteen club members attending the meeting that day. I must say, I was a bit taken aback by the quality of the reading, which included some bits of French language, which the women seemed to relish getting their teeth into. I was also impressed by the amount of information that the women knew about the play. I was told that many of them act in local productions. The home where the meeting was held belonged to member Lydia Lord, who, after the meeting, showed me the club's bookcase of Shakespeare reference books and plays that she keeps on the second floor of her home.

No refreshments are served at the club's regular meetings, but there is always a pitcher of ice water on the table, as there was on Lydia's dining room table downstairs, within view from where the group had been meeting in Lydia's living room. The ice-water-only rule is a tradition, but the club does have parties three times a year where food is served, including an April celebration of Shakespeare's birthday with a special cake, and a *Twelfth Night* party in early January with wassail and a Yule log.

On a food-related subject: one longtime club member, Madge Lorwin, who died in 2003 at the age of ninety-six, was the celebrated author of *Dining with William Shakespeare* (Atheneum, 1976), which has long been considered *the* reference book on Elizabethan cookery. She worked on the book for nine years after giving an Elizabethan feast for the Shakespeare Club in 1967 and being encouraged to take the research she had done for that meal even further.

I attended the regular meeting of Eugene Fortnightly from 1:00 p.m. to 2:00 p.m. on Thursday, April 5, filling in my time between the meetings on April 2 and April 5 by doing research in the three clubs' archives. Fortnightly is a large and thriving group with fifty active members. About forty of them filled the meeting room of the First Congregational Church, entering quickly a few minutes before 1:00 p.m. and seating themselves immediately in rows of folding chairs. There are no refreshments at these meetings, so the meeting began efficiently at 1:00 and ended efficiently at about 2:00. The president, Julie Whitmore, began by moving quickly through the business at hand and onto the program. Sandra Piele, a member since 2004, was the speaker for the day. She was introduced by a club member, Jane Powell, who gave a brief bio of Sandra, mentioning that Sandra had two aunts who had been members of Eugene Fortnightly. This type of biographical introduction of the speaker given by another member is a tradition I found in several of the groups I visited. Sandra gave an excellent, in-depth exploration of her assigned topic, "Environmental Law—Going Green Is Not Just a Good Idea," by discussing the specific case of "The Spotted Owl vs. Old Growth Controversy." At one point, to show how emotional the subject was to people in Eugene, she unfurled a huge scroll of paper that reached from one side of the room to the other. On it, she'd pasted all of the articles about the spotted owl controversy recently printed in local papers. She finished at 1:55, and questions from club members followed.

After the meeting, I spoke to my great helper in the group, Nancy Kibbey, who had researched and written a very professional history of Fortnightly in 2010. This is another feature I found in several of the groups: self-trained or university-trained club historians who took great pains to dig into the group's past, using primary source documents, and then wrote a thorough history of the group. When I asked Nancy if she were a trained historian, she said that she was a fabric artist and had completed only two years of college. She also told me that she loved doing the papers and would hate to give up her active status in the club. Clearly, she is a woman who loves history and who likes to learn and challenge her mind—the perfect candidate for membership in one of these historic study clubs.

After thanking Nancy for her help and being greeted by a few women I'd met in other groups, I drove to the airport and flew to San Francisco for my meeting with the Santa Cruz Shakespeare Club, which was to take place the next morning. Unfortunately, I'd been turned down by the FRFG Women's Study Club in Gilroy, California, and would not be allowed to visit them, so my so-called cluster in Northern California was reduced to one actual visit with the Santa Cruz group. But I had the permission of the Gilroy club's historian to use her prizewinning history of the club to put together a summary of the group, which follows.

Snapshot Summary of the Fortnightly Club of Eugene

1. **Official name of the club:** Fortnightly Club of Eugene.
2. **Date founded:** December 13, 1893.
3. **Founder's name:** Dr. Alice Hall Chapman, MD, wife of the second president of the University of Oregon. Twenty-one women joined her as charter members.[1]
4. **Size of club as limited by bylaws:** Fifty active members, unless a temporary excess of actives is caused by the return of a reserve or associate member.[2]
5. **Actual size of club today:** Fifty-one active members and twenty-eight associates. No reserve members are listed in the 2011–12 yearbook. The reserve category is for members who are unable to attend meetings because of health problems or job commitments.[3] When I asked member Carol Hildebrand before the April 5, 2012, meeting why there were so many associate members, she said, "Because we live forever." After working on this book, I could almost believe it - having come to believe in the longevity of women's literary society members.
6. **Meeting schedule:** Fortnightly meets from 1:00 p.m. to 2:00 p.m. on the first and third Thursday of the month, October through May. Unlike all other literary societies and study clubs covered in this book, they do meet twice in December (one meeting being the holiday coffee). They meet only once in January, strictly on the third Thursday. Their first meeting is their fall luncheon, held at the Eugene Country Club in 2011, and their final meeting in May is the spring luncheon, which takes place at 11:30 a.m.[4]
7. **Where they meet:** Virtually all meetings, except for the fall luncheon and possibly the holiday coffee and the spring luncheon, are held in the First Congregational Church. The holiday coffee is typically held at a member's home.[5] The venue of the spring luncheon is decided by the social committee.[6]

8. **Election of new members:** Prospective members are usually invited to a meeting on guest day.[7] Nominations for membership are made to the executive board on a prospective member form, which must be signed by three active or associate members, one of whom must be a member of the board.[8] Letters describing the nominee's achievements and attributes, written by club members, accompany the application.[9] The board votes on member nominations by written ballot at the executive board meeting in December or May, with their presentation to the board having been done in April or November. The number of votes allowed each board member corresponds to the number of vacancies. A simple majority is required to elect a woman to membership.[10]

9. **Object of the club as stated in bylaws:** The original object was "to bring together women interested in artistic, economic, philanthropic, literary, and scientific pursuits with a view of rendering them helpful to each other and useful to society." The 1935 constitution and bylaws shortened this to, "To bring together women interested in cultural and social pursuits."[11] Recently, this was changed to, "To bring together women interested in cultural pursuits and fellowship."[12]

10. **Dues:** $45 for active members; $25 for associate members.

11. **Club motto:** None. **Club flower:** None, but a red rose is given to new members at the induction, as well as to new officers. In addition, members who have reached the twenty-five-year mark and thirty-year mark, etc., receive a red rose at the spring luncheon.[13] **Club colors:** None, but **Club pledge:** Many clubs share the same prayer, "The Collect for Club Women," written in the early 1900s by a Colorado woman, but this group has a nonreligious pledge, found at the beginning of their yearbook and taken from their original constitution. No longer recited at meetings, but recited by new members, the pledge consists of five sentences. Its final sentence is, "I will be a member of the Club as long as I can be useful to it and receive benefit from it."[14]

12. **Paper and hostessing assignment rotation schedule:** There are no traditional (rotating) hostesses, as the group meets in the First Congregational Church, not in homes.

However, there is a room and hospitality standing committee to manage the setup of the church's meeting room with chairs, a lectern, etc. The social committee manages the fall and spring luncheon and the holiday coffee. As for the assignment of nine papers to members each year and the choice of topics, that is done by the program committee, whose rotation schedule results in a paper assignment every three to four years for every member, except for the president and program chairwoman,[15] but they may choose to participate and give a paper.[16] There are usually three guest speakers each year, spread out during the year.

13. **Length of papers or programs:** "Programs shall not exceed 45 minutes in length, and the material used shall be varied and flexible."[17] A Q&A session should follow each paper, and the meeting, which begins at 1:00 p.m., should end at 2:00 p.m. sharp.

14. **Location of the club's archives:** Special Collections, Knight Library, University of Oregon, Eugene.

15. **Civic achievement of the group or its members:** In 1904, Fortnightly agitated for a Carnegie Library, like so many of its sister literary societies. In 1906, the new library opened. To thank them for their help, Fortnightly was given a meeting room there,[18] which they later had to relinquish once the library had a need for it. The Fortnightly's 657 volumes were the "nucleus" of the new library's collection.[19] Prior to the founding of the Eugene Public Library, the club had started a circulating library with its own books. Its librarian, Fortnightly member Mrs. Adelaide Lilly, who trained to be a librarian at the age of forty-seven, after her husband's death, was chosen to be city librarian in the new public library. She "held that position until her death"[20] in 1933.[21] In 1959, Fortnightly also funded the library's first bookmobile.[22]

16. **Special events of the year:** A fall luncheon to open the club year, a holiday coffee, and the spring potluck luncheon. These are the only "social meetings."

17. **Refreshments:** For all but the three special events mentioned above, there are no refreshments.

18. **Special traditions:**

- A "silver offering" (loose change) is collected at the holiday coffee in December and is earmarked for a project chosen each year by the executive board.[23]
- The public library is seen as the "principal project"[24] of the club. A book chosen to honor each deceased member is donated to the library.[25]
- The archives chairwoman takes her successor to the Special Collections department of the Knight Library at the University of Oregon, introduces her to the staff, and shows her the procedures for accessing club archives. The new club archivist is in charge of placing in the archives two copies of that year's yearbook and a copy of papers presented by members during the preceding year, as well as fully filled scrapbooks.[26]
- There are three guest speakers each year. Members may invite guests to those meetings.[27]
- New members are inducted at the holiday coffee or the spring luncheon. They are presented with a red rose "at an appropriate ceremony."[28]
- Small teas are given in members' homes, usually by a sponsor in honor of a new member, possibly when the new member gives her first paper.[29] Small luncheons at a number of homes are also encouraged. Those attending get to know each other better by drawing seating/destination assignments from a hat. Small potlucks are also encouraged for the same reason.[30]
- The tradition of maintaining a low-tech approach to the club's life was abandoned by a vote of the membership at the April 2012 meeting I attended, when members approved the funding of a Fortnightly Club of Eugene website. A member will act as webmaster; another, as a backup. I only encountered a few groups that maintained a web site, probably due to their very private nature.
- One member introduces the speaker for the day, giving a brief biography.

19. **Example of an overall yearly theme or topic:** In 2011–12, the topic was "Court Decisions that Affect Our Lives."

20. **Example of an individual paper for the topic:** The paper I heard presented by member Sandra Piele on April 5, 2012, was "Environmental Law: Going Green—Not Just a Good Idea."

21. **Particularly colorful or interesting member, present or past:**

    - The club's founder, Alice Hall Chapman, MD, was a practicing physician and was the wife of the second president of the University of Oregon. She studied medicine in New York and Europe and had been active in New York City's Sorosis club,[31] the mother of all women's literary societies. She also worked to establish women's sports at the university.[32]
    - Charter member Luella Clay Carson was the University of Oregon's first dean of women and, later, the president of Mills College.[33]
    - Charter member Helen Bushnell started the first local chapter of the Women's Christian Temperance Union. She also served as librarian in "the first public library in Eugene, upstairs in a store building on Willamette Street."[34] This was a subscription library opened by the Eugene Library Association in 1874.[35]
    - Charter member and businesswoman Idaho Campbell at the age of 64 was a passenger in the cockpit of a Boeing air transport on July 6, 1928 on a cross-country mail route for twenty-six hours, during which the plane lost its way in the Midwest, but she remained thrilled throughout, flying over country her parents had traveled in a covered wagon. Her grand home, built for her by her father, who was a pioneer, a gold miner, and a timber owner, is now a bed-and-breakfast called the Campbell House.[36]

22. **Legacy members and longest-active members:**

    - Regarding legacy members: Sandra Piele, who delivered her paper at the meeting I attended, had two aunts who were members of Eugene Fortnightly.

Another member, Molly Stafford, is related to a founding member, Cornelia Straub, by virtue of the fact that Molly's mother-in-law, Sally Stafford, was Cornelia's daughter-in-law.[37]

- Regarding the longest-active members: two associate members, Hope Pressman and Jane Thomas, joined Fortnightly in 1955, sixty years ago. As for longest-still-active member of Eugene Fortnightly, that honor goes to Anne Carter, who joined in 1978, thirty-seven years ago. Anne is also a member of Monday Literary Club. She hosted me in her home to review that club's archives.

Snapshot Summary of Monday Book Club of Eugene

1. **Official name of the club:** Monday Book Club of Eugene, Oregon.
2. **Date founded:** Fall (probably November) 1911.[38]
3. **Founders' names:** Eleven women met at the home of Mrs. Guy Davis on South Willamette Street. They were Mmes. Currie, Davis, Deifel, Eberhardt, Flint, Gilbert, Gullion, Magladry, Matlock, McMorran, and Roberts.[39]
4. **Size of club as limited by constitution or bylaws:** Sixteen women, "proposed by individual members and elected by vote of the club."[40]
5. **Size of club today, including all categories of membership:** Sixteen active members and three honorary members.
6. **Meeting schedule:** The club, obviously, meets on Mondays, and their start time is 1:00 p.m. The meetings begin for the season in October and end in late May or early June, taking place twice a month, for a total of sixteen meetings. For a large chunk of time—from four to six weeks during the Christmas and New Year holidays—the club doesn't meet.[41]
7. **Where they meet:** In members' homes.

8. **Election of new members:** Members propose two or more names to the membership committee for each vacancy. Two anonymous ballots are required. The first lists all names submitted and asks if anyone objects to any of them. A single no vote removes a name. The second ballot, with the remaining names, requires that members choose a first, second, and, possibly, third choice. The candidate with the highest number of votes is invited to join. If she declines, then the next in line is asked.[42]

9. **Object of the club as stated in the constitution:** "The purpose of this club is to share friendship and our mutual interest in good books."[43]

10. **Dues:** The club abolished dues in 1975.[44] If a need arises, then a collection is taken. A small account is kept for occasional expenses. For instance, the club donates a $100 shelf at the library—actually, a plaque on a shelf—in memory of each Monday Book Club member who dies. At the meeting I attended, the president, Karen Warren, said she had found some change under her couch cushions, which she was donating to the tiny treasury. This was a bit tongue-in-cheek. The group chuckled knowingly.

11. **Club motto, flower, and colors:** The motto was "Work" before it was discarded in 1921.[45] If there ever were a club flower and club colors, they have been lost to time.

12. **Paper or program assignment schedule and hostessing assignment rotation:** There are sixteen members and sixteen papers or reports, so each member is expected to give one book report per year. As for hostessing, the same holds true. Prospective new members are asked, "Are you willing to give a book report once a year, and can you serve a sit-down lunch to sixteen people in your home?" Longtime member Anne Carter told me, "Program scheduling and hosting is accomplished by passing around a clipboard listing next year's schedule, which begins in October and goes through June." Sign-ups are voluntary and are often changed as personal schedules change.[46]

13. **Length of papers:** Forty-five minutes to an hour.

14. **Location of the club's archives:** The archives are currently kept in the home of Anne Carter, who acts as the club's historian. I visited her at her home during my visit to Eugene so that I could plow through the boxes and scrapbooks. I did find a note in the archives claiming that a summary of the club's history done in 1985 was given, along with some of the pertinent research material, to the Lane County Historical Society (LCHS).[47] However, I never received a confirmation of this bit of information from the LCHS. Anne was puzzled to hear of the alleged summary.

15. **Civic achievements of the club or its members:** Anne Carter said, "Though in the beginning the club was established to 'delve into literature during the indoor season,' the ladies did involve themselves in advocating and promoting civic issues and concerns of the day." Anne listed the club's involvement in ballot measures; fund-raising for public building and causes; Red Cross efforts during the world wars; fighting for public cleanliness in Eugene; raising funds for Chinese relief; university scholarships; support of orphans; sending money for Biafran relief; and the perennial practice of donating books and funds to the Eugene Public Library. (See "Special traditions," below.[48])

16. **Special events of the year:**
    - There is a holiday luncheon with wine—the only luncheon at which wine is served. This new tradition began when the program for a particular December meeting was about the establishment of Oregon wineries. Club members enjoyed sampling the subject matter so much that the tradition has been continued.[49]
    - In the summer, the new president hosts a morning coffee, where the program booklet for the upcoming year is usually handed out. At this time, members might also discuss what books they plan to review.[50]

17. **Refreshments:** Meetings start with a seated lunch, with members usually divided, some sitting at a dining room table and others at a breakfast room table or something similar, as it would be difficult to get fourteen to sixteen women around

one normal dining room table. After a salad lunch—usually a chicken salad recipe (accompanied by a fruit salad on the day I attended)—See's chocolates are passed. Many members have a set of at least sixteen tiny plates for these candies, to be used with each place setting for a Monday's lunch.

18. **Special traditions:**

- My favorite tradition of this group, and possibly of any of the women's study groups in this book, is the passing of the See's chocolate candy at the end of the meal and the set of sixteen tiny plates that Anne Carter, meeting hostess Liz Hall, and other members have in their sideboards for serving this special Monday Book Club treat.

- For the club's hundredth anniversary, Anne Carter collected "reading memories" from each of the members—memories of their first book reviews and favorite reading experiences. I suspect that this will continue in the years to come.

- In 2006, different members took different club minutes from different eras and summarized them in printed reports for the archives. My guess is that the club will continue to do this for each decade to come—a new tradition.

- Club members have wine with lunch at holiday time, another new tradition.

- The usual salad served at lunch is chicken salad. One member told me that a good cookbook for the group to publish would be called *A Hundred Years of Chicken Salad.*

- A member introduces the member who is about to give her book report. I saw this custom in many of the groups I visited.

- Although the club uses no prayer today, "The Collect for Club Women" was a part of its history and was traditionally used in the early days. I saw this prayer being used in many groups which have no knowledge of each other. I feel that is probably a remnant of early study club federation memberships, when groups shared information through a central organization.

- Members' dietary concerns and allergies are listed in the club yearbook to help the hostess plan the menu.
- No "hostile or strained conversations takes place amongst" members.[51] Anne Carter told me several times that the club members try not to talk about politics or religion, so as to keep the atmosphere congenial.
- See "Special events of the year," above, for information about the club's traditional holiday meeting and summer coffee.

19. **Example of a yearly topic:** There is no overall topic. Each woman delivers a very in-depth book report on a work of nonfiction or fiction, a play, or poetry, but I was told that the books covered are almost always nonfiction. No one else in the group needs to have read the book. Several women stressed that this group does not give book reviews, saying that they give *reports* that tell the whole story of the book when it is their turn to present the program. In the 1980s, former member Lucile Aly delivered a report on six historical novels by the same author about Mary, Queen of Scots. Longtime member Marian Wilson, now deceased, would do readings of entire plays or musicals and might have included recordings of bits of the corresponding score.

20. **Example of a paper based on that topic:** The book report delivered by member Shirley Clark on April 12, 2012, thoroughly covered Ken Ballen's *Terrorists in Love: The Real Lives of Islamic Radicals.* I have a printed copy of the report. It is nine and a half single-spaced pages long—very detailed, presenting a complete and complex picture of the book, a list of characters, a list of terminology, and an overview.

21. **Particularly colorful or interesting member, present or past:** I repeatedly found newspaper stories about and photos of fifty-five-year member Marian Wilson, who was the wife of the president of the University of Oregon. She joined the club in 1956 and was a member until the day she died in 2011. She is said to have had a keen mind, to have

been extremely gracious, and to have been the mother of six, grandmother of twenty-five, and great-grandmother of thirty-five.[52] In every photo I saw of her—into her ninety-fourth year—she was smiling a smile that reached from ear to ear. Her specialties were poetry and drama, and she was known to play all the roles in a drama or give the most startlingly vivid descriptions of the books she chose.[53] In one obituary, Marian's community activities were described: "Art, theater, and hospital boards; faculty women, service and study groups; book and bridge clubs benefitted equally from her energy, ideas, appreciation and participation. She took great joy in opera, symphony, and ballet; and she treasured the Oregon Bach and Oregon Shakespeare Festivals. The University of Oregon Ducks never had a greater fan."[54]

22. **Legacy members and longest-active members:**
- Active member Anne Carter joined in 1992, twenty-three years ago, and honorary member Sue Keene Malott has been a member since 1978, for thirty-seven years. Beloved former member Marian Wilson was a member for fifty-five years.
- In a report of the club minutes from the 1990s, it is noted that member Jari Byard gave her thirty-fourth book review in May 1997.[55] She was a member from 1963 to 2000—thirty-seven years.
- As for legacy members: new member Natalie Newlove had two aunts who were members, one whose wonderful name was Eupheme Culp.

Monday Book Club, Eugene, Oregon
Photo by Karen Warren

Snapshot Summary of the Shakespeare Club of Eugene, Oregon

1. **Official name of the club:** The club is called "the Shakespeare Club of Eugene, Oregon," in the preamble to its constitution, which was updated in 2004, but the club is not mentioned by that name or any other in the rest of the document.[56] However, the cover sheet for this updated document and all other documents refer to the club as the Eugene Shakespeare Club. When it was first founded, its name was Monday Afternoon Shakespeare Club.[57]

2. **Date founded:** 1909,[58] but the club feels that it is the direct descendant of a men's and women's study group started in 1893 and disbanded in 1899. The club includes that earlier group's archives with its own in the Knight Library of the University of Oregon.[59] To further complicate matters, Eugene Shakespeare Club did not adopt a constitution until 1912.[60] On May 13, 1912, they elected a president and secretary for the first time—Ms. Mabelle Gilstrap and Mrs. P.K. Hammond, respectively.[61] Until that time, from 1909 to 1912, they simply met to read or act out the plays without taking notes or having bylaws.[62]

3. **Founded by:** Mrs. Hammond, the wife of Eugene's Episcopalian rector.[63] Other charter members were Mrs. Tromp, Mrs. Buoy, Mrs. Dillon, Mrs. Loomis, Mrs. McGladry, and Mrs. Frink.[64]

4. **Size of club as stated in bylaws (size limit):** Twenty-five.[65]

5. **Size of club today:** Twelve active members, one honorary member, and eleven life members.[66]

6. **Meeting schedule:** Meetings are held on Monday afternoons, from 2:00 p.m. to 4:00 p.m., roughly every two weeks from early October to late April. There is one meeting in December—the Christmas tea.[67] In all, there are three special, social events each year: the Christmas tea, Shakespeare's birthday luncheon, and a Twelfth Night celebration. (See below in Refreshment highlights.)

7. **Where they meet:** In members' homes,[68] but off-site for special occasions. (See "Refreshment highlights," below.)

8. **Election of new members:** Prospective members are invited to Shakespeare's birthday party, as was discussed when I visited, and members may be added at any time.[69] The club's constitution specifies that a possible new member be proposed by a member and then have her name presented to the membership for approval.[70]

9. **Object of the club as stated in bylaws:** "Organized for the study and fuller appreciation of the works of William Shakespeare, and pledged to faithful cooperation and regular attendance."[71]

10. **Dues**: $20 a year.[72]

11. **Club motto, flower, and colors:** None found.

12. **Paper or programming schedule and hostessing arrangement:** The president passes around a sign-up sheet at the final meeting—the business meeting—and members volunteer for hostessing dates. Another sheet is passed for volunteers for the job of facilitator of the play readings, once the four plays for the season are announced at the Oregon Shakespeare Festival, as those are the plays the group usually studies.[73] Member Lydia Lord explained to me, "In the event that no one volunteers to host a meeting (or to lead a play discussion and reading), the program/hospitality chair asks for volunteers, usually by phone."[74]

13. **Length of programs:** Meetings last exactly two hours. A half hour is spent on business, and an hour and a half is spent on a discussion of one of the four plays studied each season and the reading of some portion of that play. A member who has volunteered for the job of facilitator researches her commentary on the play and assigns the roles to fellow members.

14. **Location of the club's archives:** An active scrapbook is kept by the club historian, but the club's archives are kept in the Knight Library of the University of Oregon.

15. **Special events:** See "Refreshment highlights," below.

16. **Refreshment highlights:**

- No refreshments are served at most meetings. At the meeting I attended, there was a pitcher of ice water and some glasses sitting on the dining room table of hostess Lydia Lord's home, and I was told this is traditional. However, there are three social events during the year, and there are refreshments at those.
- The Christmas tea lasts for at least one hour, and the hostess—a life member who has hosted the event for many years—contributes tea and coffee. Members bring cookies and seasonal treats. A second hour is usually spent on the club's business.[75]
- On the Monday closest to January 6, the club holds its *Twelfth Night* party in a life member's home, with Shakespeare-related games or funny poems written by club members and music by members or guests.[76] A Yule-log cake and wassail are featured. When the cake is marched into the room, the club members sing "Here We Come a-Wassailing" or "Here We Come a-Shakespearing." Sprigs of evergreen are thrown into the fireplace, in which there is a roaring fire reflecting the spirit of the season. The *Twelfth Night* party was a big social event in the club's early days, with men invited and coverage in the local newspaper.[77]
- In April, the club holds a luncheon to celebrate Shakespeare's birthday. In recent years, this event has been held at the Eugene Country Club or Lane Community College. There is always a birthday cake, a guest speaker, and a drawing for a small bust of Shakespeare, which gets passed around from year to year among the winning members.

17. **Special traditions:**

- See above for the club's three social events of the year.
- Eugene Shakespeare Club maintains the tradition of a lending library—which includes books about Shakespeare and his plays—housed in the home of

member and club librarian Lydia Lord. New books are offered to members to "check out" on loan. The lending library includes a complete set of Shakespeare's plays and a set of *Hollinshed's Chronicles,* a history that Shakespeare used to write many of his plays, especially his historical plays.

- No one arriving at a meeting ever knocks on the front door of the home where the meeting is to take place. Members are expected to arrive promptly at 2:00 p.m., to let themselves in, and to be ready to depart promptly at 4:00 p.m. There are no refreshments other than ice water, which is offered at the end of the meeting.

- The group maintains an informal relationship with Ashland's Oregon Shakespeare Festival. Most members travel to Ashland to see Shakespeare productions. The club gives money to the festival in honor of recently deceased members.

- Meetings are held in a somewhat formal manner, following the same agenda that the members have followed for much of their life as a group. However, the atmosphere is relaxed and very friendly, especially during the reading of the play, when laughter breaks out at intervals.

18. **Example of a yearly theme or topic:** Club members read and study four Shakespeare plays per year.[78] These are usually the same ones chosen by the Oregon Shakespeare Festival in Ashland, Oregon.

19. **An example of a paper or program presented on that theme:** One member leads the group in a discussion of the play—one out of four plays studied per year—a section of which will then be read quite dramatically and professionally by club members who have been assigned a part. Plays usually take three meetings to finish,[79] and members often read the same part at each of the three meetings. When I visited the group on Monday, April 2, 2013, they were reading and discussing *Henry V,* acts 4 and 5. The woman who led the discussions and gave a well-prepared report on the play

(themes, historical significance, etc.) was Sigrid Lambros. The line readings were extraordinary. I was told that many of the members have acted in local theater productions.

20. **Particularly colorful or interesting member, present or past:** Madge Lorwin (1907–2003) was a gourmet cooking teacher and a member of Shakespeare Club who was able to brilliantly combine these interests. Starting in the 1960s, she began to research and test recipes for dishes mentioned in Shakespeare's plays, sometimes with the help of her husband, Val. Val Lorwin, a professor of history at the University of Oregon and also a labor activist,[80] had, early in his career, been wrongly embroiled in a series of McCarthy-era witch hunts.[81] In 1967, Madge presented a dinner—an Elizabethan feast—featuring these dishes to her beloved Shakespeare Club. Then, after nine years of testing and tinkering, trying to determine measurements (as there were none in the early 1600s), researching, and writing, Madge oversaw the publication of her cookbook of these recipes, *Dining with William Shakespeare* (Atheneum, 1976),[82] which is still referred to today as a sort of gold standard for cooking of that era and is used in a wide range of programming. It is also mentioned in other cookbooks. In fact, as I was searching online for information about Madge, I found a query letter dated 2010 from a rights and permissions officer at Yale University Press. The officer was looking for relatives of Madge to whom to send the cookbook's royalty checks.[83] Copies of the cookbook are available today through Amazon.com, with new copies selling for $53.77, so-called collectible copies for $35, and used copies for $4.70.[84] While Madge was researching the book, her husband was so supportive of her project that he is said to have Xeroxed all cookbooks of the Elizabethan period that were available in the British Museum when he was in London.[85] In addition to leaving the legacy of this acclaimed book, Madge and her husband established and endowed a lecture series at the university, the Lorwin Lectureship on Civil Rights, which lives on today and which features "world-class activists, scholars, and writers."[86]

21. **Legacy members and longest-active members:** There seem to be no legacy members at this time. As for the longest-active member, that is Phoebe Staples, who has been a member since 1955—sixty years.[87]

CHAPTER 5

Northern California

The Friday Shakespeare
Club of Santa Cruz

(With Mention of FRFG Study Club of Nearby Gilroy, California)

I flew from the Eugene airport to San Francisco International Airport immediately after the Eugene Fortnightly meeting. After picking up a rental car and driving thirty miles to my sister's new home in Portola Valley, California, I found it just as night fell. After an overnight stay, I drove on Friday morning, April 6, 2012, to the 10:30 meeting of the Friday Shakespeare Club of Santa Cruz, California, forty-four miles from Portola Valley. My carefully plotted route took me through the Santa Cruz Mountains, mostly on the crazily winding and oddly driveway-intersected Route 17, which is often cited as one the most dangerous roads in California.[1]

However, I arrived safely in Santa Cruz, a socially active university town also blessed with beaches, a giant amusement park called the Boardwalk, and prime surfing spots along its Pacific Ocean shoreline. But in spite of Santa Cruz's youthful, left-leaning, freewheeling reputation and vibe, I was there to visit a little-known, far quieter, and far less demonstrative sector of the community. I felt this alternate vibe as soon as I walked into the meeting room in the city's large First Congregational Church complex and met sixteen of the nineteen active members of the Friday Shakespeare Club. This is where the club members, whom I was told range from sixty to ninety years of age, typically gather to look back in time and celebrate the writings of a literary genius of the Elizabethan Age.

I spent several hours with the group. We all enjoyed a member-led program centered on a partial reading and discussion of *The*

Two Gentlemen of Verona. Member Kris Lee, who was running the program and doing the overview sections, emphasized that the role of the dog in the play, a mutt named Crab who belongs to the character Launce, has always been adored by audiences. After the members read select sections of the play and provided a report on the background, Kris showed a film clip from the movie *Shakespeare in Love,* in which the characters watch a production of *The Two Gentlemen of Verona.* After this, two of the characters—the lovers, played by Gwyneth Paltrow and Joseph Fiennes—go home and perform part of the play.

The group typically breaks for coffee after an hour or so and then continues with the program, a second paper, perhaps. However, in honor of my visit, a potluck lunch had been organized after the program. The food had been set up on the pass-through to the kitchen on one side of the meeting room. President Grace Gerbrandt, who had been running the meeting, invited us all to fill our plates and visit, which I happily did, balancing a plate, my pen, and my notepad.

The club's annual Shakespeare birthday party was in two weeks, and there had been a discussion during the meeting I attended of trying to get as many to attend as possible, with guests and prospective new members being welcome. The club had been struggling to find new members. This yearly social event is one way they advertise what they do. They are looking with some difficulty for women who feel they can commit to doing at least one paper or program a year, who are willing to actively participate and be vocal in meetings, and who want to devote time to the study of Shakespeare. To this end, the club has a very good public website put up by Deborah Cardillo, a member who calls herself "Mistress Quickly" on the website, where she is the website administrator and contact. It was her website and her response to my query that led me to Santa Cruz. Friday Shakespeare was the only group I found that created a website as a way of spreading the word about what they do, as most groups are deeply private. I later found Syracuse's Portfolio Club's website and Eugene Fortnightly's website, both meant for members only, except for the home pages, which give basic information about the clubs.

After I'd eaten some of the lunch that the club members had kindly provided, I was asked to stand and talk about my book. I followed my explanation with a dialogue with club members. Among other things, I asked them if they thought their small and aging club would "still be here in ten years." They answered with an unequivocal yes.

The meeting closed with a recitation of the club's version of the prayer that I heard in most of the groups I visited—"The Collect for Club Women" by Mary Stewart—although this group calls it their closing poem, giving a nod to those who would like to keep religion out of the study of Shakespeare. In fact, there had been some past dissension among Friday Shakespeare members about the mention of God. The club had even tried reciting Shakespearean sonnets for a while in lieu of Stewart's poem, but they had changed back to "The Collect," with the mention of God removed from the first and last lines and also with a change in the title. I spoke to my great helper and contact in the group, Gail Olson, as I was about to leave, and she said that she liked the final words of "The Collect" ("let us not forget to be kind.") She said she had been upset to have to read a sonnet, including, once, a "dog sonnet," and was happy that the club members were again reading "The Collect," even if they did call it "the closing poem," at the end of meetings. (See the snapshot summary of Friday Shakespeare for the text of the closing poem.) Another member told me that the women who had objected to "The Collect" were no longer members. This was the only tempest I ever heard discussed when I visited the groups I studied for this book.

Gail Olson also took a moment after the meeting to share her feelings about why Friday Shakespeare was formed in 1903. She said that "women were so isolated here, with the mountains on one side and the ocean on the other."

I was unable to do research into the club's archives, which are housed in UC Santa Cruz's McHenry Library's Special Collections, as I was told that they are not processed and not available for research. So, with the meeting at an end and my thank-yous completed, I drove back over those mountains that had isolated the early settlers of Santa Cruz, drove away from the ocean that further isolated them, and ended up in the San Jose International Airport, where I eventually boarded my plane for Los Angeles.

If I had been able to combine this visit with a visit to Gilroy's historic FRFG Study Club, then I would have tried to visit both clubs in one day, as they are a scant forty-one miles apart. But the members of the Gilroy club had decided that they did not want a writer visiting and observing them. However, I was told that I would be welcome to make use of the material that appeared on the Internet about their history, which was the way I had found them in the first place. The material that led me to FRFG was a profile of the group that member Elizabeth Barratt had entered in the Pioneer Californians of Santa Clara County's 2011 Essay Contest and that had won an honorable mention. Accordingly, you will find the group's description and background in one of the snapshot summaries that follow this chapter's introduction. FRFG's snapshot summary is based on information in that essay, which I used with Ms. Barratt's permission. FRFG has a rich and well-documented history, and its founder, the formidable Miss Emily Wilson, whom you will read about in the snapshot summary, is another of those larger-than-life women who established many of the literary societies during the women's club movement. Her life story is worthy of its own book.

However colorful the Gilroy group's history or its founder might have been, when I mentioned the FRFG Study Club to a few women in the Santa Cruz Shakespeare Club, they told me that they had never heard of it. This was what I typically found as I traveled around the country. I discovered that these wonderful groups know little or nothing of the virtually identical study clubs within a short commute from their home base, not to mention that they do not know anything about the other virtually identical clubs around the country. Hopefully, *Smart Women* will change that.

Snapshot Summary of Friday Shakespeare Club of Santa Cruz, California

1. **Official name of the club:** The Friday Shakespeare Club of Santa Cruz.

2. **Date founded:** October 2, 1903,[2] as the Pierian Club. The group became the Friday Shakespeare Club in 1907 and, as such, was a part of the Bay View Study Club's continuing education program.[3] Although the record of when the club severed ties with the Bay View organization was – when I tried to see the files - tied up in unprocessed and, therefore, inaccessible archives at the library of UC Santa Cruz, it is a fact that their association with the Bay View Study Club could not have lasted later than 1921, when this educational organization, based in Michigan, was disbanded. It is interesting to note that a neighboring study club, founded in 1898 and still in existence today—the Gilroy, California, group calling itself FRFG Women's Study Club—was also a Bay View Study Club and followed its curriculum.[4] When I visited one group and corresponded with the other, neither was aware of the other's existence, although a mere forty-one miles separate them.

3. **Founded by:** Mrs. Della Perry, a former schoolteacher, who invited a few friends to her home on what was then Davis Avenue and is now Escalona Drive to form a reading and study group initially called Pierian Club, to reflect an interest in classical themes. (I'd seen at least one other Pierian Club and a Junior Pierian Club while researching this book. In ancient Greece, Mt. Pierus was a sanctuary for the worship of Orpheus and the Muses.) Mrs. Perry was elected the group's first president.[5] Other founding members were Mrs. L. K. Andrews, Mrs. Addie C. Miller, Miss Mabel Martin, Mrs. Francis Gordon, Miss Constance Gordon, Mrs. Nellie L. Hinds, Mrs. Blanche A. Rittenhouse, and Mrs. Emily Philbrook.[6]

4. **Size of club as stated in bylaws (size limit):** Currently, there is no limit, but there is a requirement of seven members to constitute a quorum for conducting business.[7]

5. **Size of club today:** Nineteen active members and nine inactive members.[8]

6. **Meeting schedule:** They meet on the first and third Friday of each month, starting on the first Friday in October and ending on the third Friday in May.[9] There is also a picnic in early June.

7. **Where and what time they meet:** First Congregational Church, Santa Cruz, 10:30 a.m.–12:30 p.m.

8. **Election of new members:** A prospective member attends two meetings to learn about the club. She is then asked if she would like to join.[10] Once she accepts, there is another meeting at which her bio is read and she is welcomed into the club.[11]

9. **Object of the club as stated in bylaws:** "The study of William Shakespeare, his life, his works, and his time."[12]

10. **Dues:** The annual dues are $25, but a new member who joins after February 1 has to pay only half of this amount.[13]

11. **Club motto, flower, and colors:** The club flower is the red carnation, or gillyflower, said to be Shakespeare's favorite. The motto is "Influence Is Responsibility."[14] The club also has a club prayer, "The Collect for Club Women," which members have recited since 1910. There are members who consider this tradition to be a bad idea and others who think that "The Collect" is inoffensive. This group calls it their closing poem. After some controversy and an attempt to read a sonnet in place of the prayer, the club is back to reciting this somewhat amended collect at the end of their meetings. There is no mention of God in the current version (see below). To backtrack a bit, a collect is a type of short prayer with a certain structure. As I explained earlier, the original version was written by Mary Stewart, who was at one time the dean of women at the University of Missouri. Stewart wrote this prayer after she had just graduated from college and was about to start her first job as a high school principal in Longmont, Colorado, in 1904.[15] She was a member of a

women's study group in Longmont, and they used the prayer, which led to its being reprinted by a local printer. It became much used by American women's clubs that were members of a national federation of women's clubs a hundred years ago and is one link that binds them together, although none of the clubs I've studied belong to that federation today or have any other current connection to, or often any knowledge of, most of the other groups. Please see the snapshot summary for Birmingham's Cosmos Club for the original collect, as recited by many women's clubs today. Here is the collect as it is recited by Friday Shakespeare at the end of their meetings (their closing poem):

Closing Poem
Keep us from pettiness; let us be large in word, in thought, in deed.
Let us be done with fault-finding and leave off self-seeking.
May we put away all pretense and meet each other face to face, without
self-pity and without prejudice.
May we never be hasty in judgment, and always be generous.
Let us put into action our better impulses, straightforward and unafraid.
Let us take time for all things; may we grow calm, serene, and gentle.
May we realize that it is the little things that create differences; that in the
big things of life we are one.
And let us strive to touch and to know the great common woman's heart in
all of us; and let us not forget to be kind.

12. **Paper or program rotation schedule and hostessing rotation schedule:** A ballot is passed to every member of the club during the final meeting in May. On it, members indicate what plays they want to read and whether they would like to chair the play's reading and discussion. They also use the ballot to indicate which of the four social events they'd

like to help out with or if they would like to chair them. After the three plays for the year have been determined, members are asked to indicate their first, second, and third choice of a play to work on. They are then assigned to be a part of a play committee. The chair of the committee organizes the members into readers and researchers, etc., and together they decide how they will present the play and what materials they will use.

13. **Length of papers or programs:** About thirty minutes each. There are two papers at each meeting, plus a reading, and possibly a film clip or other visual aid.

14. **Location of the club's yearbooks or archives:** The Special Collections section of the library at UC Santa Cruz, but, when I requested access, I was told that the archives were "unprocessed" and couldn't be accessed for research.

15. **Civic achievement of the group or its members:** Like every other women's study club of this age and history, Friday Shakespeare remembers proudly that its members volunteered to sew and knit for the Red Cross during WWI and WWII.

16. **Special events:**
    - There is a president's luncheon in October, usually held at a restaurant.
    - Club members celebrate Shakespeare's birthday with an April lunch—usually, between April 15 and April 20—at a restaurant, and they top the meal with a big birthday cake for William Shakespeare. Guests are invited to this, especially those who might be interested in membership.
    - They have a holiday party in December. Members bring potluck dishes to the Congregational church's meeting room.
    - There is a picnic in early June, and this is also potluck. There is usually music at this event, or short plays or games. High school students may perform.

17. **Refreshment highlights:** There are no refreshments other than coffee during regular meetings.[16]

18. **Special traditions:**
    - See "Special events," item 16, above, for the club's four traditional annual parties.
    - They visit the Ashland Shakespeare Festival, and, at the time of the writing of this book, they supported Shakespeare Santa Cruz, a professional repertoire company then in residence at UC Santa Cruz, which put on a yearly summer festival of plays.
    - If a website can be called a tradition, then Friday Shakespeare can claim one in this category. Syracuse's Portfolio Club and the Eugene Fortnightly also have websites (which can only be accessed by members), but they are almost alone among the hundred groups in this book. Most don't see the reason to have a website. After all, these groups are private and small and are adept at sharing information the old-fashioned way and by e-mail. However, the Santa Cruz group is so small now that they are looking for members. They were lucky enough to have Deborah Cardillo as a technically proficient member. As "Mistress Quickly," she put up an impressive website for the group so that possible members might find out about it. Find the site at www. fridayshakespeare.org.
    - See item 11 for a discussion of "The Collect for Club Women," which the members of Friday Shakespeare Club call their closing poem and which has been the traditional prayer of many American women's clubs from their early days in the first part of the twentieth century. The Friday Shakespeare Club has worked to remove any mention of God from the poem's lines, but there are still some members who complain about the implications of maintaining this particular tradition.[17]
19. **Example of a yearly theme:** The club's yearly studies revolve around the three Shakespeare plays the members chose the preceding spring. In 2010–11, they studied *Love's Labour's Lost; Troilus and Cressida;* and *The Merchant of Venice.* In 2011–12, the three plays the members chose were

The Comedy of Errors; King Lear; and *The Two Gentlemen of Verona.*

20. **Example of an individual topic or paper on that theme:** Members leading the discussion for a meeting—the play chairwomen—are urged to cover and identify the main theme of the play, its subthemes, the nature of the language of the play, its history, the development of several of the key characters, and the play's universal message. Group readings and discussions or presentations follow this.[18] When I visited the group, there was a paper and a discussion of the use of Crab, the lovable dog in *The Two Gentlemen of Verona,* and an eight-minute clip of *Shakespeare in Love,* in which the main characters, Viola and Will, watch a rehearsal of *The Two Gentlemen of Verona* and then go home and perform some of the play. We also had a reading from *The Two Gentlemen of Verona* delivered by designated club members. Refreshments were offered during the intermission in between the presentation of the paper on Crab the dog and the presentation of the film clip and group reading.

21. **Particularly colorful or interesting member, present or past:** Marguerite Brewster, who died in 1996, was an internationally renowned poet who won several poetry contests and whose work was included in an anthology.[19]

22. **Legacy members and longest-active members:**
    - Barbara Lewis, who joined the club in 1981, is currently its longest-active member. She is also their longtime historian.
    - Until this year, the club's one legacy member was Grace Gerbrandt, whose mother was a member. Grace was the president when I visited the group, but she resigned the following year.

The FRFG Women's Study Club, Gilroy, California

This club did not want to actively participate in my book and was unwilling to have me visit them. However, I have the permission of the author of an essay about the group, historian and club member

Elizabeth Barratt, to draw from her essay on FRFG. Her composition was entered in the Pioneer Californians of Santa Clara County 2011 Essay Contest and won an honorable mention. Everything you see below has been extracted from that essay.

1. **Official name of the club:** The FRFG Women's Study Club. *FRFG* is an abbreviation for the club's motto, "Freely Received, Freely Given."[20] What is received and also given is knowledge. The club's founder felt that knowledge should be shared.[21]

2. **Date founded:** November 9, 1898, by an extraordinary woman, Miss Emily Wilson, at her home. She had also previously founded the Ladies' Reading Circle, also in Gilroy, to make up for the town's lack of a public lending library.[22] See below for more information about Miss Wilson, whose life is worthy of a book.

3. **Size of club today:** Club size has always been limited to twenty members.[23] By studying the Barratt essay about FRFG, counting its members posed in a 2011 photo attached to the essay, and then noting a list of those missing, I estimate that the group had fifteen active members.[24]

4. **How often they meet and where:** For the club's first forty-four years, meetings took place for two hours every Friday at members' homes, for "study and discussion."[25] Now, they meet twice a month, on the second and fourth Fridays of the month during the "club year,"[26] between October and May, from 1:30 to 3:30.[27] Their schedule includes an opening luncheon each fall, a November observance of their founder's day,[28] a single holiday meeting in early December featuring a cookie exchange and a choral concert, and a final meeting, a potluck picnic, in early June.[29] [30]

5. **Examples of yearly themes:** From 1905 to 1915, they used the Bay View Study Course as a guide to yearly themes. For the next few decades, they covered a wide range of subjects.[31] In 1945–46, their yearly topic was "Modern Science and Scientific Advancements."[32] During the 1960s and through to the 1990s, the club often chose as a theme the study of various nations of the world that were in the

spotlight. Another favorite was the study of historic women. However, there is currently no program committee. For the past twenty years, the annual theme has mostly been one of personal choice, although the members did do a two-year study of California, from 2004 to 2006. Otherwise, members choose a topic that interests them, such as a certain book they review, or something in which they have been involved, such as a trip.[33]

6. **Of note:**

- In 1899, this group adopted a club call, "Ave Roma Immortalis," meaning, "Hail, immortal Rome," and a club color, Tyrian purple.[34] The group was deeply immersed in studies of Rome and books about Rome in their earliest days.[35]

- Sometime around 1903, the club subscribed to an adult home study program also used by several other groups mentioned in this book in their early days. The program was called the Bay View Study Course, which had its roots in the Chautauqua movement.[36]

- Miss Wilson, the club's founder, blew into Gilroy in 1864 to visit her sister. On her own, she had traveled from her home state of Massachusetts and gone to New York City, then taken a ship through dangerous Union and Confederate waters to the Isthmus of Panama, where she **walked on foot** through the jungle to reach the Pacific and to board a ship to California. For forty-two years, she traveled between Gilroy, the Bay Area, and the East Coast, seemingly impressing many great names of her day with her intellect. In 1906, she settled permanently in the New York area.

  Working as a college professor as soon as she graduated from Mt. Holyoke Female Seminary (later called Mt. Holyoke College) in 1861, Miss Wilson later became, for a time, the oldest graduate of Mt. Holyoke. She died at the age of 101, having traveled all over the world on her own and even sailing in a three-masted ship in 1896, when she was 56, to islands in the South Seas whose people had never seen a white woman. She spent several days in native villages on many of the islands. Following her South Seas trip, she gave lectures during her travels to Gilroy and came up with the idea in 1898 of founding a weekly study group for the young women who seemed most interested in her talks. It was her idea to name the club "FRFG" for "Freely Received, Freely Given," to make it clear that she felt that knowledge should be shared.[37]

- At the group's June 9, 1944, picnic, a massive and ancient oak tree split and fell on club members, seriously injuring four women. One woman remained in a lengthy coma, but she eventually recovered. The other injuries were broken bones.[38]

CHAPTER 6

Upstate New York and the Greater Syracuse Area

The End of the Rainbow?
A Cluster of Twelve Historic
Groups in the Syracuse / Finger
Lakes Area of New York State

At the top of a hill, surrounded by pristine farmhouses, barns, trees decked in colorful fall foliage, and perfectly plowed fields, I steered my car carefully to the side of the freshly graveled farm road— Great Gully Road—and took in the view. There was no issue with safety, as mine was the only car on the road. I was on my way to a meeting of the historic, all-women Thursday Club in the tiny village of Aurora, on the eastern shore of one of New York State's scenic Finger Lakes, Cayuga Lake (pronounced "KAY-u-gah" by several of the locals whom I met that day). My GPS device had directed me to this sublime and intensely rural spot forty-five miles southwest of my Syracuse University–area hotel. It was October 11, 2012. After four days of visiting six other hundred-year-old women's literary societies in the area, I would be heading back home to Los Angeles the next day. Aurora was meant to be the end of the road for me and my book research. That it didn't turn out that way and that I would find more and more groups over the next year and a half, including a startling number in a small town in Illinois, remained to be seen.

What I did see from the top of the hill was Cayuga Lake spread out in front of me, shining brightly in the early afternoon sun. My immediate reaction was one of great joy at the sheer beauty of the scene. Adding to my euphoria, the number of historic women's study groups I was finding in the Syracuse / Finger Lakes area had far exceeded my expectations. It seemed at that moment that

157

this part of New York State would prove to be the pot of gold at the end of the rainbow for me. And there was the lake, shining like that very pot. The area I was finding very fertile for the formation and longevity of women's study groups was adjacent to the old "burned over district," so called during the days when the land around the then-new Erie Canal seemed to be a hotbed of new religions, sects, and utopian communities, not to mention the site of the first Women's Rights Convention, which was held in Seneca Falls in 1848, just a stone's throw from Cayuga Lake. That first convention and others that followed in the area seemed to me *still* to have some unacknowledged effect on the women who have kept these groups going—the groups that feminists of the day had urged their peers to form in order to self-educate.

I drove on and found myself in the postcard-pretty, miniscule, eighteenth- and nineteenth-century lakeside village of Aurora, home of Wells College and the MacKenzie-Childs home decor company— both of which had been saved from collapse over the past thirteen years by the deep pockets and determination of Wells alumna and founder of American Girl Doll, Pleasant Rowland. Rowland recently bought all of the buildings in the town's business district, including the now-elegant Aurora Inn, which she had earlier renovated extensively in an arrangement with Wells College, the previous owner of all of the commercial buildings in the business district. Among the town's seven hundred or so residents, three hundred of whom are students at Wells, opinions vary widely on whether Ms. Rowland's refurbishing and purchasing of so much of the town was a good thing or a very bad thing.

I thought at the time when I learned about Ms. Rowland that, in terms of intelligence and backbone, she made an appropriate modern-day match to the determined Victorian-era women who urged other women to found the literary societies that men scorned and ridiculed.

The meeting of the modern-day version of Thursday Club was scheduled for 3:30, but I met my contact, Mary Ellen Ormiston, then the president of the club, a bit earlier so she could show me around the tiny village. She walked me through the Aurora Library, where the Thursday Club archives are stored, and took me upstairs so I could look at the second floor opera house. Then we walked down the street to the United Ministry Church, once a Presbyterian church and now merged with an Episcopalian congregation. The Thursday Club often meets there. Just behind the church, Cayuga Lake lapped gently at the shoreline.

The meeting of the Thursday Club began promptly at 3:30 in the church's meeting room, with fourteen members, spanning four or five decades in age, seated in folding chairs, a few easy chairs, and a couch, all arranged in a circle. Longtime member Ann Burch was there, every bit as bright and interesting as she had been when I was interviewing her on the phone months earlier about the possibility of visiting her club. At eighty-eight years of age, she contributed smartly, with great wit and wisdom. At one point, she told the story of a humorous paper she'd written for Thursday Club about an experience her late husband had had in WWII on a desert island. The paper was entitled "How Spam Helped Win the War," but it actually had more to do with the history of tea. Ann joined in 1968 and is the club's longest-active member as well as being its one legacy member. Her mother, Elizabeth Stewart, belonged to Thursday Club from 1939 to 1972. Ann remembered the days when the dress code for meetings was considerably fussier than it is now, with Sunday-best dresses (never pants, which are almost de rigueur these days), hats, and gloves worn to meetings—and even a particular kind of corset, the Spencer corset.

On an allied subject, the program that day was the evolution of women's dress and its impact on women's lives, given by an outside speaker, Cynthia Koepp, a professor of history at Wells. Usually, club members give the programs. A recent example of a program is "Hitsville, USA," about Motown, which was a part of the yearly theme "Remember When—Those Were the Days." Papers can be on any topic the members choose as long as they fit with the yearly theme, which is chosen by secret ballot from a list of possible choices prepared by the program committee. After this day's program and some comments and questions, the group members discussed their individual experiences in the club. They were responding to my question about how long each of them had been a member and adding their own thoughts as we went around the circle, allowing each member to speak. Several members said they were glad that the days of a "blackball" rejection of a prospective member were over. They said that now, a prospective member just has to come to a meeting to see if she likes it.

A tea table had been set up between the circle of chairs and the kitchen. After the formal meeting ended at 5:00 p.m., the members got up, helped themselves to the refreshments, and chatted with each other for about fifteen minutes. Among other offerings, I saw a seasonal hot cider, sliced cake, and cookies. After enjoying the chatter and refreshments, I drove back to my Syracuse hotel and prepared for my flight back to Los Angeles the next morning.

Before my visit to the Aurora Thursday Club's regularly scheduled meeting, I had visited with two exceptional groups in Syracuse, two in nearby Fayetteville (one of them failing and one still viable), one in Hamilton (home of Colgate University), and one in Auburn. In the process, I'd learned about five additional historic groups nearby, gotten contacts for them, and subsequently researched and included them in this book, although I was unable to meet with the members face-to-face. These additional groups included a club in Manlius, a second group in Auburn, a club in Union Springs, and two groups in Skaneateles, another picturesque Finger Lakes village. I have their descriptions organized in separate snapshot summaries at the end of this Syracuse section. These additional groups brought my number of historic women's groups in what I call "the greater Syracuse commuting area" (within an hour's drive) to twelve. I know there are more out there. While chatting with members of the groups I was able to contact and visit, I'd heard about a Wednesday Morning Club in Utica, possibly two study clubs in Oneida, an Alpha Study Club in Ogdensburg, and the Outlook Club in Sandy Creek, but I had no contacts in any of these. Given that all of these towns and their seventeen historic study clubs are within an hour's commute from Syracuse or else inside Syracuse, I'd say that this general area is the most fertile area overall for these historic women's literary societies of any area in America. If one expands the area to include the rest of New York State, from far western New York to far eastern Long Island, then one realizes that there are even more (27 in all), as you will find in the last two chapters of this book.

I did find a small town in Illinois—Jacksonville—with six historic women's study clubs. Jacksonville would win the prize of most literary societies in any town that I could uncover during my three-plus years of research. See Chapter Nine for more Jacksonville revelations.

At the beginning of my five-day visit to Syracuse, I landed at the Syracuse airport, rounded up my rental car, and drove to the impressive Women's Rights National Historical Park in Seneca Falls. I spent a few rather emotional hours, bringing myself up to speed on the historic first Women's Rights Convention held there in 1848. I was also looking for any connection to "my" groups, which were meant to self-educate women who were then largely excluded from American colleges and universities. In subsequent meetings of the Association for the Advancement of Women's congress, women were urged by such luminaries as Julia Ward Howe (prominent abolitionist, social activist, poet, and the author of "The Battle Hymn of the Republic") to form groups to self-educate.[1] Among those activists who were helping young women organize into study groups was an extraordinary secondary school art teacher, Mrs. Mary Dana Hicks. Mrs. Hicks subsequently founded both of the Syracuse clubs I visited: Social Art Club and Portfolio Club. Many of the young women in her groups had been her students in secondary school but had since graduated to face a future involving a quiet domestic life. They were eager to help start clubs in order to expand their horizons.

I met with six members of today's Portfolio Club on my third day in Syracuse, October 9, 2012. I'd been given great and detailed assistance in connecting with this group and others. I was also assisted in learning about their history by member Mary Beth Hinton, a professional editor who had been Portfolio's president in 2011–12. Mary Beth also picked me up at my hotel and drove me to the imposing Century Club downtown for my meetings with Portfolio and Social Art. Her demeanor and that of her equally highly intelligent fellow club members was professional, friendly, and helpful.

I had just missed Portfolio's regular meeting while I was in Syracuse, ergo the informal one organized by their president, Rosalia –"Zalie" - Linn, and Mary Beth, with six members for me to interview. I was most impressed by the very unique portfolio, or packet of information, about the coming year's programs that was given to every member to equip them for the coming year. These portfolios are dreamed up and executed by each Social Art president in her turn. Zalie Linn had picked the topic of symbolism and had produced a stunning purple portfolio for the twelve subtopics of her choosing, which were to be the subject of each member-given paper in the coming year. The descriptions of the topics for each paper included directions for the women who would give these papers, recommending how to proceed and what to include. Zalie had included for the first time in recent years a roster of the membership in the portfolio, which she had designed, written, and produced. All of the club's most important information was in one handsome and beautifully designed booklet. This portfolio was unique in my experience with historic study clubs, but also unique were two other facts: this group never has guest speakers, and they have a website. I found only three clubs that had websites, as most groups are quite small and need not advertise or publicize what they do.

Each incoming president of The Portfolio Club has very big shoes to fill, taking on the job of most other clubs' program committee, formulating a subject and course of study for the entire year. Mary Beth's portfolio and choice of that year's study when she was president had been "American Utopias," separatist communities established in this country, mostly in the 1800s, in which residents lived by a religious or moral set of rules. Mary Ellen shared her utopia portfolio with me, and she shared much of the information from an extensive exhibit about the Portfolio Club that she and another club member, Michele Combs, curated in 2009 at the Syracuse University Library, where Michele is employed as librarian and lead archivist in the Special Collections Division.

Following the Portfolio meeting and interview, I hurried downstairs at noon to the regularly scheduled meeting, luncheon, and program of the Social Art Club. There, I heard an extraordinarily well-researched, finely written, thirty-minute-long paper, with accompanying slides, about philanthropist Harriet Lane Johnston. Johnston was a niece of the only bachelor US president, James Buchanan, and she often served as his hostess in the White House. Her later life was one of tremendous philanthropy. She founded several Washington, DC, area institutions: a branch of Johns Hopkins Hospital, the nucleus of the collection of the National Gallery of Art, and St. Albans School. The paper was very ably delivered by club member Rocha Folger. She had an attentive and large audience, forty-eight members and guests, which Jeanette Mattson, that year's president, explained by telling me, "Well, it's the first meeting of the year, but probably also they came because you are here." I enjoyed an excellent lunch, which included carrot and ginger soup, popovers, and chicken with cavatelli pasta, prepared by the Century Club kitchen staff. Jeanette, who had already been a tremendous help to me in organizing my visit, drove me back to my hotel after the Social Art meeting was over at 2:30 p.m. Of course, during the meeting and before the program, Jeanette had asked me to address the group and tell them about my book project, which I did.

The two Syracuse groups were very impressive—healthy, still learning together, full of women who are loyal to the friendships and the history of their organization. These are very old clubs, both dating from 1875. Both were founded with the help of an inspirational teacher, Mary Dana Hicks, who had attended at least one meeting of the Association of the Advancement of Women's congress at the Wieting Opera House in 1875 in Syracuse. Hicks would have heard Julia Ward Howe and other women speakers like her urge women to form study clubs for purposes of self-culture.[2] The influence of these Women's Rights Conventions seems to have lasted in this area to today.

On Columbus Day, Monday, October 8, the day before I met with the two Syracuse clubs, I'd driven seven miles southeast of Syracuse to meet with members of Philomath and Coterie - two smaller, but still historic, women's groups in the small town of Fayetteville, New York, the boyhood home of US President Grover Cleveland. His family's house is directly across the street from the Trinity Episcopal Church, in the parlor of which I met members of both groups—one at 10:00 a.m. and one at noon. After these two meetings, I drove about thirty-five miles southeast of Fayetteville to Hamilton, New York, to meet with yet another group, Hamilton Fortnightly, at 3:00 p.m. Along my route, I passed through scenic farm country and the old-fashioned and charming village of Cazenovia on the shores of Cazenovia Lake.

The home of the hostess of the meeting of Hamilton Fortnightly Club, Carol Bergen, was in a neighborhood of comfortable, old-fashioned homes about a block from the Colgate University campus. Both Fayetteville and Hamilton seemed like *Our Town*–era villages, products of a quieter, simpler time. There was nothing contemporary about either one, and that was refreshing to me, coming from the noise, traffic, and constant change of Los Angeles. However, the women I met from both groups were contemporary and sharp, while being dedicated to the history and traditions of their clubs and the warm friendships within them. Both of the Fayetteville clubs were very proud that their town was the home of noted suffragette Matilda Josyln Gage, who was also the extremely supportive mother-in-law of L. Frank Baum, author of *The Wizard of Oz*.

My first meeting of the day was in Fayetteville, with Nancy Bond, the president of Philomath, a slowly dying club. She had been a member since 1996, and she told me that she was mostly retired from thirty years of music education and choir directing, but she was still working as a church organist. I was expecting several members to attend the interview, but Nancy came alone and began her interview by saying, "This is a sad story. We are struggling, struggling." The club's membership, once consisting of twenty-five active members, had grown smaller and older, to the point that they were now down to "five to seven members" and were ready to cease meeting. They finally did so while I was writing the book. Nancy said that the group had tried recruiting new members and even made it easier to belong, excusing members from writing a paper if they didn't want to do it, but this had not helped. She had also tried something new, helping to organize a book-gifting operation for local schools at Christmastime, but the original idea of a club founded on the idea of self-education through the writing of research papers was no longer appealing to prospects.

Finally, on February 5, 2013, I received an e-mail from Nancy in answer to several of my questions. She ended it by writing, "Regretfully, we are winding up this club and its activities due to a lack of members—it has outlived its purpose."[3] She had shared an interesting fact with me when we were talking face-to-face in the preceding October, namely that Philomath had, at one point, explored trying to unite with Fayetteville's other study club, Coterie, but nothing had come of it. Philomath was the one group I met with or contacted by phone or e-mail that was on its last legs and died while I was working on the book. A few other clubs, while actively looking for younger members, were determined to keep going.

After interviewing Nancy, I met with three bright and enthusiastic members of Coterie, who were also extremely well versed in their club and town history. These were Ann Moore, Marian Loosman, and Nancy Wilson. As it was noon, they brought a light lunch of very elegant and tasty finger food for all of us to share while I interviewed them. The women of the groups I encountered were almost always great hostesses, complete with the social skills and know-how needed to produce and present the right kind of spread for any occasion.

Ann Moore, a librarian in the public library system and the historian for her church, was able to bring me an archived copy of a 1996 PhD dissertation on adult education written for Syracuse University by a nonmember, Jane Hugo. The dissertation was also about Coterie, from its beginnings in 1885 and through to 1985. This copy is normally housed at the Fayetteville Free Library with the rest of the Coterie archives. I had been connected to Ms. Hugo many months before my Fayetteville interviews by Mary Beth Hinton of the Portfolio Club in Syracuse, and Jane then became the beginning of my chain of discoveries of historic women's study clubs in the greater Syracuse commuting area.

I left the Coterie meeting in Fayetteville. After driving for forty-five minutes on rural roads (hooray for my GPS!), I found myself in Hamilton, New York, in time for a 3:00 p.m. meeting of eight members of Hamilton Fortnightly. We met at the home of former club president Carol Bergen. It was in Carol's home that Meika Loe, Colgate University associate professor of sociology and women's studies, and director of women's and LGBTQ studies, had rented a room seven years ago and subsequently discovered, to her delight, the women of Fortnightly through her landlady, a club member. As the subject of aging was of great interest to Ms. Loe and one that she would write a book about in 2011, she researched and wrote an article called "The Women's Academy Down the Hill," which was published in The Colgate Scene in May 2007. This piece popped up five years later in my Internet research. After I contacted Meika and explained my project, she put me together with Carol and the club president at that time, Joanne Geyer. Together, we organized an informal meeting at Carol's home, as I would be missing the group's regular meeting at the Hamilton Public Library.

The nine of us sat around Carol's dining room table on that October afternoon. Over cookies and coffee, we discussed the club, with the women eagerly answering my questions, which were mostly based on the questions for the standard snapshot summary I was then organizing for each group. Along with providing factual responses, the women did a lot of reminiscing about past members, some of whom sounded like *grandes dames*, but even these social queen bees were said to have been the machinery that got things done in what was for many years the male-dominated society of Colgate and Hamilton. There are examples of these formidable women in the group's snapshot summary at the end of this chapter.

Toward the end of my fact-finding session, Carol said that there had been three recent obituaries in the local newspaper in which the deceased's family had mentioned her membership in Fortnightly. "It is very important to all of us," she added. Another woman, Corrine Honkalehto, said, "It's the bylaws that keep us together. They are the framework of the group's activities." This was followed by a funny memory from another member who said that few people know what *fortnightly* means and that this led recently to a humorous display on the announcement board at the local inn where the club was having lunch. The sign read, "Welcome Fort Knightly." The word, meaning "once every two weeks," has fallen out of use, but the clubs with this name—and there are many—are still going concerns in many towns across the country, although they are in no way connected to each other. Interestingly, I found that the towns where there were Fortnightly Clubs dating from the days of the women's club movement were usually college towns. Another Syracuse-area women's study club I visited, Auburn Fortnightly, is in a town with a junior college and a branch of the State University of New York.

But what Auburn, a city of almost twenty-eight thousand residents, is best known for is its connection to William Seward, who lived there for many years. Seward was at one time a New York State senator, a US senator, and the governor of New York State. He served as both Abraham Lincoln's and Andrew Johnson's secretary of state. It was one of his daughters-in-law, Janet Seward, who, as president of Auburn Fortnightly for sixteen years (1897–1913), held club meetings in the imposing Seward House in the heart of Auburn—now a trust-operated historic site at which many Fortnightly members volunteer. I was able to drop into Seward House for a quick look on my way out of town after my meeting with Auburn Fortnightly. The most imposing room was the large front parlor, very ornately Victorian, where I imagine the Fortnightly meetings would have been held. I could visualize the women in the dress of the day, decorously sitting and listening to a fellow member deliver her paper.

Earlier that day, six totally modern women from Auburn Fortnightly met me in the imposing Seymour Library in downtown Auburn for an informal meeting and information-exchange session. It was ten o'clock on the morning of Wednesday, October 10, 2012, and I had been in the Syracuse area doing research since Sunday. The meeting was largely organized by one of two helpful contacts in the group. One of these was Barbara Clary, who was vice president of the club when I visited and is now serving a two-year term as president. The other was Carol Contiguglia, who was the president when I visited. She was equally helpful in pulling together the facts and lore of Auburn Fortnightly. Both of these women were among the six who attended the meeting in a tiny upstairs room at the library. One other attendee, Ann Blauvelt, who is a triple legacy member, having three different relatives who have belonged to Auburn Fortnightly, had driven thirty miles to our meeting from her home in Fair Haven, on Lake Ontario. Diane Windsor, another member who met with us that day, said in the course of the meeting that the group has survived because they are actively working at getting younger members, women in their fifties. We talked. I pumped them for information for my snapshot summary of the group. At noon, most of us went to lunch at a little restaurant across the street. After lunch, Barbara walked me back to the library and showed me the trunk in a storage closet upstairs that holds the group's archives. We took out some of the earliest ledgers—handsome, leather-bound books—so I could look through them. I read about Janet Seward and about club member Edith Dulles, the mother of Secretary of State John Foster Dulles and the daughter of another secretary of state, John W. Foster.

The next day would bring my meeting with the Aurora Thursday Club, and then I would fly back to Los Angeles. Unbeknownst to me at the time, I was not as near the end of the book as I had thought on that sunny day in October when I stopped to enjoy the view of Cayuga Lake in upstate New York. More and more historic study groups would pop up through personal connections or research for another year and a half, and I would chase them down, either calling on the phone or sending e-mails. Then, all of the information I accumulated had to be organized, written, and edited. But I knew that nothing like this book had been attempted for over a century, and that thought kept me going. No one knew about these historic groups, and the groups didn't know about each other. What made the long haul of the book research and writing bearable were the friendly connections with smart, helpful women that I made while doing the work. The phrase "It takes a village" certainly applied to my project. I couldn't have done any of this work without the help of a long list of dedicated and thoughtful women's study club members. I can't thank them enough, but I thank them here.

"Author's Trip to the Greater Syracuse Area"

Seneca Falls, NY,
October 7, 2012

Members of Coterie, Marian
Loosman, Ann Moore, Nancy Wilson,
Fayetteville, NY, October 8, 2012

Members of Hamilton Fortnightly,
Hamilton, NY, October 8, 2012

Meeting of the Social Art Club,
Syracuse, NY, October 9, 2012

Members of Auburn Fortnightly,
Auburn, NY, October 10, 2012

Meeting of Thursday Club,
Aurora, NY, October 11, 2012

Photos by Ann Costello

Snapshot Summary of Auburn Fortnightly

1. **Official name of the club:** The Fortnightly of Auburn, New York.
2. **Date founded:** January 28, 1884.
3. **Founded by:** Thirteen women who met at the home of Mrs. James G. Knapp, who was elected the group's president and served in this position for thirteen years.[4]
4. **Size of club as stated in bylaws (size limit):** Twenty-five active members and any number of honorary members.[5]
5. **Size of club today:** Twenty-three active members, with two openings for new members in 2012. There are also thirty-five honorary members;[6] however, honorary members don't attend meetings unless they are invited. Also, they do not pay dues.[7]
6. **Meeting schedule:** October through early May, from 3:00 p.m. to 5:00 p.m., once a month in the winter and the spring and twice a month in the fall, on alternate Thursdays. This includes a holiday party in early December. There is no meeting in March.[8] In 2010–11 and 2011–12, there were nine meetings. Eight featured some kind of original paper or program. One additional meeting was the holiday party.[9]
7. **Where they meet:** In members' homes, with exceptions specific to the program being presented.
8. **Election of new members:** The member who proposes a candidate asks the candidate to attend a paper presentation and tea and also gives the candidate a copy of Fortnightly's history and procedures. A two-thirds vote is required to admit a prospective member. The club secretary extends an invitation to the candidate who has been approved by the membership.[10] Privacy is stressed in regard to all matters discussed at meetings.[11]
9. **Object of the club as stated in its bylaws or constitution:** "The mutual improvement by a systematic course of reading or study of some category in history, literature, art, or any topic which the club may select."[12]
10. **Dues:** $15 a year.
11. **Club motto, flower, and colors:** None.

12. **Paper or program assignment schedule and hostessing rotation schedule:** Members hostess one year and present a paper the next.[13]

13. **Length of papers:** One paper is presented at each meeting, and it should be no longer than forty-five minutes in length. The usual length is thirty to forty-five minutes.[14]

14. **Location of the club's yearbooks, minutes, scrapbooks, and archives:** The local library in Auburn, New York, the Seymour Library, where the archives are beautifully bound and kept in an old trunk, in a second-floor archive closet, which I saw first-hand.

15. **Civic achievements of the group or its members:**

    - This year, the club donated its original ivory gavel to Seward House, a grand Auburn home now open to the public, once belonging to William Seward, Abraham Lincoln's secretary of state. That gavel had been used by one of Seward's daughters-in-law, Janet Seward (Mrs. William H., Jr.), who was an Auburn Fortnightly member and the longest-serving president of the club (1897–1913). She would use it to call meetings to order in the parlor of Seward House. To replace the historic gavel, now deceased member Eleanor Blauvelt's husband, Pete, donated a "monster gavel" once used by one of his relatives who had been a justice of the Superior Court. This huge gavel is the one used by the Fortnightly president to open meetings today. The group also donated the round, silver bowl used during Janet Seward's time to the Seward House,[15] as well as a silver vase used during Mrs. Seward's time.[16]

    - Members who played an extraordinary part in the civic life of Auburn and of our country in an earlier day include Mrs. Eliza Osborne, Mrs. Edith Dulles, and Mrs. Janet Seward (see item 21, below). Current members have served on many boards and headed numerous local civic organizations. Among these are the following:

        o Carol Contiguglia served for eighteen years as Auburn's parks and recreation commissioner and was vice-chair of the Cayuga County Industrial Development Agency for eight years. She served at that agency for a total of twelve years, in addition to performing many other jobs in the community.

o Many of Fortnightly's members were involved in the Auburn Children's Theater, which evolved into the Merry-Go-Round Playhouse, as well as with the Musical Theatre Festival, Inc.

o Member Joanne Foresman's family has given a gift to the Cayuga County Community College's Schwartz Family Performing Arts Center, which will name its lobby after her. She has also been involved in the children's theater mentioned above since the late 1960s.

o Barbara Clary served three elected terms as town councilor of the town of Owasco. She was the first and only female elected in Owasco.[17]

16. **Special events:** A Christmas party is held in early December. This can take place in different locations, which can be a surprise. It features a guest speaker and tea.

17. **Refreshment highlights:** Every meeting ends with tea, coffee, and finger food provided by the hostess. A silver tea service is often used. A member told me, "We try to keep up that tradition and femininity."[18] (See "Special traditions.")

18. **Special traditions:**

• The group rotates the jobs of vice president and president in keeping with each woman's order of admission. Also taken in order of admission is the job of being recording secretary. A woman becomes secretary in her second year of membership.[19]

• The group always holds a Christmas party.

• Two favorites that almost always make an appearance on the Fortnightly tea table are lemon squares and cucumber sandwiches.[20]

- Auburn Fortnightly members never say no to a request.[21]
- They absolutely start each meeting on time.[22]
- Many Fortnightly members volunteer at or support the Seward House, partly because of their club's connection to it.[23]
- Members still dress nicely for meetings, although some wear slacks. "People respect the hostess and dress accordingly," I was told at my meeting with six club members.[24]
- See the above "Civic achievements" entry about the tradition of using a particular gavel to call the meetings to order.
- Longtime members, disturbed by the more modern attitude toward absences, remind members of an old Fortnightly saying that warns that the only two occasions for which one may be excused from a Fortnightly meeting are when a member's husband is handing out cigars or when there is a black wreath on a member's door—in other words, if a member has had a baby or else someone in her household has died.[25]

19. **Example of a yearly theme or topic:** In 2010–11, it was "The Role of Industry in the Development of Auburn." In 2012–13, it was "Contemporary Women World Leaders."[26]

20. **Example of individual paper or assignment based on that topic:** For "The Role of Industry in the Development of Auburn," the program "Got Milk?", with a visit to the O'Hara Agriculture Museum, was presented. For "Contemporary Women World Leaders," there was a program on Hillary Clinton. For this season's "Outstanding Women and Their Fields," members will report on Beverly Sills and Lady Gaga.[27]

21. **Particularly colorful or interesting member, present or past:**
- Edith Dulles (1863–1941) was the mother of John Foster Dulles, secretary of state under Dwight Eisenhower. (Auburn Fortnightly seems to be uniquely connected to secretaries of state of the

past.) She was married to a Presbyterian minister and was the mother of five children. Her father, John Foster, was *also* a secretary of state, under President Benjamin Harrison. Her son's uncle by marriage, Robert Lansing, was also a secretary of state, under President Woodrow Wilson.[28]

- Janet Seward, wife of William H. Seward Jr. and daughter-in-law of Secretary of State William H. Seward, presided over Auburn Fortnightly for an unrivaled sixteen years and held meetings in the still-grand Seward Home's ornate side parlor.[29]

- Mrs. D. M. Osborne (Eliza) (1829–1911) was a member of a family long involved in the fight for the abolition of slavery, during which family members' homes were way stations for the Underground Railroad. Eliza and her family were friends and supporters of Harriet Tubman and helped to settle her in Auburn. Eliza was also active in the fight for women's suffrage and was the founder of the Women's Educational and Industrial Union of Auburn. This organization's goal was to provide women with practical training and vocational advice. It later became the Auburn YWCA–WEIU.[30]

- Current member Bourke Kennedy is an artist and also an amateur actress, director, and playwright. She has been actively involved in the Auburn Players Community Theater for the past forty-two years. She has also volunteered for "nonviolent opposition" in the Palestinian conflict with an organization called the Christian Peacemaker Teams, serving for fifteen years in Hebron, Palestine, in the occupied West Bank. For her Fortnightly program on the conflict between Palestine and Israel, she wore a border-crossing guard's uniform and subjected members, as they entered her home in Skaneateles, to an unnerving scrutiny. Bourke is the longest-active member at this time, having joined Fortnightly in 1975. She describes herself as a Buddhist Unitarian and is on the board of the Auburn Universalist Society.[31]

- Club member Gillian Sheen Donaldson, when she was a twenty-eight-year-old British dental surgeon, won the gold medal for Great Britain in fencing (individual foils) in the 1956 Olympics. She went on to win the British Empire and Commonwealth title in 1958, and in 1960 she won her tenth and final British championship. Britain's only Olympic fencing gold medalist continued competitive fencing until 1963, and then, once she married and became Mrs. Donaldson, she settled in Auburn, New York, where she joined her husband in a dental practice.[32] She has been a Fortnightly member twice: beginning in 1971, and, after a pause, recently resuming her membership in 2005.[33]

22. **Legacy members and longest-active members:**
- The longest continuously active member is the above-mentioned Bourke Kennedy, who joined in 1975. Carol Contiguglia joined in 1977, and Diane Brownlie in 1978.[34]
- As for legacy members currently on the Fortnightly rolls, Ann Blauvelt, who was one of the members who met with me in October 2012, having driven down from her home on the shore of Lake Ontario, is a triple legacy. Her mother-in-law, Eleanor Blauvelt, was a member, as was her cousin Elizabeth Berg and her husband's cousin Nancy Eldridge.[35]

Snapshot Summary of the Roundabout Club of Auburn, New York

I'm left with many unanswered questions about Roundabout, but I felt they should be included.

1. **Official name of the club:** The Roundabout Club of Auburn, New York.

2. **Date founded:** 1888.[36]
3. **Founders:** The founders were said to be a group of women who "wished to pursue the study and discussion of a wide variety of subjects."[37]
4. **Size of club today:** Ten active members and nine inactive members. Some of the inactives still present papers. My contact, Jackie Alexander, was uncertain that the club would continue, as its numbers were dwindling and its members were aging. But she stressed that they greatly "enjoy each other's company and the opportunity to learn and discuss many topics which [they] might not otherwise do."[38]
5. **Meeting schedule:** September through May.[39]
6. **Where they meet:** In members' homes, but mostly in a handicap-accessible senior living facility in the Auburn area.[40]
7. **Special events:** A final luncheon and a summer picnic. The picnic in 2011 was held on the shores of nearby Lake Cayuga and was catered by a local restaurant.[41]
8. **Refreshments:** Tea or coffee is still poured and offered along with other refreshments, which member Jackie Alexander says are less formal than in earlier times. She added that these come at the *beginning* of the club's meetings.[42]

Snapshot Summary of The Thursday Club of Aurora, New York

1. **Official name of the club:** The Thursday Club of Aurora.
2. **Date founded:** The club's first year was 1895–96, as an outgrowth of a local men's group, whose members had shared magazines and the information found in them. The Thursday Club's first topic for their first year was "Glimpses of Germany."[43] The new women's club would often meet on the front porch of the Aurora Inn,[44] which still exists today in the heart of the village, on the eastern shore of Lake Cayuga. Today, the inn has been renovated, as have other buildings and businesses in the village of Aurora, by Pleasant Rowland, the founder of American Girl Dolls.

3. **Founder's name:** Unknown to the club at this point. In my own research, I found a local *Union Advertiser* newspaper blurb about the club written in April 1896, naming the officers of the club, who were surely among its founding members, as Mrs. Waters (president), Mrs. Freley (vice president), Mrs. Russell (secretary), and Miss Morell (treasurer). The next earliest member I could find was a Mrs. Mandel, mentioned in an 1897 *Union Advertiser* newspaper blurb as being the hostess for a Thursday Club meeting that year. During the club's founding year, the local paper usually referred to its first members as an anonymous group, for example, "The Thursday Club, of Aurora, is in a nourishing condition and is supported by the first ladies of that pleasant village by the lake. The program for 1897-8 has for its subject 'A Winter in Florence and Venice.'"[45]

4. **Size of club, as limited by bylaws:** Twenty-five active members.[46]

5. **Size of club today:** Eighteen, with no official honorary or associate members, but club members report that they have "several ladies who have retired from active membership due to health or distance [and who] are often invited to attend as guests, and [club members] call them honorary members, [as] they participate with no responsibilities." The club also reports having had unofficial associate members who pay their $10 dues and receive the schedule of events, but attend either no meetings or very few.[47]

6. **Meeting schedule:** The club averages nine meetings per year, but that can vary. Club President Mary Ellen Ormiston answered my question about the meeting schedule by writing, "According to the by-laws, [we meet] 'at intervals from September through May with a winter break as determined by the program committee.' We have lately had a June meeting also. We meet on Thursday, naturally, 3:30–5:00, with one evening meeting, also on Thursday, but at 7 p.m."[48] When I visited their meeting on October 11, 2012, I was told that they always take a winter break, which is understandable, as they are in the snowbelt of central New York State. There are no meetings in December, January, and February.[49]

7. **Where they meet:** In member's homes, in the Aurora Free Library, or at the United Ministry of Aurora's social room.[50]

8. **Election of new members:** A prospective member is invited to attend a few meetings. If she is interested and the group reciprocates her interest, then a letter proposing her name for membership, signed by three members, is presented, probably at the business meeting in May. Usually, a show of hands or a voice vote is used. If the prospect is accepted for membership, then the secretary sends her a letter officially inviting her to become a member. If there might be any controversy about her approval, then, rather than a public vote, a secret ballot is used.[51] At the meeting I attended, the members laughed at, but were slightly scandalized by, the now frowned-upon practice of blackballing a prospective member, as was done in the past. They indicated to me that all that was really needed these days was a prospective member who wanted to join.

9. **Object of the club as stated in bylaws:** Currently, there is no object stated in the club's constitution or bylaws, which were revised in 2006.[52]

10. **Dues:** $10 per year.[53]

11. **Club motto, flower, and colors:** Unknown at this time, and—if they ever existed—no longer in use. Members of the meeting I attended said that such things were "too frivolous."[54]

12. **Paper or program assignment schedule and hostessing schedule:** The bylaws state, "Each member shall expect to be asked each year to give a paper or serve as a hostess. Each member shall submit a copy of her paper to the program chair for placement in the Aurora Free Library."[55] I was told at the meeting I attended that a sign-up sheet is passed around for papers and hostessing duty alike. If there are still holes in the calendar, then the vice president (who is also the program chair) will call members to fill in the blanks[56] or the group will get a guest speaker. The list of possible yearly topics is generated by the program committee; they come up with eight to twelve possible topics. These are discussed and voted on at a business meeting, and then the top three are voted on by secret ballot at the final meeting of the year.

After the winning topic is announced, the sign-up sheet is circulated. The vice president constructs a program booklet for each member once the assignments and dates are in place.[57]

13. **Length of papers:** About thirty minutes long.

14. **Location of the club's archives:** The Aurora Free Library.

15. **Civic achievements of the group:**
   - The group donates equally to the Aurora Free Library and its upstairs neighbor, the Morgan Opera House,[58] both housed in the same Tudor Revival, half-timbered, two-story building on Aurora's Main Street, built in 1898 as a gift of long-ago Thursday Club member Louise Morgan Zabriskie.[59]
   - Longtime member Ann Burch recalled that during WWII, the group rolled bandages,[60] as did many other literary societies during wartime.

16. **Special events of the year:** None, other than the annual meeting at the end of the year.

17. **Refreshments:** There is always a tea table, as described in item 16. At the end of the meeting I attended, the table, set up adjacent to the institutional-style kitchen, which was visible from the church's social room where we were meeting, was spread with cookies, finger foods, a very rich sliced cake, and hot cider, among other offerings. This meeting was in early October, so the cider was seasonal. One member told me that for the tea table after a paper about the Devil, the hostess produced only black-and-white food and drink.[61] At another meeting, where the paper delivered was on Scotland, the hostess served scones.[62]

18. **Special traditions:**
   - There is a tea table at the end of each meeting. It features finger foods, sweets, and beverages. I was told that one former member always served two kinds of pie, one apple and one without crust. For years, many members used a local woman who was a caterer who turned out beautiful crustless tea sandwiches.[63]

- The annual meeting was mentioned as a tradition. It is held at the end of the year and features, among other things, a vote for the yearly topic by secret ballot.
- Another tradition is that there is no meeting in December, January, or February.[64]
- The members have just begun a new tradition: having one evening meeting a year, at 7:00 p.m. on Thursdays, so that working members can attend without taking time off from work.[65]

19. **Example of an overall yearly theme:**
    - Longtime member Ann Burch explained that this is the only topic that is assigned—an overall theme or topic for the year. Members may cover it any way they wish. In other words, there are no individual assignments, just volunteered paper topics somehow related to the yearly theme. Ann said that one of her favorite papers was one she had written about her husband's WWII experiences on a South Pacific island. She called it "How Spam Helped Win the War," although it was really about the history of tea.[66]
    - One overall topic from a recent year was "Remember When—Those Were the Days."

20. **Example of an individual paper from that topic:** "Hitsville, USA—Motown."

21. **Particularly colorful or interesting member, present or past:**
    - Former member Judy Kenyon is said to have appeared at meetings barefooted.[67] She was also a key player in opposition to the recent purchasing and renovating of many of Aurora's and Wells College's historic buildings by American Girl Doll tycoon and Wells graduate Pleasant Rowland. Ms. Kenyon, herself a 1952 graduate of Wells College, helped organize anti-Rowland floats for two annual parades during the rebuilding process.[68]

22. **Legacy members and longest-active members:**

- Current member Ann Burch, who was my first contact with the group and who answered my questions diligently and with good humor and referred me to the group's president, is a legacy member. Her mother, Mildred Stewart, was a member from 1939 to 1972. Ann, who is now ninety years old, has been a member since 1969—forty-six years—and so is the oldest member of the group and its longest-active at this point.[69] Ann remembers that her mother attended every meeting wearing her Spencer corset, a dress, a hat, and gloves. Happily, Ann added, "Club members have been wearing pants to meetings for years."[70] However, she said that she thinks her group should be a tad more formal. "The early members would have a fit at such attire!"[71]

- Elsie Torres has been a member the second longest, from 1980 to 2013, and Charlotte Moser, now an honorary member, had been an active member for fifty-eight years, from 1951 to 2009.[72]

Snapshot Summary of The Coterie of Fayetteville, New York

1. **Official name of the club:** The Coterie of Fayetteville. (*Coterie* means "an intimate and often exclusive group of persons with a unifying common interest or purpose."[73])
2. **Date founded:** October 26, 1885. The group broke away from a men's and women's Shakespeare Club and first called themselves the Social Art Class. They became the Coterie on the above date in October 1885.[74]
3. **Founders' names:** Mrs. Harriet (Andrew J.) Wilkin, Mrs. D. S. Evans, Mrs. Bartlett, Mrs. Sarah (Huntington) Beard, M. B. Birdseye, Mrs. Mary Louise (Edward) Collin, Mrs. Charles Collin, Miss F. E. Ecker, Mrs. N. M. Gillette, Miss Mollie Hoyt, Mrs. B. N. Hurd, Mrs. Charles Larkins, Mrs. Julia Osborn,

Mrs. Searles, Mrs. F. N. Severance, Mrs. N. L. Seward, and Miss Wood.[75]

4. **Size limit of club as stated in bylaws:** Thirty-six active members and any number of honorary members.[76]

5. **Size of club today:** Eighteen active members and twelve honorary members[77] when I met with members of the group in October of 2012. In December 2014, their historian, Nancy Wilson, wrote to me and said the following:

> Our group has had a resurgence of membership. We had three new members last year and currently have three women awaiting approval into the group. The credentials of some of these women are impressive. One is an architect, and several are award-winning and retired teachers. Of course, we are having the usual departure of the older members who find they can't host meetings or travel easily from house to house. We did broaden our area of membership by including locales east of the city of Syracuse, and this has encouraged current members to look outside our community amongst their acquaintances.[78]

6. **Meeting schedule:** The Coterie meets on the second Tuesday of the month, September to April. In May, there is a luncheon at noon. Otherwise, meetings start promptly at 2:00 p.m. and are over by 4:00 p.m.[79] The September meeting is a new addition to the schedule, which used to start in October. In September, members planned for a field trip in October—possibly a day trip to a museum or to one of the many religious communities in the area from the 1800s, such as the Oneida Group. This tour is followed by lunch.[80]

7. **Where they meet:** To quote the group's answers to my question about meetings: "Meetings are usually at the homes of members. Each hostess has an assistant hostess to share the work. Occasionally, if the home is too small, we meet at the library or one of the churches."[81]

8. **Election of new members:** To find new members, current members speak to friends and acquaintances in the Fayetteville–Manlius area[82] to see if they might be interested

in The Coterie. If they are interested, then they need to attend three meetings, but these need not be in sequence. A member must then propose the candidate. After this, a small committee meets with her to be sure she understands what her duties will be. At the next meeting, the proposer reads the introduction she's written about the new member, and then the member is welcomed into the club.[83]

9. **Object of the club as stated in bylaws:** "The club shall provide opportunity for intellectual growth and for friendship."[84]

10. **Dues:** $10 per year. Dues are used to cover the printed roster or program for the year. The balance of the funds is donated to the Fayetteville Free Library, divided between the Local History Room (which houses their archives), the Motto Music Collection (a collection of over thirty-five thousand pieces of sheet music and four hundred books donated by a local shop-owner[85]), and the Women's History Collection. Several of the founders of the library were Coterie members, with Emma Burlew Beard and her mother, Sarah Beard, also a Coterie founder, being the names most mentioned in that respect. Sarah was a Coterie member from 1885 to 1897, but the dates of her daughter's membership are uncertain, given that thirty-five years' worth of roll books were lost.[86]

11. **Club motto, flower, and colors:** There is no record of a club flower or colors, but the motto is, "In America, literature and the elegant arts must grow side by side with the coarser plants of daily necessity" —Washington Irving.[87]

12. **Paper or program assignment schedule and hostessing schedule:** Two directors—a programming director and a hostessing director—put together a schedule for the year. They use a spreadsheet to show what each member has done over the past few years. The rotation of papers and hostessing is usually on a three-year cycle. Those members who are scheduled to give a paper will meet with the directors and come up with a theme and subject for the individual papers. Hostessing assignments are made at the last meeting of the year for the next year, with a sign-up sheet being passed around and cohostesses being chosen from the remaining members. Usually, the newest members are

allowed to learn the ropes by being cohostesses. Directors and officers are usually not required to host, cohost, or give a paper, although when the membership drops below twenty, they must perform one of these jobs. Sometimes, members may have to double up on their assignments.[88] The bylaws state that "members will be expected to be a hostess one year, to prepare and present a paper and to be an assistant hostess the alternate year, and to hold office when requested."[89]

13. **Length of papers:** Papers take about thirty to forty minutes, followed by a teatime of about forty minutes.[90]

14. **The location of the club's archives:** The archives have been stored in the Fayetteville Free Library's Local History Room since 1970. However, there is a gap of thirty-five years, from 1909 to 1944, in The Coterie's roll books stored there, so some membership dates are unknown or estimated.[91]

15. **Civic achievements:** Several Coterie members were part of a group of citizens who started the first library in Fayetteville in 1906.

16. **Special events:** The Coterie is now taking field trips during its September meeting. Among other places, members have visited the Susan B. Anthony House, the Women's Rights National Historical Park in nearby Seneca Falls, and the Erie Canal Museum in neighboring Canastota. The group has also hosted outside speakers and used to invite husbands to an occasional holiday meeting, although that custom has faded away.[92]

17. **Refreshments:** Tea and any kind of tea table the hostess cares to offer.[93]

18. **Special traditions:**
    - A donation is given each year to the Fayetteville Free Library, usually being divided between the Women's History Collection, the Motto Music Collection, and the Local History Room.[94]
    - The Coterie honors members who have reached twenty-five years of membership. A member volunteers or is assigned to write an overview of those twenty-five years, sometimes in verse. Those

papers are a part of the club's archives stored at the Fayetteville Free Library.[95]

- Another tradition is the "blue book," in which each member has a page showing the record of her participation.[96]
- For special observations, like the group's hundredth birthday, papers detailing each twenty-five-year segment of the history are researched and presented. On the hundredth birthday of the group, many members dressed in period costumes specific to their twenty-five-year period.[97]
- The pouring of tea is a tradition. The member who was honored as being the one who poured tea in the club's early days was mentioned in the local newspaper's society column. Today, there is still a member stationed at either end of the tea table, helping pour either tea or coffee. And, of course, the offering of tea sandwiches, cookies, and other delicacies is another beloved tradition.[98]
- It is traditional to mention in the minutes the weather at the previous meeting, "perhaps to indicate the hardiness of the membership who venture forth in 'intense heat' or 'blustery' cold afternoons to attend these gatherings."[99]

19. **Example of an overall yearly theme of study, and who assigns the papers:** The two directors organize the paper and the hostessing schedules. One recent topic was "New York State."[100] However, the group doesn't always have a unifying theme.

20. **Examples of individual papers for "New York State":** "Washington Irving," "Gems and Minerals of N.Y. State," "New York State Parks,"[101] "Oswego and the War of 1812," "A Ride through the Countryside" (about area railroad lines), "The Man Who Gave Us Central Park" (a biography of Frederick Law Olmstead), and "Their History Is Carved in Stone" (about the limestone houses north of Utica, New York, dating from the early 1800s).[102]

21. **Particularly colorful or interesting members, present or
    past:** The three women I met with suggested Emma Burlew
    Beard, Grace Bryan, and Betsy Knapp.

    • Emma Beard was a Smith College graduate, Class
      of 1895. An orphan raised by the Beard family of
      Fayetteville, she became a civic activist. Her adoptive
      mother, Sarah Beard, was also a Coterie member.
      Among her many other quiet accomplishments,
      Emma was one of the founders of the Fayetteville
      library with a group of local citizens, which included
      her mother. Having once worked in a settlement
      house in New York City, she remade a local home
      into a kind of settlement house. She died in 1943.[103]

    • Grace Bryan, who graduated from Pratt Institute
      in 1908, was active in many civic causes and was
      one of the first teachers of home economics in New
      York State, teaching in the Fayetteville schools
      after moving to Coterie's central New York village in
      1916. She died in 1988, just a few weeks shy of her
      hundredth birthday. She was married to a doctor, and
      she is remembered as being a real lady and very vital
      into her old age. She was a Coterie member from
      1945 to 1977, after which she became an honorary
      member.

    • Betsy Knapp was of the sixth generation of the Collin
      family—descendants of the founder of Manlius,
      David Collin III—to live on the property acquired
      by her great-great-grandfather in 1817.[104] Her home
      was called Indian Oven,[105] named after a unique
      rock formation on the homestead property (now a
      state park), which Indians may have used for cooking
      before the Collin family settled there.[106] Betsy, a
      member of Phi Beta Kappa, graduated from Smith
      College, probably in 1932, and later did graduate
      work at Syracuse University. In 1934, she became the
      youngest president of the Onondaga County League
      of Women Voters.[107] After working for the national
      office of the League of Women Voters in Washington,

DC, from 1935 to 1949, and for the Allied High Commission in Germany, from 1949 to 1952, helping with postwar community affairs,[108] she eventually became the head of the Maxwell School Library at Syracuse University, at which job she worked until her retirement in 1972. She also served as a trustee for that university's Library Associates. She helped to found the Manlius Environmental Council in 1973— one of the first environmental councils in New York State—and was its chairwoman for ten years.[109] Ms. Knapp founded and was the first executive director of the World Affairs Council of Syracuse.[110] She was the author of many articles, often about local history and the environment, and a memoir published in 1989, which focuses largely on her memories of her family's property around Green Lake, which is now a state park.[111] Ms. Knapp stockpiled family memorabilia and memories, and she established the Collin Room at the Onondaga Historical Association to house the records of the Collin, Park, and Knapp families.[112] She was a member of The Coterie from 1973 to 1990,[113] and she died in 1993 at the age of eighty-two.[114]

22. **Legacy members and longest-active members:**
- Currently, the longest-active member is Ann Moore, one of the three members who met with me to discuss Coterie. She has been a member for thirty-five years.
- In recent memory, the longest-active member was Harriet D. Wilkin, who was active for fifty years, although the exact years of her membership have been lost along with the missing roll books.[115]
- Carol Gridley just became an honorary member after being an active member for forty-nine years. Her mother, Cornelia Kerslake, was a member from 1945 to 1974.
- Margot Bourke also just became an honorary member. She has been a member since 1982— thirty-three years. Her mother, Margaret Ogg, was a member from 1959 to 1980.

- Hilda Broad was an active member from 1947 to 1979. She became an honorary member in 1980 and recently died at the age of 107. She had graduated from Bryn Mawr and had taught classes at the prestigious Oldfields and Madeira schools before marrying and moving to Fayetteville.[116]
- Dorothy Ashley was a member from 1950 to 1988. Her daughter, Jo Anne Ashley, was an active member from 1966 to 1994 and is now an honorary member.[117] Dorothy's husband, Carlyle M. Ashley, held sixty-seven patents for work he did during his forty-three years at Carrier Corporation, the biggest name in business in the Syracuse area. Also, Carlyle Ashley was the president of the Syracuse Museum of Fine Arts.[118]

Snapshot Summary of Philomath, Fayetteville, New York

1. **Official name of the club:** Philomath. The word means "a lover of learning, a seeker of knowledge."[119]
2. **Date founded:** Friday evening, April 11, 1884.[120]
3. **Founders' names:** Mrs. Charles Noble, Mrs. William Austin, Mrs. L. J. Welles, Mrs. T. B. Robinson, and Miss Luella Dunham,[121] meeting in Mrs. Austin's home.
4. **Size of club as stated in bylaws (size limit):** No more than thirty members.
5. **Size of club today:** Seven participating members when I met with their president; however, they have since disbanded.
6. **Meeting schedule:** The most recent pattern had been to meet monthly, starting in October and concluding in May. There was no meeting in January or March. Philomath met on the second Tuesday of the month at 1:00 p.m.—a "dessert meeting."[122] However, with the sharp drop in their membership numbers and the illness of a key member, their meeting schedule for 2012–13 had been disrupted and shortened when I interviewed their president, Nancy Bond, in person

in Fayetteville in early October 2012. In early February 2013, she wrote to me and said that she and her fellow members were regretfully "winding up this club and its activities due to lack of members. It has outlived its purpose."[123]

7. **Where they met:** In members' homes, except for the annual meeting, which was also the final meeting, which might have been held at a local restaurant or inn.[124]

8. **Election of new members:** Prospective members' names were submitted with a brief biography, and then active members voted.[125]

9. **Object of the club as stated in bylaws or constitution:** Their constitution states that the club's object was the "systematic study of countries, their history, art, and literature by readings, discussions and such miscellaneous work as may be suggested."[126] However, minutes from the group's first meeting say that the members were meeting to "form a society for mutual advantage and improvement by means of the study of works of travel."[127]

10. **Dues:** $10 per year.

11. **Club flower and colors:** None known. What seems to be an unofficial **club motto** is "128 years of progress," or however many years had passed when the new roster was printed.[128]

12. **Paper or program assignment schedule and hostessing schedule:** Members gave a paper one year and served as hostess the next year.[129]

13. **Length of papers:** Papers were at least fifteen minutes long, sometimes twenty minutes.[130]

14. **Location of the club's archives:** The Local History Room of the Fayetteville Free Library.

15. **Civic achievements of the group or its individual members:** The purchase, wrapping, donation, and distribution of books to a classroom of needy students at Christmastime. The club also made annual donations to charitable and civic organizations.[131]

16. **Special events of the year:**
    - There was always a final luncheon in May, with a speaker on the topic for the year.

- There was usually a covered-dish luncheon for the opening meeting in October, but it had to be cancelled in 2012 and moved to another month after one of the key members, the chairwoman of the reading committee, became ill.
- The Christmas book-wrapping meeting had lately become a festive tradition, with holiday treats for dessert.[132]

17. **Refreshments:** Until this year, the opening meeting in October had always been a luncheon, with every member bringing a covered dish or other item. The other meetings during the year featured dessert, tea, and coffee. The final meeting was a luncheon, with the most recent one held at a local inn and conference center.[133]

18. **Special traditions:** Meetings were called to order with a big bell mounted on a marble slab or stand. A member's husband made a wooden case for it, and the heavy bell and box were carried in a blue velvet bag to meetings.[134]

19. **Example of an overall yearly theme:** One example of a yearly theme was the 2010 choice, "First Ladies: Influence and Mission."[135] The theme of study was chosen by a reading committee.

20. **Example of individual papers for that theme:** Papers on Abigail Adams, Eleanor Roosevelt, Edith Wilson, and Jackie Kennedy were given during the study of first ladies.[136]

21. **Colorful or interesting member, present or past:** Agnes Cook, who died in 2003 at the age of eighty-nine, whom Nancy Bond described as "very interesting, very well-read, did work for political parties, and she gave wonderful papers, was great on local history. I always learned something when it was her turn. She was a great speaker. She served as president of Philomath, and she organized the 100-year celebration in 1984."[137] Agnes was an alternate delegate to the Republican National Convention in 1972.[138]

22. **Legacy members:** None at this time.

Snapshot Summary of Hamilton Fortnightly Club

1. **Official name of the club:** Hamilton Fortnightly Club.
2. **Date founded:** January 23, 1894.[139]
3. **Founders:** The first preparatory meetings were held at the home of Mrs. Eugene Sisson (Jennie). Mrs. William J. Russell was elected president at the first official meeting on January 23, 1894. Other names mentioned as founders include Mrs. Sylvester Burnham, Lottie Andrews, Gusta Berry, and Mrs. Albert Perry Brigham.[140] However, current club members stress, "Our records don't show much emphasis on founders per se. The village was very small in those days, and [we] think they thought of founders as everyone who showed up for the early meetings."[141] Fifty percent of the members were traditionally from the Colgate community ("gown"), and fifty percent were from the town. Professional women joined—the heads of the Hamilton Female Seminary and Emily Judson Prep School—as did women whose husbands had occupations. These included two doctors, a school principal, a bank director, a grocer, a bookseller, a lawyer, an engineer, a dentist, and members of a civic improvement association.[142]
4. **Size of club as stated in bylaws (size limit):** Thirty-five regular members.
5. **Actual size of club today:** Thirty-two regular members and seven honorary members.
6. **Meeting schedule:** From 3:00 p.m. to 4:00 p.m., every other Tuesday, from September to April. The initial meeting, which is a guest meeting, is held on a Sunday. There are seventeen meetings in all, including a final luncheon and a holiday meeting.[143]
7. **Where they meet:** They used to meet in members' homes, but, as of the 1990s, they now meet in the community room of the Hamilton Public Library.[144]
8. **Election of new members:** "The by-laws revision of 2009 eliminated the election of members. Anyone who wants to join may now do so after attending two regular meetings as a guest of two sponsoring members."[145]

9. **Object of the club as stated in bylaws:** "Intellectual and general improvement."[146]

10. **Dues:** $15 per year.

11. **Club motto, flower, and colors:** No motto or flower is noted, but the club colors are yellow and white. The club has used a beautiful monogram on the front of its program roster and other printed matter since the club was, at the most, twenty-five years old.[147]

12. **Paper or program assignment schedule and hostessing schedule:** "Members are asked to state when they would like to give papers, and the program chairwoman then makes the assignments. The same is done with hostessing, which involves only setting up chairs."[148]

13. **Length of papers:** Two papers are given at each meeting, and they are each twenty minutes long. Time is allowed for questions. Including the opening business portion of the meeting, the entire meeting is only one hour long.[149]

14. **Location of the club's yearbooks, minutes, scrapbooks, and archives:** "Members' papers are stored in the Hamilton Public Library, along with copies of program booklets and recent minutes. Books of minutes (1894–2000), a complete set of program booklets, early newspaper clippings, and other items which need archival-quality care are stored with the archivist at the Case-Geyer Library at Colgate."[150]

15. **Civic achievements of the group or its members:**
    - Hamilton Fortnightly's members were instrumental in starting Hamilton's public library in 1902 and its hospital in 1952. One of their current honorary members, Ruth Hartshorne, and now-deceased member Gwen Todd were the founders of a local cooperative nursery school, Chenango Nursery School, in 1948. Ruth also was a cofounder of Education Unlimited, a continuing education program, in 1979.[151]
    - The club funds a journalism award at the local high school.
    - Margaret Miller, a current Fortnightly member, is the mayor of the village of Hamilton. Member Carolyn

Todd serves the town of Hamilton on its board, and Deborah Kliman is a trustee of the village board.[152]

16. **Special events during the year:** There is a guest meeting, the first meeting of the year, which is held on a Sunday and features a speaker. A holiday party, usually with entertainment, and a year-end luncheon are both held in a spot like the Colgate Inn. The year-end luncheon also features a speaker. Men may be invited to any meeting.[153]

17. **Refreshments:** *No refreshments,* except at the events mentioned in item 16. The meeting takes exactly one hour—from 3:00 p.m. to 4:00 p.m.—and then the women are out the door.[154]

18. **Special traditions:**
   - Roll is always called at the beginning of the meetings.
   - The one-hour time limit for the meeting and the twenty-minute time limit for each of the two papers delivered at each meeting are strictly adhered to.
   - No refreshments are offered, except for at the three meetings at the beginning and the end of the club's yearly schedule, and at holiday time in December.[155]
   - Several old traditions have died out, e.g., using "Mrs." or "Miss" during meetings and answering the roll call with a quotation or fact relevant to the day's two papers or the yearly theme.[156] The fifty–fifty town–gown membership split is no longer observed, and the group stopped meeting in members' homes in the 1990s.[157]
   - The secretary is in charge of keeping the old-fashioned secretary's ledger pasted up with copies of each set of minutes plus the roll-call list.[158]
   - Presidents usually serve two consecutive one-year terms.[159]
   - New members do not give a paper during their first year of membership.[160]
   - Guests may attend two meetings per year, unless they are on a "membership track," in which case they might attend a guest meeting or luncheon in addition to meeting the requirement of attending two

regular meetings. Once they do this, they declare their intention to join. After that, they meet with the membership committee and then attend the next meeting as a full member.[161]

19. **Example of a yearly theme of study, and who assigns the theme and paper topics:** "The 2012/2013 subject was 'The Sound of Music.' The program committee presents three topics, and members vote on their preferences. Presentation topics are then chosen by the members."[162] Members are given their assignments in March for the coming year so that they have the summer to do their reading and preparation.[163]

20. **Examples of individual papers or programs based on that topic:** "Shostakovich: Life into Music,"[164] "Music as an Agent of Social Change," and "Music of the Harlem Renaissance."[165]

21. **Particularly colorful or interesting member, present or past:** I was told several times that Hamilton Fortnightly's ranks had, at one time, included several *grandes dames*, especially Gwen Todd, mother-in-law of current member Carolyn Todd, and Molly Ramshaw. Both Gwen and Molly died in 2000, perhaps marking the end of a certain era for the club.

- Gwen Todd, a Smith College graduate and the wife of a biology professor at Colgate, was very active in community affairs and cofounded Chenango Nursery School with current honorary member Ruth Hartshorne. She was a stickler for being on time, was said to "scare [members] to death," and "could have been a CEO" in other times. However she also had a warm and friendly side and presented wonderful papers into her old age. She died at the age of ninety-three. She is remembered as being at the top of the local social hierarchy. At least one member said that Fortnightly was reflective of a "snobby" social scene in the 1960s, which is not true of the town or the club today. Mrs. Todd was a Fortnightly member from 1966 to 1980.[166]

- Molly Ramshaw, whose husband was also a Colgate professor, was interested in dramatics and was a very dramatic individual. She always did her papers on the theater. Before Colgate went coed in 1970, Mrs. Ramshaw sometimes starred in their productions when a woman was needed. She funded an award, one that still bears her name, for a local graduating high school senior who has excelled in the dramatic arts. She is described by current members who knew her as having been "like someone from another century," dressing beautifully and grandly. She was Fortnightly president during 1979–80 and 1980–81. She died at the age of seventy-four.[167]

22. **Legacy members and longest-active members:**
   - Present member Carolyn Todd's mother-in-law, Gwen Todd, mentioned above, was a member and was president between 1983 and 1985, when the women decided to start using their own first names, instead of their husbands', in the directory.
   - Current member Debbie Kliman's great-aunt Mrs. Samuel Burhans (Mabel) was president from 1927 to 1929.[168]
   - As for longest-active member, club members say that Hamilton Fortnightly has "four active members who joined between 39 and 46 years ago."[169]

Snapshot Summary of Monday Evening Club, Manlius, New York

1. **Official name of the club:** The club started life as the Monday Night Club, but the name was changed in the 1950s to the Monday Evening Club.[170]
2. **Date founded:** 1884.
3. **Founders:** The prime mover was Mary Babcock. She was the daughter of the rector of Christ Episcopal Church in Manlius. She was joined by Mrs. Moulter, Miss Jenny Clark, Mrs. Neely, Miss Jenny Cook, Miss Eugenie Scoville, Miss

Louise Davis, Miss Florence Scoville, Mrs. Frances Hudson, Miss Minnie Sinnamon, Miss Grace Moulter, Miss Martha Smith, Miss Nellie Moulter, and Miss Charlotte Stimson.

4. **Size of club as limited in bylaws:** A total of twenty-five women.

5. **Actual size of club today:** Fourteen active members and six honorary members. President Kelly Garwood, whose mother was also a member, said that although the club has three members who still work, most of the members are in their seventies and eighties. "It's hard to get the younger ones to join. They're too busy," she added.

6. **Meeting schedule:** The club meets every other Monday, on the first or second Monday of the month, from September to early May, at 7:30 in the evening. There are ten meetings per year. There is only one meeting in December (the Christmas meeting), one meeting in January,[171] and no February meeting, as "so many members are in Florida."

7. **Where they meet:** Members' homes or in a local church or another spot conducive to a particular event.

8. **Election of new members:** A current member brings a friend whom she thinks would be interested to a meeting or two to see if she is, in fact, interested. If she would like to join, the current member sends a note to the president listing the prospective member's abilities and activities and saying how these would benefit the club. Then, the club votes. There is no set time of the year for bringing in new members. Kelly wrote to me to say that in recent years, there have been few members and many vacancies.[172]

9. **Object of the club:** The club's constitution states, "The object of the club shall be the study of special and general information and social interaction for its members."[173]

10. **Dues:** $10 per year. This pays for the roster, which lists the hostesses for the day and the papers to be given. During the Christmas season, the group also donates to the local historical society, or to the library, or the food bank. In honor of recently deceased members, the group sends flowers and a card to the family.

11. **Club motto, flower, and colors:** None on record.

12. **Paper or program assignment schedule and hostessing rotation schedule:** Members alternate between hostessing and presenting papers, hopefully being a hostess one year and giving a paper the next, but it sometimes happens that members do both in the same year. (There are ten meetings and fourteen members.)

13. **Length of papers:** There is one paper per meeting, and each paper is twenty to thirty minutes long.

14. **Location of the club's archives:** The Manlius Library. This library also stores a quilt made by the club in 1975–76 to observe the American bicentennial. Each square in the quilt was created by a member and shows a scene from Manlius's or Monday Evening Club's history. This was the first quilt of this type I ran into while researching this book.

15. **Civic achievements of the group:**
    - In 1899, the group received a certificate of registration from New York State, recognizing them as a study group.
    - They started the first Girl Scout troop in Manlius (the exact date is unknown, but it would have been after 1912, when the Girl Scouts were founded.[174]).
    - In 1929, the club started a petition for a village curfew.
    - As mentioned above, in 1975–76, the group created a quilt for the country's bicentennial celebration. For the club's hundredth anniversary, the quilt was raffled off to one of its members, who later bequeathed it to the club (and thence to the library for safekeeping).

16. **Special events:** The annual banquet is a dinner in May, and the group also holds potluck suppers at 6:00 p.m. twice per season. At their evening Christmas meeting, members sing carols and exchange Secret Santa stockings. They also eat sundaes, slices of a traditional Yule log, and cookies, which are provided by the program committee. They might enjoy a talk about Christmas in Manlius in the 1800s or hear another short report on an equally historic and seasonal subject.

17. **Refreshment highlights:** Every meeting ends with tea, coffee, desserts, nuts, and mints. The Christmas meeting

has the most elaborate desserts: a Yule log, sundaes, and Christmas cookies, plus hot beverages.

18. **Special traditions:** See "Special events" and "Meeting schedule," above, for Monday Evening Club's traditional way of celebrating Christmas and of holding their annual meeting and their potluck suppers. Also traditional is the organization of each meeting: each starts with the minutes and roll call, moves onto old and new news, and then resumes with the program, which is followed by refreshments. A dessert is provided by the hostess, as are nuts and mints, which are *always* offered, along with coffee and tea, or perhaps hot apple cider during apple season.

19. **Example of a yearly theme or topic:** In 2011–12, the theme was "Old Forts of New York State."

20. **Example of an individual paper based on that topic:** "Theodore Roosevelt and the Forts of Eastern New York State."

21. **Particularly colorful or interesting member, present or past:** In 1935, a member named Mrs. Curtis attended a dinner in Syracuse for Amelia Earhart and met the colorful heroine and foremost aviatrix of her day.

22. **Legacy members and longest-active members:**
    - The mother of current club President Kelly Garwood was Joyce Vedder, who was a member. The mother of current member Marge Edwards, Rhoda Edwards, was also a member.
    - The five members who have been active members of the group for the longest time are Shirley Mapstone, who joined in 1956, fifty-nine years ago (she recently became an honorary member); Harriet Helsher, 1964, fifty-one years ago; Betty Hopkinson, 1968, forty-seven years ago (Betty wrote a history of the group); Beverly Gilmore, 1972, forty-three years ago; and Myrna Benedict, 1973, forty-two years ago. All of the other members mentioned still present papers.

Snapshot Summary of The Leisure Hour Club, Skaneateles, New York

1. **Official name of the club:** The Leisure Hour Club.
2. **Date founded:** November 28, 1892.[175]
3. **Founder's name:** Mrs. Justin Howard.[176]
4. **Size of club as stated in bylaws (size limit):** Twenty-five active members.[177]
5. **Size of club today:** Twenty-five active members, plus twenty-three honorary or associate members.[178]
6. **Meeting schedule:** Members meet promptly at 2:00 p.m. every Monday (except during Christmas week and Thanksgiving week) from early October to the first week of April. One exception is the opening luncheon, which is held at noon on the first Tuesday of October, as the country club where the luncheon is held is closed on Mondays. Meetings consist of a long reading, a condensed and smoothly transitioned continuum of various passages from a book chosen by a reader, which takes one hour. Then comes a formal tea, with tea, coffee, sweets, and tea sandwiches. This lasts thirty minutes. Then comes a short business meeting followed by a thirty-minute "short reading," which can be from a magazine or short story.[179]
7. **Where they meet:** In members' homes.[180]
8. **Election of new members:** When there is a vacancy, names are suggested at one meeting and then revisited and perhaps added to at another meeting. After the members vote on the short list of names, the prospective member with the most votes is asked to be a member by the member who sponsored her. The prospect accepts or declines by giving her answer to that sponsor.[181]
9. **Object of the club as stated in bylaws:** "Intellectual and cultural stimulation."[182]
10. **Dues:** $10 per year. This pays for memorial flowers and the yearly roster.
11. **Club motto, flower, and colors:** None.[183]
12. **Program assignment schedule and hostessing assignment schedule:** Every woman serves as hostess once each year. Each woman also gives a long reading and

presents a short reading each year. The program committee sets up the schedule, but members may swap dates with each other if a certain date is difficult for them.

13. **Length of papers or programs:** Long readings last one hour, and short readings last thirty minutes.

14. **Location of the club's archives**: The Skaneateles Public Library.

15. **Civic achievements of members, past or present:** Shotwell Park, which contains a war memorial said to be one of the most beautiful in the country,[184] was developed on land paid for by the family of author Louisa Shotwell. Its maintenance fund was endowed by Louisa as a gift to the town.[185] Louisa's mother was a member of the club.[186] Also, see item 21, below, for a description of still-active member Louise Robinson's involvement in the founding and nurturing of the Skaneateles Festival, an annual music festival.

16. **Special events during the year:** Other than the opening luncheon, there are no special events. After all, there is a meeting and a tea every week from October to April!

17. **Refreshments:** A full tea table between the long reading and the short reading. This is unique among the groups I studied.

18. **Special traditions:**
    - Using "Mrs." or "Miss" rather than a member's first name during the meeting. During teatime, first names are used.[187]
    - Members come nicely dressed, never in jeans, although they may wear slacks.[188]
    - Other traditions revolve around the meetings and their organization, e.g., tea in between a long reading and a short reading, and a meeting almost every Monday from October to early April.[189]

19. **Example of an overall yearly theme:** The club used yearly themes and was more of a traditional study club in its early days. Now, it has no yearly theme, but each member picks the book or magazine from which she will do her long and short readings.[190]

20. **Example of an individual paper or program:** Phyllis Clark delivered a reading on October 29, 2012, from *The Elephant*

Whisperer, by Lawrence Anthony. She often picks books about wildlife for her readings. Other members may choose a favorite author or subject.[191]

21. **A particularly colorful or interesting member, present or past:** After consideration and some confusion over a mother and daughter with the same name—Shotwell—one of whom was thought to be the club's most interesting member, I found that the lead turned out to be a dead end when it was discovered that the famous daughter, Louisa, who was an author and educator and was not a member, although her mother had been. My great helper with all of the Leisure Hour Club information, Phyllis Clark, wrote me after this discovery and said that she felt that she could not single out any one "most interesting member," as she believes that all of the members are interesting and colorful—and that is why she and the other members look forward to seeing each other every Monday.[192] I then discovered that the club's longest-active and oldest member, Louise Robinson, was a cofounder of the Skaneateles (music) Festival in 1980. I have added her as an "interesting" member, and Phyllis agreed wholeheartedly with my choice, adding that many volunteers—from the club's ranks and otherwise—make the festival work as well as it does. (See below, item 22.)

22. **Legacy members and longest-active member:** The group calls its legacy members "heritage members," and there are three, as follows:

   - Member Peggy Manring, a talented artist whose mother, Louise Robinson, is still a member; Sally Holbein, whose mother, Marion Holbein, was a member; and Peggy Bennett, whose mother, Marge Evans, and sister, Ginny Longacre, were members.[193]
   - The longest-active member and oldest member in the club today is Louise Robinson, who joined in 1979. Louise and her husband, David, were cofounders in 1980 of the Skaneateles Festival, an internationally renowned music festival, for which they opened their home, Brook Farm, to house and feed the musicians. They also opened their home's rolling lawn for

concerts. Many of their family members pitched in and helped with every conceivable task. Some of the biggest names in classical music play at this festival each summer.[194]

Snapshot Summary of the Monday Evening Club, Skaneateles, New York

Unless otherwise noted, all answers come virtually verbatim from an e-mail written by club member Phyllis Clark and sent to me, on March 13, 2013, with minor additions in following e-mails. Phyllis was assisted by the club's historian, Nancy Tiedemann, in gathering the information. Phyllis is somehow able to fulfill her responsibilities of membership in both the Monday Evening Club and the Leisure Hour Club, although both meet on Mondays, one in the afternoon and one at night. Two Mondays a month, she attends club meetings in the afternoon and the evening!

1. **Official name of the club:** Monday Evening Club.
2. **Date founded:** September 1908.
3. **Founder(s):** Miss Elizabeth Cobane, who was said to be an outstanding high school teacher, was afraid that her niece Gertrude Platt was not reading enough, so she invited a group of six of her niece's contemporaries—women in their early twenties—to meet once a week and read together. They literally read aloud from each woman's choice of material. They met informally in each other's homes until 1912, when they organized formally into the club's present format.
4. **Size of club as limited by its bylaws:** There are no bylaws. However, it appears that the membership number is kept at a maximum of twenty-five, perhaps for the purposes of accommodating everyone inside the members' homes.
5. **Size of club today:** Twenty-four members. There are no membership categories.
6. **Meeting schedule:** The first and third Monday evenings, October through April.
7. **Where they meet:** In members' homes.

8. **Election of new members:** New members are elected at the September dinner meeting. Names of a new member and an alternate are proposed and voted on by ballot.

9. **Object of the club as stated in bylaws:** There are no bylaws, but the members who answered this question for me said that the club's object is "intellectual and literary stimulation in a social setting." (See the above statement of attribution for this quotation and for all information in this snapshot summary.)

10. **Dues:** $10 per year.

11. **Club motto, colors, and flower:** None.

12. **Program assignment and hostessing assignment schedule:** Each member chooses a date to present her program. She also chooses a date either to host the meeting in her home or cohost by bringing the dessert.

13. **Length of papers or programs:** Meetings begin at 8:00 p.m. with a short business meeting. Then, two programs of about thirty to thirty-five minutes each are presented by members. This is followed by dessert.

14. **Location of the club's archives:** All old minutes and scrapbooks are locked in a storage cabinet in the Skaneateles Library, and the club historian keeps the current scrapbook.

15. **Civic achievements of members, past or present:** None noted, although a little sleuthing turned up one of the original members of the club, Katherine Willets, who grew up in a grand Greek Revival mansion, now called Roosevelt Hall, overlooking the lake. Katherine lived her entire life in Skaneateles, except for a brief period during her school years, and she produced three sons, all of whom died in their infancy. The most stunning photographic portrait I've seen of the era when she was a child can be found on the website for the history of Skaneateles. The portrait is called *Katherine by the Window,* and it gives a sense of what a privileged Victorian childhood may have been like. Katherine died at the age of seventy in 1956.[195] The link to the photo and to Katherine's story is http://kihm6.wordpress.com/2012/04/12/katherine-by-the-window/.

16. **Special events during the year:** There is an opening dinner at a restaurant in September and a closing banquet with a special program in May.
17. **Refreshments:** Dessert is served, accompanied by nuts, candy, coffee, and tea. Members are seated at tables to enjoy these treats.
18. **Traditions:** See "Special events" and "Refreshments."
19. **Example of a yearly theme:** Although the club had yearly themes in its early days, there is none today. Each member now chooses a book or a topic she is interested in. The presentations often include handouts or posters.
20. **Example of an individual program or paper:** In 2012, Nancy Tiedemann reported on the book *The Greater Journey,* by David McCullough.
21. **Particularly colorful or interesting member, present or past:** Mary Simpson, a retired teacher who died in 2010 at 101 years of age,[196] was a member of Monday Evening Cub until the age of 95.
22. **Longest-active member and legacy members:** Lynne Bennett has been a member for forty years, and Barbara Evans has been a member for forty-one years. No legacy members are noted.

Snapshot Summary of The Portfolio Club of Syracuse, New York

1. **Group name:** The Portfolio Club of Syracuse, New York.[197]
2. **Date founded:** October 30, 1875, at the home of Helen Plumb on East Genesee Street.[198] This was one month before the founding of Social Art Club, making Portfolio today, at 140 years of age, the oldest still-active women's literary society in Syracuse, New York,[199] and one of the oldest groups I found. Only the Sorosis club of Jacksonville, Illinois, is older, having been founded the same year as the original Sorosis in New York City: 1868.
3. **Founders:** Portfolio was founded as a sketching club (ergo, the Portfolio name) by nine young women, new high school

graduates, with guidance from their high school art teacher, Mrs. Mary Dana Hicks. The charter members of the club were Amelia L. Didama, Hattie S. Curtis, Emma E. Smith, Helen C. Waters, Ella J. Barber, Hattie R. Dingman, Willa L. Hasbrouck, Helen A. Hudson, Mary L. Van Meter, Hattie M. Rowe, Mary B. Hurst, Louise Albro, Jenny Bennett, Ellen Samson, Ella Eager, Emma Soule, Helen Plumb, Mattie Arnold, Fannie I. Noxen, Fannie H. Hopkins, Aria S. Huntington, and Florence Smith.[200] Their first president was Amelia Didama.[201] Mrs. Hicks, who later became Mrs. Louis Prang, wife of the noted art education publisher,[202] had attended a congress of the Association for the Advancement of Women at the Wieting Opera House in 1875 in downtown Syracuse. "At these conferences, which were held in many American cities, Julia Ward Howe (prominent American abolitionist, social activist, poet, and the lyricist of "The Battle Hymn of the Republic") and others encouraged women to form study clubs for self-culture."[203] Miss Hicks also founded Syracuse Social Art Club in November 1875 and served as its first president. Eleven years after the club's founding, Portfolio members moved from the exclusive study of art as outlined in the reportedly stultifying *Outlines of the History of Art,* by Dr. Wilhelm Lübke, to studying a wide range of subjects of their own choice.[204]

4. **Size of club as limited by bylaws:** A maximum of thirty-five members in three categories: preliminary, five members; regular, thirty members; and associates, no maximum (one can request to become an associate after having served as president).[205]

5. **Actual size of club today:** Twenty-eight regular members, plus sixteen associate members and one preliminary member.

6. **Meeting schedule:** The club meets the first and third Mondays of every month from October through April, with just one meeting, the holiday celebration, in December, and no meeting held on the first Monday of January. These meetings start with lunch at 12:30.[206] This is followed by a

fifteen- to twenty-minute business meeting and a twenty- to thirty-minute paper, with discussion afterward.

7. **Where they meet:** Mostly in members' homes, but also in a restaurant chosen by the hostess or else in the Century Club of Syracuse, which requires that at least one member be the sponsor of the event.[207]

8. **Election of new members:** A prospective member attends a meeting as a guest and then is nominated for membership, with one member writing a letter to propose her and with two other members cosigning the letter. The letter is read at two consecutive meetings, and the vote is done by secret ballot. A new member begins by being a preliminary member. She becomes an active member when a spot opens up and, usually, after she's given at least one paper. Membership status is decided by the membership committee.[208]

9. **Object of the club as stated in bylaws or constitution:** "To effect the organization of a society for more thorough culture and education in art."[209]

10. **Dues:** Currently, dues are $20, but this may change in the near future.

11. **Club motto, flower, and colors:** There is no known club flower or color, but a club alma mater is noted in the archives. The alma mater is sung to the tune of "Drink to Me Only with Thine Eyes." There is a motto often used in headlines and histories referring to the club: "A Goodly Heritage of Study." On the front of the Portfolio Club roster, a date-sensitive motto is always printed, which would read this year: "One Hundred and Forty Years of a Goodly Heritage."

12. **Paper or program assignment schedule and hostessing schedule:** Papers, based on the topic for the year, are assigned by the current president. She also assigns hostessing duties to members who will not be presenting a paper.[210] Regular members do a paper every other year, except for the president, recording secretary, president-elect, and membership chair. Preliminary members give a paper every year until they become regular members.[211]

13. **Length of papers:** Papers tend to be long enough to make for a twenty- to thirty-minute presentation (roughly, eight to twelve double-spaced pages).[212]

14. **Location of the club's archives, yearbooks, and old minutes:** Syracuse University Special Collections Research Center.

15. **Civic achievement of the group or its members:** Club member Mary Beth Hinton said that although "the club has generally focused on mutual edification, there have been times, such as during WWII, when the club undertook a charitable project or two."[213] Records show that these projects were the same ones undertaken by hundreds of other women's literary societies during wartime: preparing bandages and volunteering for the Red Cross, and donating money for orphans. The Portfolio Club also contributed to the YWCA over the years.[214]

16. **Special events:**
    - A holiday celebration in December includes a holiday program, the singing of carols, the wearing of red and green, and the reading of the Christmas story from the book of Luke. No business is conducted. There is no paper unless the topic can be related to the holiday season.[215]
    - There is a president's luncheon or annual meeting in mid-April, for which the vice president supplies the table decorations and place cards. The corresponding secretary invites associates to that meeting and to the holiday celebration.[216]

17. **Refreshment highlights:** A silver tea service is often used to serve tea and coffee in members' homes, and tea sandwiches are a favorite luncheon item.[217]

18. **Special traditions:**
    - There is one guest day in November, but members may bring guests to other meetings after clearing this with the hostess.[218]
    - Rather than having one yearbook or roster each year—i.e., a single, small booklet, as other groups have—Portfolio Club presidents have, in recent

history, produced not only a yearbook, but also a folder full of useful materials, including a list of officers, a list of past topics, and the year's scheduled papers,[219] plus an essay introducing the topic and research suggestions.[220] The year I visited, President Zalie Linn combined all of these documents into one larger-than-usual roster, which also contained the constitution, a list of succession, and more.

- Every year, the new president begins her administration with the sentence (adapted to reflect the current year), "This is the 140th year of a goodly heritage."[221]
- Associate members write a newsy annual letter every year. This is read at the annual meeting.
- The club sends a $50 donation to a member's designated charity when she dies.[222]
- In order of the date of their joining Portfolio, members automatically become recording secretary and then have a year off to prepare for the coming year, when they will be president and decide on and write up the yearly topic and subtopics for paper assignments.[223]
- Club members traditionally wear red and green to the holiday party.[224]
- The woman with the longest membership reads the Christmas story from the book of Luke at the annual holiday party.[225]
- Preliminary members help the hostess of the day by serving food and clearing away dishes.[226]
- Members always say yes to all assignments and requests.[227]
- Place cards are used on the luncheon tables for the annual meeting only.[228]

19. **Examples of yearly theme or topic:** Each year's president decides the topic for that year and announces it at the annual meeting. In 2011–12, Mary Beth Hinton chose "American Utopias." In 2012–13, Zalie Linn chose "Symbolism."[229]

20. **Individual paper assignments for these yearly topics:** For the topic "American Utopias," members delivered papers

on the Shakers, the Roycroft community, and Brook Farm, among others. The topic in 2012–13 produced assignments for papers on "Symbols Found in Everyday Life," "Symbolism in Our Capitol," and "Symbols of the Dance," among others.[230] For the 2014–15 season, President Beecher Graham chose "The Future of the 1980s," which led to papers on Chernobyl, the Human Genome Project, overpopulation, and HIV/ AIDS.[231]

21. **Particularly colorful or interesting member, present or past:** Bette Maltby (Mrs. Charles) was a brilliant club historian, an accomplished artist, the possessor of a keen mind, a professional-level researcher and writer, and a contributing author of a book about the club's history, *Portfolio Club: A Goodly Heritage, 1875–1975.* In 2000, she was coauthor of a subsequent history of the club's next twenty-five years, *The Portfolio Club of Syracuse, The Years 1975–2000.* Bette died in 2010 at the age of ninety-eight.[232] One of her most famous Portfolio presentations included her own chalk portrait of the first Canadian prime minister, John A. Macdonald, to accompany her paper on Macdonald, the opening salvo of the 1982–83 season, the chosen topic for which was "The Political History of Canada: Its Prime Ministers." That portrait was recently included in an extensive exhibit on the Portfolio Club at the Syracuse University's Bird Library in 2009—a show that was cocurated by two Portfolio members, Mary Beth Hinton and Michele Combs. Mary Beth, now an editor, was then assistant to the director of Special Collections[233] at Bird. Michele was an assistant librarian at the time of the show, but she is now librarian and lead archivist of Syracuse University's Special Collections.[234]

22. **Legacy members and longest-active members:**
    - According to Michele Combs (the librarian mentioned in item 21), who is one of two Portfolio historians, the club's most senior member when I visited the club was active member Mary Ten Eyck, who joined in 1960, giving her fifty-five years in the club as of this year, "almost half of its existence."[235] Between 1979 and 1990, she was an associate member, as she had

moved for this period to Beaufort, South Carolina, where she was also a member of the historic Beaufort Clover Club, a women's literary society founded in 1891.[236]

- As for legacy chains, the only one in the club when I visited was in Mary Ten Eyck's family. Her grandmother Genevieve Stevenson McChesney was also a Portfolian, as was her great-grand-aunt Mary Redfield Bagg, who is said to have worked hard to induce the Association for the Advancement of Women to hold its historic conference in Syracuse[237] at the Wieting Opera House.[238] I met Mary at a meeting with several Portfolio members in October 2012, and I was impressed by her mental acuity, memory, and good humor, not to mention her stunning vitality and good health. I believe that she is something of an icon to the women of the club and to all younger women who know her. She wrote the following to me in an e-mail after I met her:

> We come from many different geographic areas, as well as backgrounds, work, interests, etc. Yet we are amazingly sensitive and supportive, with caring concerns for each other, and their often challenging needs. This is accomplished quietly, with dignity, complete sincerity and selflessness. These feelings are truly deep-felt. In all my years with Portfolio, I have never heard a derogatory remark about others, their participation in the Club, or their presentations. We seem to always find and embrace the good qualities of each other. I think this is quite remarkable.[239]

Snapshot Summary of Social Art Club of Syracuse, New York

1. **Official name of the club:** Social Art Club of Syracuse.
2. **Date founded:** November 30, 1875.
3. **Founder's name:** The extraordinary Mrs. Mary Dana Hicks, later to become Mrs. Louis Prang. She also served as the first president of Social Art, from 1875 to 1879. See the snapshot summary of the Portfolio Club of Syracuse for more information about Mrs. Hicks.
4. **Size of club as limited by bylaws:** The number of active members is limited to forty-five; the number of associates, to twenty-five. (Associates are actives who have given at least three papers and who apply to the executive board for this designation.) Corresponding members (who have not lived in the area for at least a year) are not limited in number. Honorary members, so designated by the club, are not limited in number, either.[240]
5. **Actual size of club today:** Thirty-seven active members, eleven associate members, two corresponding members, and four honorary members.[241]
6. **Meeting schedule:** Meetings begin with lunch at 12:30. They are held on the second and fourth Tuesday of each month, from October until the last Tuesday in March, with only one meeting in December. The annual meeting is the final March meeting.[242]
7. **Where they meet:** The Century Club of Syracuse, New York.[243]
8. **Election of new members:** A prospective member must visit first as a guest. A letter proposing her and signed by two sponsors who are members is submitted to the club's secretary. The executive board votes on the applicants and then presents the names of approved applicants to the club at the next meeting for a second ballot vote.[244]
9. **Object of the club as stated in bylaws:** "The purpose of this organization shall be the study of art and its various relationships by written papers prepared and presented by

members plus illustrative materials and/or such methods as shall be approved by the Club. It is organized and operated exclusively for pleasure, recreation and other more profitable purposes, no part of the net earnings of which inures to the benefit of any individual."[245]

10. **Dues:** $20 per year.

11. **Club motto, flower, and colors:** None of these are recalled today, but the club does have a symbol used on its yearbook and other publications. This consists of "three intertwining rings, suggested by the quotation from Michelangelo: 'Architecture, Sculpture, and Painting are like three rings, each of which passes through the other two. Each is complete in itself, but linked together, they form a triple chain of Beauty, Symmetry, and Order.'"[246]

12. **Paper or program assignment schedule and hostessing schedule (rotation of assignments):**
    - Active members are required to present a paper according to a schedule kept by the program committee, which consists of the second vice president, the ten members who will be giving a paper in the coming year, and possibly other members. The membership votes on an overall topic for the year. Active members must also write a short synopsis of their paper and give it to the secretary, who passes it on to the historian, who will store it in the club's archives at the Onondaga Historical Association.[247]
    - "No member shall be required to present a second program until every active member has taken part in the program."[248]
    - Hostessing is assigned by the hostess committee, which creates the schedule.[249] The head of the hostess committee is the first vice president.[250]
    - Hostessing in this group means being responsible for part of the cost of the Century Club luncheon meeting. There are at least three members splitting the cost at most meetings. At the holiday luncheon, there are five. The hostessing assignments are rotated among the actives and associates.[251]

13. **Length of each paper:** Thirty to forty minutes.

14. **Location of the club's archives:** Onondaga Historical Association.

15. **Civic achievement of the group or its members:** Although the group has always steered clear of community issues and has tried, instead, to improve its members' lives culturally,[252] the club has, in the past, supported the Syracuse Museum of Art and other community art projects. Members also donated to the war effort during WWI.[253]

16. **Special events of the year:** The annual meeting is the last meeting of the year in late March, with the presentation of next year's program and the election of officers. The Christmas meeting at the end of the year is also a guest day. There are five hostesses for this, who plan the menu. Each member who brings a guest is responsible for her luncheon cost. The Century Club provides the decorations.[254] At other, regular meetings, three hostesses are responsible for the cost of the luncheon and for table decorations.[255]

17. **Refreshments:** All meetings begin with a catered luncheon at the Century Club in downtown Syracuse.

18. **Special traditions:**
    - A guest day is traditionally held on the second Tuesday of December. At this holiday meeting, the president presents a "short paper on some aspect of the Social Art Club."[256] Members may also bring guests to other regularly scheduled meetings. Members introduce their guests during roll call.[257]
    - The president, first vice president, secretary, treasurer, and historian serve for terms of two years. They are eligible for reelection after their first term. The second vice president serves for a one-year term and is eligible for reelection. The president and treasurer are elected in odd-numbered years, and the first vice-president, secretary, and historian, in even-numbered years.[258]
    - Along with the usual officers and committees, this club has four directors, who are named by the nominating committee and serve for one year.

Directors serve on the executive board and also help the first vice president arrange the guest day (the Christmas meeting). My favorite Social Art committee name is "Friendly Concern." The chairwoman of this committee sends cards and sympathy notes, when needed.[259] This type of job exists in all other groups mentioned in this book, but I found this particular job title charming.

19. **Example of a yearly theme or topic:** In 2012–13, the topic was "Fearless Visionaries."

20. **Example of an individual paper or program based on that topic:** When I visited Social Art Club's first meeting of the year, on October 9, 2012, the beautifully researched and masterfully written paper delivered by member Roscha Folger was "Harriet Lane Johnston: The Philanthropist Whom No One Has Heard Of."

21. **Particularly colorful or interesting member, present or past:** The somewhat mysterious but quite brilliant club member Irene Sargent (1852–1932) was at various times an instructor of French, architecture, art history, ornamentation, aesthetics, literature, Italian, Latin, and fine arts at Syracuse University. She became a professor of the history of fine arts in 1922 and taught the subject for thirty-seven years. She was an internationally acclaimed critic of art and architecture and also a translator, but what she was most famous for in her day was being a spokeswoman for the arts and crafts movement. For her contributions to the field of architecture, she was awarded an honorary membership to the American Institute of Architects. She was the second woman in the institute's history to receive this honor. Irene Sargent belonged to several clubs with an intellectual purpose in Syracuse and was also revered by her students. She never married and was gradually forgotten, except by an occasional biographer.[260]

22. **Legacy members and longest-active member:**
    - A corresponding member, Gwen Birchenough, who lives in Asheville, North Carolina, joined forty-three years ago. An associate member, Barbara Collum,

joined thirty-nine years ago. Of the active members, Joyce Bird is the longest-still-active member, having joined thirty-four years ago. Cynthia Stevenson and Lucia Whisenand joined thirty-three years ago. Social Art seems to have done a good job of recruiting over the years, as they have many more recently joined members than long-timers.

- The current treasurer, Lucia Beadel Whisenand, is a legacy. Her mother, Lucia Maria Chapman Beadel (1905–1993), was a member from 1945 to 1993.[261] Maria was a 1927 graduate of Vassar and a 1932 master's graduate of Syracuse University Library School. She was, for a time, the president of the Syracuse YWCA.[262] Her daughter is a retired lawyer, a trustee of the Everson Museum of Art, a member of the board of the Friends of the Central Library, the incoming president of the Syracuse Garden Club,[263] a former cochair of the Syracuse Symphony Association,[264] and the 2012 recipient of the Spirit of Mary Harriman Award, given to her in 2012 by the Junior League of Syracuse, of which she is a member.[265] Lucia B. Whisenand has been a member of Social Art since 1982—thirty-three years.[266] To add to this list of achievements and responsibilities, Lucia is also now a provisional member of the Portfolio Club,[267] which also appears in this book.

In an e-mail sent to President Jeanette Mattson on April 11, 2013, Lucia described her vivid memories of Social Art functions at her house when she was a girl, as her mother and aunt were both members. They were also both Vassar graduates. Lucia's mother joined Social Art in the late 1930s or early 1940s; her aunt, in the late 1920s or early 1930s. Lucia wrote that she feels that she's been going to Social Art meetings since she was five, as she would often pass cookies at meetings as a little girl and would be keenly aware of the fine tweed suits, hats, and white gloves that the women wore. As a girl,

Lucia loved poring over the art books her mother and aunt often used as references for their papers. The papers that her aunt or mother were working on were frequently the topic of conversation in her home. "There was always the agony of working on a paper—and the joy when it was well received."[268]

Snapshot Summary of The Leisure Hour Literary Club, Union Springs, New York

Unless otherwise noted below, the following information was provided by Club President Pat Deller, primarily in e-mails to me between November 20, 2012, and January 2013. Some of my questions were answered with the assistance of longtime members Millie Lewis and Betty Shockey.

1. **Official name of the club:** The Leisure Hour Literary Club.
2. **Date founded:** October 1896.
3. **Founder:** Eunice Wooley Yawger, at the age of sixty-seven, invited six other women to meet at her house at 64 Cayuga Street in Union Springs, New York, to form a literary club. The other charter members were Georgianna Yawger, Mima Yawger, Estella Yawger, Abbie Fordyce, Alice Bowen, and Rose Yawger. They were all related to each other by blood or marriage. In following years, members who were not Yawgers joined.[269]
4. **Size of club as limited in bylaws:** Eighteen members at this point, although the club's membership limit has fluctuated and has been as high as thirty-six at other times.
5. **Size of club today, including all categories of membership:** Sixteen active members and four honorary members.
6. **Meeting schedule:** The club meets from 7:30 p.m. to 9:30 p.m. or 10:00 p.m. on the first and third Monday evening of September, October, November, April, and May. They also meet on the first Monday of December and the third Monday in March. They always have a winter break from

mid-December to mid-March, and a summer break from June through August. They begin their meetings with a short business meeting, which is followed by the paper and a discussion period. That is followed by dessert and a social hour.

7. **Where they meet:** In members' homes.

8. **Election of new members:** Pat Deller wrote to me and said that when a member wants to suggest a new member, the current member needs to ask the hostesses of the next two meetings if she may bring the prospective member as her guest. After attending these meetings, the prospective member is asked if she would like to join. If her answer is yes, then her membership is voted on at the next meeting. Pat said that as long as she's been a member, the votes have been unanimous. A formal invitation to join the club is sent by the secretary, and a formal reply by the new member is sent to the club in return. Pat added that this process is often done at the end of the season so that the new member may be included in the annual dinner that opens the new season.

9. **Object of the club as stated in bylaws:** "Mutual improvement and a broader social and intellectual life."[270]

10. **Dues:** $10 per year. Members also pay for their own meal and for their guests' meals at the annual dinner meeting, which is always the first meeting of the year, held in September at a local restaurant.

11. **Club flower:** Daffodil. **Club colors:** Gold and white. **Club motto:** "They must upward still and onward who would keep abreast of Truth." —James Russell Lowell. **Club pledge:** "Prizing highly my membership in The Leisure Hour Club, and holding it worthy of unfailing loyalty, I will sustain the Club in its good work, and guard its reputation as long as I am a member."[271]

12. **Paper or program assignment schedule and hostessing schedule:** Each member can expect to be asked to hostess one meeting each season and also to present a paper at a different meeting during the same year. The schedule is set by the program committee (see item 19).

13. **Length of papers or programs:** These last for thirty to sixty minutes and were even longer in earlier years.

14. **Location of the club's archives:** The club's archives are stored in the Frontenac Historical Society and Museum in Union Springs as a permanent loan, not an outright donation. The secretary of the club keeps a book with a section for each year that contains a copy of the club's roster or yearbook, a list of member attendance at meetings, and the secretary's annual report, which is delivered at the last meeting of each season.

15. **Civic achievements of the group or its members:**

    • Margaret Pimm Getman (1886–1968) was a club member from 1923 to 1961. She was vitally interested and deeply involved in the life of her hometown. She researched and wrote a history of Union Springs titled *A History of Our Town,* published in 1948. A talented pianist featured in musical programs in the area for many years, she was also the force behind the inclusion of the Springport Free Library of Union Springs in the Finger Lakes Library System.[272]

    • As the village of Union Springs is a small one (population: approximately twelve hundred people), the members of the club have been involved in "nearly every civic activity" (to quote president Pat Deller).

    • Recently, the officers of the Frontenac Historical Society and Museum were all Leisure Hour members, were all good friends, and were all named Pat. Pat Kimber was president, Pat Deller was secretary, and Pat Hill was treasurer. They became known as "the Pats" and were a perfect example of the importance of club members in the civic life of the town. In fact, Ms. Deller, who was an executive in the IT division of American Airlines before her retirement, is now the hardworking board member of four associations dealing with the area's civic, historic, and cultural life. She is also on the board of a local home for the elderly. Her specialties are grant-writing and fund-raising. (Author's Note: Pat, as my contact and researcher for this snapshot summary, never took more than a few hours to respond to any of my requests for information or clarification, and she always wrote with great clarity and precision.)

16. **Special events of the year:** To open the club year, Leisure Hour holds an annual dinner at a restaurant, always on the Monday following Labor Day (September). This always includes a program.

17. **Refreshments:** Meetings are always in the evenings, at 7:30 p.m. After a short business meeting, a paper, and discussion, the hostess serves dessert, chocolates, mixed nuts, tea, and coffee—always using her best china, silver, and linens, with all guests seated at a table.

18. **Special traditions:**
    - See item 17, above, for the group's tradition of having formal dessert.
    - When a member—and sometimes a member's husband—dies, the club donates a book to the library in line with that person's interests or background. For instance, when Helen Fricano died recently at the age of eighty-eight, the club remembered her stories about her life in the Marine Corps Women's Reserve in WWII, so they donated a book about women troops in Iraq.
    - Each meeting has a director who neither presents a paper nor acts as a hostess, as those jobs are filled by others. Her job is to take over from the president after the preliminaries are finished, to thank the hostess, and then to introduce the paper for the evening.
    - At the final meeting of the year in May, the secretary gives her report, an overview of the year; dues are collected; officers are installed; and the program committee for the next year, which has been appointed by the president, is announced. Over the summer, the program committee plans the programs around a topic selected by the members during the last two meetings of the year. Each member receives a booklet or roster with the assignments and topics

at the first meeting of the new year, the September dinner meeting.

- President Pat Deller explained that club members are supposed to refer to each other as "Miss [or "Mrs."] So-and-So" during meetings—for example, "I know that we all thank Mrs. Komanecky for inviting us into her lovely home"—but she says that they "keep forgetting to do this."

- Another tradition is the roll call, which, for this club, is a kind of topical roll call. Each member is assigned a topic and asked to give a two-minute exposition when her name is called in the usual alphabetical order. The club's first roll call of the year was "Voting Experiences." President Deller, when she wrote me, said that she feels that this tradition is dying out.

- Another tradition that has died out in this club and all others I found is formal dress. The trend of dressing more casually for meetings is a development in society as a whole and not just in club life. The longest-active members, Millie Lewis and Betty Shockey, who have been members for fifty-three and fifty years, respectively, remember when each member attended every meeting in her best dress, heels, hat, and gloves. For long-ago annual dinners in September, the women wore "floor-length gowns, and their husbands wore tuxedoes. "Today," says Pat Deller, "we haven't seen a skirt at a meeting in years," although members are usually dressed in a good pair of slacks and a dressy top.

19. **Example of an overall yearly theme, and who assigns the paper or program topics:** During the club's last two meetings of the year, members are asked to suggest possible topics for the next year. A vote is taken on these, and the president picks a program committee of three members for the new season. The program committee meets over the summer to create a program schedule for the upcoming year. After that, they have a program booklet printed with the dates, the hostesses, the director for each evening, and

the topics. At the annual dinner, which is the season's first meeting in September, every member receives a copy of the booklet, which reveals to them the date when they will be a hostess, when they will present a paper, and what the topic of their paper will be. At the next meeting—the first regular meeting—the program committee presents the topic for the year and explains why they chose it. In 2012, their topic was "Women in Politics." One year, according to Pat Deller, their topic was "Understanding Cultural Conflicts through Fact or Fiction." Pat said that it was "one of the most depressing years we ever had. The next year, we deliberately picked a very light topic to change the mood."

20. **Example of an individual paper or program based on that topic:** For the 2012 topic, "Women in Politics," the papers covered, among other things, "Women's Political Organizations," "State Governors," and "Women Leaders in Countries Where Women Are Oppressed."

21. **Particularly colorful or interesting member, present or past:**

- Although Pat Deller said that she felt that "all of our members are colorful and interesting," she pointed out that current member Chris Moulton worked at the nearby Women's Hall of Fame in Seneca Falls and, in her capacity as organizer of the induction of honorees, met many impressive individuals like Hillary Clinton, Ruth Bader Ginsburg, and Senator Barbara Mikulski of Maryland.

- In the 1940s, member Annabel Schenck Dillon, who lived five to seven miles north of the village, was worried about getting her car stuck while driving to a nighttime Leisure Hour meeting in the village after a particularly bad snowstorm, so she drove a tractor with an open cab to the meeting. She may have been nicely dressed, sporting hat, gloves, and heels - but bundled up against the wind and cold - and she would have presented quite a sight when parking her tractor in front of the hostess's house and climbing down to make her entrance.

- Zobedia Alleman, who joined Leisure Hour in its first year of existence, traveled around the United States while lecturing on temperance and the suffrage movement.[273] Nine of her letters dealing with suffrage issues, written between 1897 and 1911, are preserved in the Library of Congress.[274]

22. **Legacy members:**

- Pat Deller was careful to point out that everyone undertakes the same steps to become a member. So-called legacies are not given special consideration. That being said, many of the founders and first members of Leisure Hour had family members in future generations who also belonged to the club.[275]
- The recently deceased mother-in-law of current member Midge Fricano was club member Helen Fricano.
- Many of the women of future generations of the founder's family—the Yawgers— were members over the years. Their last names were all Yawger for at least part of their lives, and their first names were Eunice (the founder), Estelle, Georgiana, Rose, Mima, Alice, Henrietta, Jennie, Claire, and Elsie. Astonishingly, Jennie (also called Jane) Yawger joined Leisure Hour in 1909 and *was a member for seventy-one years.* Elsie was the last Yawger to join, in 1936, and was a member for only fourteen years, but Jennie was a member until 1980, so there was always at least one woman from the Yawger family in the club from its founding in 1896 until 1980. That has to be some kind of record. It is certainly a record as far as the groups I've researched are concerned, especially the length of a single membership—seventy-one years. Member Pat Deller believes it is possible that Jennie, or Jane, lived in Florida in her final years but continued to pay her dues to Leisure Hour.
- As for the current crop of longest-active members, those would be Millacent (Millie) Spring Lewis, who joined in 1959 (fifty-six years ago), and Elizabeth

(Betty) Shockey, who joined in 1962 (fifty-three years ago). Millie and Betty were invaluable to me, as they filled in the blanks when Pat Deller could not find answers to my questions by searching available materials. Millie and Betty remember a great deal of local history and, with a little help from their collection of old rosters, Leisure Hour's history.

CHAPTER 7

Indiana

Indianapolis and Elkhart, Indiana, Including Some Confusion about the Names of Two Groups

I did all of my research on the two, and possibly three, historic women's study clubs in Indianapolis by e-mail during the summer of 2013. Long before that, I'd seen that there was tremendous similarity among the historic study clubs I was aware of. I felt I had seen enough to be able to continue working on this book without traveling to meet with the clubs. Once I'd finished in the Syracuse area in early October of 2012, I took no more research trips, as I was able to conduct my interviews by telephone and e-mail.

I first found public radio producer Nora Hiatt by searching through the collected documents of the Indianapolis Woman's Club online. The Indiana Historical Society, which holds the club's archives, had posted the information on the Internet. I spotted Nora's name in a piece mentioning that she was the author of some very interestingly titled papers that are now on file online. I saw that she'd delivered them in recent years. From that point, I was able to track her down. She proved to be very helpful in filling me in on her club and on two others in Indianapolis, one that fit my parameters and one that did not.

Nora said that the Woman's Club is so large, with a hundred members, that she said she only has to give a paper every other year. Two papers are given at each meeting. Meetings are held on the first and third Friday of the month, from October to early June.

I was very grateful to Nora for getting me started in her city. After all, it was the Woman's Club—really, a literary society or study club and not a typical woman's club—whose principal founder, Martha

Nicholson McKay, had come up with the perfect, but very ladylike, retort to a rabbi who expressed his displeasure about women's organizing in 1875 to get out of the house and learn in a group. I so admired her reply and the sentiment in it, as it pertained to the women of that day who were still walking on eggshells as they organized, that I used the anecdote at the beginning of this book, after the title page. As the story goes, the rabbi "shook his head, saying, 'Sarah's place is in her tent.'"

Mrs. McKay is said to have retorted, "Oh, yes, we know. We just want her to have a window in it."[1]

Nora led me to Nancy Fyffe, who sent me a copy of the club's history and was able to answer my questions about the racial integration of the Woman's Club in 2000. Nora also led me to a friend, Cathy Gibson, who belonged to a similar group in Indianapolis called Fortnightly.

And this is where things got murky. There proved to be two groups with either the same name or virtually the same name in Indianapolis: one that was founded in 1885, called Fortnightly Literary Club or Indianapolis Fortnightly Literary Club, and one that was founded in 1923, also called Fortnightly Literary Club or Indianapolis Fortnightly Literary Club, which was then and still is an African-American group. I could find no contact for the latter group. Its founding less than a hundred years ago eliminated it from consideration for my book, but the club is of great interest to me, as I found very few African-American women's literary societies that were not civic-minded groups. I can't really be sure that this women's group is still active, as my three local contacts did not know. The club's archives at the Indiana Historical Society cover the years from 1927 to 1990.

There were other groups in Indiana, too—at least the three I found in Elkhart. I discovered this interesting cluster of historic women's groups by good luck stemming from a casual conversation. In the spring of 2012, my back was killing me. I thought this was a result of sitting at my computer all day, working on this book. Two years later, I learned that I had blown a disc in my lumbar vertebrae, but at the time I thought my back pain was a result of the chair I sat in while I typed on my computer. I went to my local franchise of Relax the Back, a chain store that sells furniture and accessories to help those who have achy backs. While a salesman was writing up my order for a special desk chair, the office manager asked me to describe the subject of my book. When I told her I was looking for and finding virtually unknown women's study clubs still surviving from the Victorian era, she said, "Oh, like my sister's Thursday Club in Elkhart, Indiana?"

Her sister, Uyen Dugle, became a cheerleader for the historic clubs in her area, finally convincing me that there were three in her town alone and that they were all at least a hundred years old. She even found me contacts in the other two clubs. I was able to get the information I needed for those clubs via e-mail and telephone conversations with Progress Club member Celia Kirk and Riverside Club member Judy Kelly.

Snapshot Summary of The Progress Club of Elkhart, Indiana

The content of this brief snapshot summary comes from two e-mails written to me in January 2013 by Celia Kirk, club member and author of *The History of The Progress Club.* This book commemorated her group's hundred-year anniversary in 2001. Her mother, Mary (or Meege) Williams, was then ninety-five and the longest-living member of Thursday Club, another Elkhart literary society or study club, and was one of the authors of that club's history in 1957.

1. **Official name of the club:** The Progress Club of Elkhart, Indiana.
2. **Date founded:** Saturday, March 2, 1901.
3. **Size of club today:** The club is limited to thirty active members and ten associate members. There is no limit to the number of honorary members. Today, there are twenty-nine active members and ten associates. Celia Kirk said that she was ready to "go associate, but, alas, no vacancy."
4. **How often the club meets, and where:** The club meets fourteen times a year, from October through May, on the first and third Wednesdays of the month, at 12:30 p.m., except for the opening and closing luncheons, which begin at noon. Usually, meetings are held in members' homes. Members host one year and give or sponsor a program the next year.
5. **What kind of topics or yearly themes the group covers:** The club now uses broad topics, such as "Wit and Wisdom," the theme several years ago. The topic in 2013 was "Food for the Soul." One member chose to read the poems most important to her when she delivered her paper. Over the years, the annual themes have been widely diverse.
6. **Of note:**
   - The following is a quotation from Celia Kirk, describing today's Progress Club members in her 2001 book about the club:

     They all have been married, have children, and many have grandchildren ... many have degrees beyond a Bachelor's degree. They have all worked at some point in their lives, and currently over one half work outside the home, either full or part-time. They are business owners, teachers, counselors, artists, photographers, musicians, saleswomen, interior designers, and librarians. Those who do not have formal jobs outside the home are incredible volunteers, giving thousands of hours to the community—heading up foundations, boards, and innumerable fundraisers.

- Celia Kirk's great-grandmother and several of her aunts were founding members of Progress Club. Her mother, Mary Jean "Meege" Williams, has been a member of Thursday Club of Elkhart for fifty-eight years. (Thursday Club does not allow mothers and daughters to be members at the same time.)

Snapshot Summary of The Thursday Club, Elkhart, Indiana

This information comes almost entirely from two telephone conversations with, and a detailed e-mail from, club member Uyen Dugle. As noted above, because of a chance conversation in a furniture store near my home in Los Angeles, I was able to reach out to Uyen by phone and - with her help - found three Elkhart groups, a pretty impressive number for a city with a population of fifty-one thousand.[2]

1. **Official name of the club:** The Thursday Club.
2. **Date founded:** 1890.
3. **Size of club today:**
   - There is a limit of twenty-eight active members, and that is how many members the club has today. Associate members are limited to twelve and currently stand at twelve. (Associates must have served for at

least ten years. They may attend meetings, but they do not vote.) Honorary members number nine at this point. To become an honorary member, one needs to have been a member for at least ten years. Honorary members might attend only a few meetings a year.

- An interesting rule of membership states that a candidate for membership may not be a daughter or daughter-in-law of a current member. I've since found the same thing in the Springfield, Illinois, group Sunnyside Literary Circle. This would explain why my contact for Progress Club, Celia Kirk, belongs to a study club different from her mother's. Her mother, Mary Jean - "Meege" - Williams, was the longest-active member of Thursday Club when I wrote this section in 2013, having joined in 1955.

4. **How often they meet and where:** From October to May, on the first and third Thursday of the month. They meet in members' homes, starting at 12:30 p.m. with a dessert social. The program begins at 1:15 p.m.

5. **What kind of study papers the group presents:** "General and literary studies."

6. **Of interest:**
   - In 1957, after one year of membership, Meege Williams helped compile a history of the club and a collection of its creative output from 1890 to 1957. She called her history "Thursday's Child." It was privately printed and was distributed for years to new members.
   - The age range of members in the group is from their forties to their nineties.
   - A charming tradition: in preparation for the holiday meeting, all members draw a name for a Secret Santa gift exchange *and* are asked to write a poem about that person, which is to be read to the group. These poems have been saved and collected for many years.
   - Also of interest: this year, the Thursday Club and the Progress Club—the latter being another historic

Elkhart study club—joined together for a spring luncheon on May 9, 2013. They nicely invited me to join them and even volunteered to put me up for the night, but I declined because I'd stopped traveling and started writing. I truly appreciated their kindness as conveyed by my persuasive and peppy contact, Thursday Club member Uyen Dugle.

Snapshot Summary of The Riverside Club, Elkhart, Indiana

All of this information comes from an e-mail from member Judy Kelly written on January 19, 2013.

1. **Official name of the club:** The Riverside Club, although for its first six years its name was the Riverside Reading Circle. The group was founded in Elkhart, Indiana.
2. **Date founded:** 1902.
3. **Size of club today:** Twenty-two active, four associate, and two honorary members.
4. **How often they meet, at what hour, and from what month to what month:** They meet at 12:00 noon on "designated Tuesdays"[3] and hold a "maximum of 12 and a minimum of 10 meetings each year, September through May."[4] They meet in members' homes, except for the first and final meetings of the year, which are held in restaurants and include a full lunch. Only light refreshments are offered at other meetings.
5. **What kind of yearly topics this group studies:** Riverside is a book club without a yearly theme. A rotating panel of member-reviewers choose a book for each meeting, which members may read before the meeting, if they wish. Discussion follows the book review presentation.
6. **Of interest:**
    *   Here is another historic women's study club with the old-fashioned, but stimulating, practice of a roll call for brief topical presentations. In the Riverside Club, this happens after the opening business session of

each meeting. Members are asked to be prepared to respond in alphabetical order to a question printed in the roster or yearbook that always relates to the book being discussed that day. "When the book was *American Passage: The History of Ellis Island,* the roll call was 'Thoughts on Immigration Now and Then.'"[5]

- Also of note is present member Helen Free, who, with her husband, Al Free, had worked at Miles Laboratory for fifty-three years. The two were awarded the National Medal of Technology and Innovation by President Obama in 2010. They helped develop diagnostic test strip technology. Helen was inducted into the National Women's Hall of Fame in Seneca Falls, New York, a town I visited on this trip, as it was the site of the first Women's Rights Convention in 1848.[6]

- Riverside's colors are gold and white. Their motto is "From Height to Height." Their club flower is unknown at this time, if there ever was one.

Snapshot Summary of Fortnightly Literary Club, Indianapolis

(Not to be confused with the Indianapolis Fortnightly Literary Club, founded in 1923)

1. **Official name of the club:** Fortnightly Literary Club.
2. **Date founded:** February 24, 1885.[7] The club was the brainchild of young Mrs. Albert Baker, who, early in 1885, had just returned from a visit to Crawfordsville, Indiana. While there, she had attended a meeting of the Athenians, a women's literary club. On her return, she mentioned to her mother-in-law, Mrs. Conrad Baker, how impressed she had been with the club. She asked, "Why can't we have a club like that?"

   Mrs. Baker Sr., wife of a former Indiana governor, replied, "Well, why don't you start one?"

On February 24, 1885, eight founding members met at the home of Mrs. Charles Warren Fairbanks to form the Nameless Literary Circle.[8]

3. **Names of founders:** Cornelia Cole (Mrs. Charles Warren) Fairbanks, Charlotte Chute (Mrs. Conrad) Baker, Anna Campbell (Mrs. Albert) Baker, Kate Noble (Mrs. E. H.) Dean, Alice S. (Mrs. H. C.) Allen, Annie Holton (Mrs. J. T.) Dye, Ida Linn (Mrs. Charles E.) Henderson, and Miss Laura Ream. A ninth potential member, Miss Alice Finch, had been invited, but, because of illness, she was unable to attend. However, her name was later included in the list of founders.[9]

4. **Size of club today:** The club membership is limited to a hundred members and currently stands at ninety,[10] with fifty to sixty of those being active members.[11] Active members give a paper every three years.[12] Privileged members must have been members for at least twenty years and are no longer required to give papers.[13]

5. **How often they meet and where:** They always meet in the Propylaeum, as does the even older Woman's Club,[14] which is another venerable literary club. The Propylaeum, a landmark building, was once a private home. It now houses a women's club of the same name. The clubhouse serves tea and luncheon, and hosts events and parties.[15]

   Despite its name, the Fortnightly does *not* meet every two weeks! Its members meet on the third Tuesday of the month from September to December. Skipping January, they resume meeting February through May.[16] When there is a luncheon scheduled, the club meets at noon. There are four luncheons each year: in September (for their president's day), October, April, and May. When there is a tea scheduled, the club meets at 1:00 p.m.—in November, December, February, and March.[17]

6. **Examples of yearly themes and individual topics:** Members take turns delivering original papers. There is no overall theme for the year. The titles of some of the papers from the 2012–13 season were "The Mitford Sisters: Assaultive Charm," "Julia Child … Bon Appétit," "Jimmy Kennedy: An Irish Troubadour," "Winners: Title IX," "Jamestown: Miracle,"

and "Hamlet's Mom."[18] There are either two short papers of twenty minutes each or one forty-minute-long paper.[19]

7. **Refreshments:** Each meeting includes either a high tea or a luncheon (see explanation under item 5), while the Woman's Club, to which Fortnightly Literary Club is often compared, has "one luncheon a year and a short water break between papers."[20]

8. **Of note:**

   - The bylaws and standing rules of this club and the Woman's Club are said to be "almost identical,"[21] with the clubs having many similarities.
   - Both the Woman's Club and Fortnightly are integrated, with the Woman's Club being first to accomplish this.[22] The first African American member of Fortnightly was Sheila Little, PhD, who was inducted in 2010.[23]
   - There are currently "about ten women who are members of both of these clubs—Fortnightly and Woman's Club."[24]

Snapshot Summary of the Indianapolis Woman's Club

1. **Official name of club:** Indianapolis Woman's Club
2. **Date founded:** February 18, 1875.[25]
3. **Founded by:** Twelve women, meeting in the home of Martha Nicholson McKay, 156 Ash Street (now Carrollton Avenue), Indianapolis, Indiana.[26]
4. **Size of club today:** Forty to forty-five members attend most meetings.[27] According to the introduction to the club's archives in the state historical society, there are about a hundred members. Aside from active members, the club includes corresponding members, who live in other parts of the country, and privileged members, who are excused from researching and writing papers.[28]
5. **When and where they meet:** They meet at the historic Propylaeum building (see description in the snapshot summary of Fortnightly Literary Club of Indianapolis), on

the first and third Friday of the month, from October to early June.[29]

6. **Type of papers/topics:** Members choose their own paper topics.[30] My contact within the group, Nora McKinney Hiatt, has three of her papers stored in the historical society's archives: "Kidnapped" (2002), "The Return of the Limberlost" (2005), and "Different and Yet the Same" (2006).[31]

7. **Refreshments:** Unlike Fortnightly, which serves a high tea or a lunch after every meeting, the Woman's Club has "one luncheon a year and, during regular meetings, a short water break between papers."[32] (There are two papers at each meeting.)

8. **How members are chosen:** Prospective members must be proposed by a member. The prospective member is vetted by two committees and passed on by both before the prospective member is notified that she is being considered for membership.[33]

9. **Of note:**
   - This club is racially integrated, as is the Fortnightly Literary Club of Indianapolis,[34] with Indianapolis Woman's Club having been the first to have begun that process in 2000 with the membership of Phyllis Adair-Ward.[35]
   - In its earliest days, the club held a reception for Susan B. Anthony and Elizabeth Cady Stanton,[36] two of the most famous supporters of women's rights in the second half of the nineteenth century.
   - Members are not to discuss religious or political topics, so as to avoid dissension.[37] This is actually a common guideline in many of the groups mentioned in this book.
   - The club's archives, up to 2007, are held at the Indiana Historical Society.[38]

CHAPTER 8

Little Rock, Arkansas, and Baton Rouge, Louisiana

Discoveries Resulting from a Random Conversation on a Cruise

In May 2012, my husband and I took a Mediterranean cruise. During a land excursion, I was randomly seated at a lunch table in a restaurant in Ravello, Italy, next to a fellow traveler who, when he found out the subject of the book I was working on, told me that his wife, seated nearby, was a member of a women's group just like the ones I was writing about. His wife, Anne Meek, would turn out to be my contact for finding two historic study clubs in Baton Rouge, Louisiana, The Study Club (her club) and Philistoria. She was able to give me some possible connections for the latter. One of these connections was journalist Carol Anne Blitzer, who was president of The Study Club when I was tracking them down. She had written articles on both venerable Baton Rouge clubs, and these proved invaluable to me, as did her help in connecting me to a very bright and interesting Philistoria member, Adele Williamson, who joined the club in 1949 and was happy to talk to me by phone.

Anne Meek, my cruise contact, also told me that there was another woman on board the ship, Lee Moore, who was in two such historic literary societies in Little Rock, Arkansas. I quickly realized that I'd already introduced myself to Lee as she stood with her husband while waiting for a shuttle bus at the end of another land excursion. Lee sent me a note by ship-mail, and we connected. Lee belonged to two hundred-plus-year-old study clubs in Little Rock: The Edelweiss, which is limited to fifteen members, and Aesthetic Club, which has a hundred and fifty-three members. Quite a contrast, but both were thriving and at capacity. Aesthetic Club was the only historic group I was able to find that still included a musical portion in its meetings. Many literary societies had music performed by members as part of their earliest meetings, but they have long since abandoned the practice.

Lee could not have been more helpful and efficient in getting me the information I needed on both Edelweiss and Aesthetic Club once we returned home. Because of a random lunchtime conversation while I was on vacation and because of the help I immediately got from Anne and Lee—two fellow cruise passengers and loyal literary society members—I was able to add four very healthy, extremely interesting historic women's study clubs in two different Southern cities to my roster of clubs. The discovery and research process was not always this easy, but the results were always worth it.

Snapshot Summary of the Aesthetic Club, Little Rock, Arkansas

1. **Official name of the club:** Aesthetic Club.
2. **Date founded:** January 16, 1883,[1] in Little Rock, Arkansas.
3. **Size of club today:** 153 members in all: 97 active members, 57 inactive members, 1 life member, and 8 associate members.[2]
4. **How often they meet and where:** Aesthetic Club meets on the second and fourth Tuesdays of the month at 2:00 p.m., from October to late April, followed by their annual luncheon in early May, which begins at noon. They meet in the MacArthur Museum of Arkansas Military History, which is housed in the historic and impressive Arsenal Building of MacArthur Park.[3]
5. **What kind of topics they cover, and some examples of yearly themes:** The topics vary widely.[4] During 2011–12, the club addressed the topic "The Passage of Time and the Persistence of Memory."[5] There are two papers on the topic presented at each meeting, plus a musical offering by a member.[6] This was one of the few groups I found in my four years of working on the book that still offered a musical selection performed by members. In the earliest days of these study clubs, the practice was more common. Aside from the speakers and musicians, there is always a chairwoman of the day who introduces the three or four hostesses and the other participants in the program.[7]
6. **Of note:**
   - Wives of five governors of Arkansas were members of the club.[8]
   - The club's archives, from 1883 to 2003, are held in the Arkansas History Commission in Little Rock, in thirty-five boxes, the contents of which have been reproduced on microfilm.[9]
   - With almost a hundred active members, the club presents an opportunity for members to deliver an original paper every three years. The business

portion of the meeting lasts for about fifteen minutes. Each paper is about fifteen minutes long, and the musical performance between the two papers lasts for about fifteen minutes.[10]

- On January 26, 1880, General Douglas MacArthur was born into a military family in the arsenal barracks on the grounds of what is now MacArthur Park.[11] Since it began meeting there in 1894, the club has maintained its presence in the Arsenal Building, with its distinctive tower, even though they were in danger of being ousted from it at different points in the 1940s and 1950s.[12]

- Many of the groups I found while researching this book have forgotten their motto, their colors, and/or their club flower. Not so with Aesthetic Club, which still proclaims all three, plus a slogan and a pledge, in the opening pages of their yearbook. The motto: "The Good, the True, and the Beautiful." The slogan: "Innocently to amuse the imagination in this dream of life is wisdom." The flower: the Easter lily. The colors are Nile green, white, and pink. And the pledge promises loyalty to the club, to its aims, and to its reputation.[13]

Snapshot Summary of The Edelweiss, Little Rock, Arkansas

1. **Official name of the club:** The Edelweiss.
2. **Date founded:** 1895, in Little Rock, Arkansas.[14]
3. **Size of club today:** The club currently has fifteen active members (the limit, according to the bylaws) and five honorary members.[15] There is no limit on the number of honorary members.
4. **How often they meet and where:** They meet on the second Friday of the month, October through May, at 10:30 a.m., in members' homes.[16]

5. **What kind of papers they do—i.e., the kind of yearly themes they study:** Past themes have included "The Celtic Heritage," "Fakes, Frauds, Scams, and Hoaxes," and "Literary and Artistic Circles."[17] From 2010 to 2012, they studied Arkansas history, with two papers on different subjects presented at each meeting. In 2012–13, they addressed the topic of travel.[18] Their papers are twenty to twenty-five minutes long.[19]

6. **Of note:**
   - This group's archives are stored at the Butler Center of the Arkansas Studies Institute, a department of the Central Arkansas Library System in Little Rock.[20]
   - The club's longest-active member when I wrote this section in 2012 was Elaine Scott, who joined Edelweiss in 1983.[21]
   - Their colors are green and white. Their flower is the edelweiss, and their mottos are "We shall not pass this way again" and "It is much better to understand little, than to misunderstand much."[22]
   - Members become officers in the order of their entry into the club, starting with treasurer and working up to president. They serve two years in each office.[23]
   - Hostesses once provided the food for the opening and closing luncheons, and the Christmas lunch was provided by one hostess. Now, hostesses provide only the drinks, tables, chairs, and table settings, and other members bring the food, which might even be "store bought."[24]
   - Three current members are daughters of former members, and two, including the 2012 President Marylyn Parins, are granddaughters of former members.[25]
   - In lieu of Christmas gifts to each other, the group makes an annual donation to a library or literacy group.[26]

Snapshot Summary of The Philistoria Study Club. Baton Rouge, Louisiana

1. **Official name of the club:** The Philistoria Study Club. (*Philistoria* is said by charter member Katherine Hill to be from a Greek word meaning "lovers of history"[27]).

2. **Date founded:** 1906, in Baton Rouge, Louisiana.

3. **Size of club today:** Twenty-five members, which has been the case ever since the club's founding.[28]

4. **How often they meet and where:** Philistoria meets on the first and third Thursday of the months between October and May, at 2:00 p.m. Their first meeting in March is always the annual luncheon at the Baton Rouge Country Club, with invitations, menus, and decorations related to the theme of study for the year. Meetings are held in members' homes.[29]

5. **What kind of yearly themes the group studies:** Each member, except for those on the hardworking yearbook committee, which researches and assigns individual topics, presents a paper on a yearly topic. Topics might range from the study of Shakespeare to great gardens of the world. Other topics include famous women, art, and deserts of the world. The topic is chosen by way of one or more ballot votes after all members have had an opportunity to suggest a topic.

6. **Of note:**
   - The club is rather famous in Baton Rouge for serving only ice water at most meetings and for running its meetings in a rather formal manner, with the president and all officers standing as they conduct the day's business. Members always refer to each other by their married names.
   - When I spoke to her in 2012, Adele Williamson, an educational consultant, was the club's longest-active member, having joined Philistoria in 1949, "when the club was studying ancient Greece."[30] Mrs. Williamson told me that she has had seven or eight family members in Philistoria, including one of the club's founding members.[31]

- Today, there are several fourth-generation members in the club.[32]
- The club shies away from publicity of any kind.[33]

Snapshot Summary of The Study Club, Baton Rouge, Louisiana

1. **Official name of the club:** The Study Club, although the club started life as the Literary Society of the Young Matrons and Maids.[34]
2. **Date founded:** November 2, 1908.[35]
3. **Size of club today:** Twenty-five active members and three associate members.[36]
4. **How often they meet and where:** From October to May on the second Monday of the month, at 2:00 p.m. in a member's home.[37]
5. **What kind of subjects the group's research papers cover:** Subjects range far and wide. In 2012–13, club members studied Louisiana's history. One paper's title was "Our Louisiana: Celebrating 200 Years of Statehood." However, in past years, they've studied such varied subjects as "Bach, Beethoven, and the Boys," "Gardens of Louisiana," and "Religions of the World." In their earliest days, they studied authors and dramatists.[38]
6. **Of interest:** A newspaper article written by Carol Ann Blitzer, a journalist who was also the club's president in 2012–13, made it clear that the Study Club's tea table, which is presented at the start of meetings, is very grand and bountiful. By comparison, the other literary society in town, Philistoria, is more serious about sticking to the study concept and does not serve anything other than ice water.[39] A Study Club member is quoted as saying that her group is serious, too, but their "primary function is social."[40]

   Carol Ann wrote to me on January 14, 2013, and said that she was one of the hostesses for a Study Club meeting when the subject was to be the Huey Long era, as a part of the club's yearlong Louisiana bicentennial theme. She said that they would be serving "red beans and rice in demitasse cups, fried chicken drumettes ('a chicken in every pot' was Long's motto), celery stuffed with homemade pimento cheese, venison sausages, biscuits with homemade pear preserves, sandwiches, chess pie, and a chocolate cake with Louisiana strawberries."[41] This would be served "in silver," at 2:00 in the afternoon.

CHAPTER 9

Illinois

Eleven Historic Groups
in Five Illinois Cities

By way of personal reference and referrals, I found two historic study clubs in Springfield, Illinois, one club in Bloomington, one in Mattoon, one in Charlestown, and an astonishing six in Jacksonville, Illinois, which has a population 19,301.[1] Six is the most historic literary societies I was able find in any single town in the country. In addition, Jacksonville also has several even older men's literary societies, plus seven literary societies with Greek letter names at the town's Illinois College in place of fraternities and sororities. These date back to 1843. (Collegiate literary societies were the beginning of fraternities and sororities in many colleges in the 1800's but have mostly disappeared.[2]) In addition, one of Jacksonville's women's study clubs – Sorosis - also has the distinction of being the longest-active literary society in the country. Another literary society in town has a club member – Gratia Coultas - who is currently the longest active member in any historic study club anywhere in the country, having been a member of Monday Conversation Club for 69 years.

To my mind, all of these newly uncovered facts put Jacksonville in a special category when it comes to historic all-women study clubs surviving in a single town. New York State has more historic groups than any other state - I was able to identify 27 groups statewide - so I thought that New York would be the pot of gold at the end of my rainbow—until I started finding out about Jacksonville and its treasures, plus the clubs in other Illinois towns.

In December 2012, my husband and I were in New York City for our annual pre-Christmas visit. We had dinner with two couples who had driven in from Connecticut and who were friends from our early married days. As often happened while I was working on this book, someone at dinner asked me about the book, which led our dinner partner Carole dell'Aquila to tell me that she had a friend back in her hometown of Springfield, Illinois, who was a member of just such a group. That led me to Sunnyside Literary Circle and to Carole's pal Carolyn Houston, who was president of Sunnyside that year—the year that the group celebrated its 125th birthday. Carolyn answered all of my questions and also led me to Mary Beaumont in Springfield's other historic study club, Anti-Rust. This contact then led me to a contact in the History Club of Bloomington.

Equally fortuitously, my connection to the astonishing six historic literary societies in Jacksonville, Illinois, came from a luncheon meeting early in 2013 with Siri Baker, a development officer for Columbia University's Graduate School of Journalism, from which I graduated. Siri asked me about the subject of the book I was working on and, learning that I was looking for and finding many historic study clubs for women, said that her grandmother Louise Bone was in such a group in Jacksonville, Illinois, a college town I'd never heard of. I was able to reach Louise by telephone. From there, my contacts and list of other groups in the area grew and grew. As always, I had to have at least one contact in each group to verify the club's existence and answer my questions.

Clearly, literary societies or study clubs are a way of life in an area I might call "downstate Illinois." The five towns in Illinois where I found historic study clubs are all in what I would describe as the middle of the state, far to the south of Chicago, and they create a significant and interesting cluster of groups practicing the historic activity of self-education combined with a social component.

I regret that I discovered Jacksonville late in the research and writing of *Smart Women,* long past the point when I had stopped traveling to do my research. The town and its women's study clubs are worth a book all their own.

Snapshot Summary of The History Club, Bloomington, Illinois

Unless otherwise noted, the information below came from club member Susan Chaney in several e-mails sent to me in September 2013. Susan also made two trips to the local museum, McLean County Museum of History, to find the archives for the group. On her second trip, she was successful. The archival material I present below comes courtesy of her perseverance.

1. **Official name of the club:** The History Club.
2. **Date founded:** January 1880, as the Philomathean Society. The group kept this name for their first year, from January to June of 1880.[3]
3. **Founders names:** Mmes. Addie Clark, S. J. DeMotte, N. O. Dyson, Rev. Dinsmore, J. A. Harris, D. Harwood, Wm. Ollis, F. Otley, Sarah Read, Sarah Schemerhorn, Rev. Simpson, and G. A. Williams. Miss Ada Laughlin was also a founder.[4]
4. **Size of club:** The club's constitution states that the number of active members may not exceed twenty-two. Currently, the membership is at fifteen, and members are "thinking of adding more." The club has five honorary members.
5. **How often, when, and where they meet:** The club meets in members' homes on the third Monday of each month of the year except for January, February, March, and July. In December, they meet on the second Monday of the month. The meetings begin at 1:00 p.m. with a dessert served by the hostess for the day, and a twenty- to thirty-minute program follows that. About once a year, they have an outside speaker.
6. **Examples of yearly themes or papers:**
   - Programs may cover anything historical. Members decide on their own what they would like to speak about. There is no overall theme for the year other than history.
   - A roster from the years 1887–88 shows the group meeting once a week and studying three challenging topics at each meeting. On December 14 of that club year, they would have heard three members deliver

papers on "Mining," "American Colleges and Their Founders," and "Our Artists and the Fine Arts," so their emphasis that year must have been on America, its history, and its art. Earlier rosters show entire years devoted to "English Authors" (the club's first year) or the authors or people of another European country.[5]

7. **Of note:** The yearly dues are $10 per member. At Christmas, half of that year's total dues money is sent as a gift to a charity of the club members' choosing.

Snapshot Summary of The Charleston Reading Circle, Charleston, Illinois

This information comes directly from Mary Jorstad, who has been a club member since 1983.

I found Ms. Jorstad through Dick Wise, a volunteer at the Coles County Historical Society, an organization that I contacted when trying to track down a member of the Mattoon Woman's Reading Club. Happily, Mr. Wise was able to give me contacts in both clubs. Ms. Jorstad answered all of the six following questions for me in an e-mail of July 10, 2014. Much of the following language and direct quotations below are taken from that e-mail.

1. **Official name of the club:** The Charleston Reading Circle (Charleston, Illinois).
2. **Date founded:** Fall 1889.
3. **Size of club today:** There are eighteen active members and two honorary members. "Membership is limited to 25 active members, and an active member may choose to become honorary after 25 years of active membership."
4. **How often the club meets, where, and from what month to what month:** The club meets twice monthly at 1:30 p.m. on Fridays, from October to March. Most meetings are held at the Charleston Carnegie Public Library, with three exceptions. The first meeting in October and the Christmas Silver Tea are both held in members' homes in the afternoon.

The last meeting of the year is a luncheon at the Charleston Country Club.

5. **Types of themes or topics assigned:**
   - The club's constitution states that "the object shall be the mutual improvement of its members in literature, art, science and the vital interests of the day."
   - Members usually read and review books they have chosen on their own, although there have been instances of presentations about movies, music, current events, etc. Books chosen are almost always nonfiction, and only the reviewer reads the book scheduled to be covered. To be selected, books must be of "literary merit" and "provide learning experiences." Each member chooses a book to review every year, and there are two book reviews at each meeting. With the exception of the three social meetings, there is no food served.
   - One book review is given at the three social meetings (first, last, and Christmas), where there are refreshments—tea at the first meeting of the year and at Christmas, and lunch at the final meeting of the year.

6. **Of note:**
   - Throughout the duration of its 125-year history, the club has had annual dues of $1.
   - As in many clubs, titles such as "Miss," "Mrs.," and "Dr." are used before last names during meetings.
   - The club's purpose and procedures have remained basically the same for 125 years, with minor changes. For instance, members are no longer fined for tardiness or absences.
   - Club members have included wives of the presidents of Eastern Illinois University (located in Charleston), such as Mrs. Livingston Lord, who was the group's president from 1908 until her death in 1924.
   - When a member dies, the donation given at the Christmas Silver Tea is used to purchase memorial books in her name for the Charleston Carnegie Public

Library. I saw a similar practice in many of the other clubs mentioned in this book.

Snapshot Summary of College Hill Club, Jacksonville, Illinois

All information in the following summary comes from two e-mails from club member Kathy English to me on April 29, 2012.

1. **Official name of the club:** College Hill Club.
2. **Date founded:** December 16, 1888.
3. **Size of club today:** Currently, there are sixteen members. The maximum allowed is twenty.
4. **How often they meet and where:** The club meets in members' homes or church parlors on alternate Mondays, September through April.
5. **Types of themes or topics for programs or papers:** The club's theme is selected each year by the members. In 2013–14, the theme was "Nineteenth-Century Biography."
6. **Of note:** The club's guest day is always its last meeting at the end of April. The secretary reads a review of the year's papers, and a guest speaker makes a presentation related to the year's theme. As the name of the event implies, members may bring guests or prospective members.

Snapshot Summary of The History Class, Jacksonville, Illinois

1. **Official name of the club:** The History Class.
2. **About its founding:** In 1896, the group began as the University Extension Club as part of the University of Chicago. It was renamed the History Class in 1901, at which point the club members were receiving study plans from the University of Illinois, from Northwestern University, and from an Illinois College professor. Then, in 1903, members

chose to make up their own study plans—"a tradition which continues today."[6]

3. **Size of club today:** Twenty-one members.

4. **Meeting schedule and meeting place:** From September to May, the club meets for two hours every other Wednesday, starting at 3:00 p.m. There are no meetings in December or during Easter week. Meetings are usually held in members' homes or in church meeting rooms.

5. **Yearly themes:** These have included a wide range of subjects. The 2012–13 topic was "Landmarks," including programs on the Great Wall of China, the great pyramids of Egypt, and the Alamo in Texas. The 2013–14 theme was "Controversial Social Issues of Our Time," focusing on such topics as climate change and stem cell research.

6. **Of note:**

   - In 1916, the group began serving tea, desserts, and finger sandwiches at meetings, after the program was delivered. The tradition of high tea continues today. However, when the United States entered WWI, members of The History Class dispensed with these refreshments and sent the money they would have spent to the wives and children of soldiers stationed in Jacksonville. They also cancelled programs during 1917–18 so that members could volunteer with the Red Cross.

   - The longest-surviving History Class member in 2013 was Margaret Bellatti, who then had been a member for sixty years. She researched and delivered a program about the group on its centennial (1996) that contained a sort of membership summary. Included in her report was the story of Gertrude Holmes Beggs, who had just become an honorary member in 1995. Gertrude joined the club in 1935 and retired from it sixty years later. She died in 2007 at the age of 103. She had been a member of Phi Beta Kappa at the University of Chicago, and she earned a Master of Arts degree in history from Tufts. In Jacksonville, she taught history, government, and economics at

MacMurray and Illinois Colleges, and world history at Jacksonville High School. She was a school board member and was a fifty-year member of the League of Women Voters, with a Susan B. Anthony Award from the league for her service.

Snapshot Summary of Household Science, Jacksonville, Illinois

Most of this information comes from e-mails from member Kathy Stafford to me on March 13, March 20, and April 11, 2013.

1. **Official name of the club:** Household Science.
2. **Date founded:** 1885.
3. **Size of club today:** Twenty-five active members and fifteen associate members.
4. **How often they meet and where:** They meet on the third Tuesday of the month, September through May, with the May meeting being a luncheon and guest day, featuring a special program. Dues are $5 a year, with an additional charge for this luncheon.
5. **Examples of yearly themes for the study papers or programs:** In 2013, the club's yearly study theme was "Celebrating First Ladies of the United States." Papers are typically twenty-five to thirty minutes long.
6. **Of note:**
   - Member Doris Hopper, author, archivist, and historian, is also an associate professor of speech communication emeritus and associate dean of students emeritus at Illinois College, where she worked for thirty-five years. In addition, she has been a member of Household Science since 1955, an impressive sixty years. She is also a member of Sorosis, another of the six Jacksonville study groups that are over a hundred years old.

- Associate member Alice Wright joined the group in 1947 and was active until 2008—an astonishing sixty-one years of active membership.
- The group has an interesting and efficient way of choosing officers and allocating assignments. They do both alphabetically, with the entire list of members taking turns in serving as president, as vice president, as secretary, as treasurer, and on the program committee (which consists of three members). The archivist serves in her position for several years.
- As for the order in which members host (provide the home for) or cohost (bring a dessert to) meetings, that is done alphabetically, too, with a member hosting one year, cohosting the next, and being assigned a paper to research and present in the third year. The program committee decides which responsibility to assign each year.
- At the May luncheon in 2013, a guest speaker came as Mary Todd Lincoln's older sister and told Mary's story from her sister's point of view.

Snapshot Summary of the Monday Conversation Club, Jacksonville, Illinois

All of the following information, with one exception, comes from several e-mails from club member Suzie Glisson to me in April 2013.

1. **Official name of the club:** Monday Conversation Club.
2. **Date founded:** 1888.
3. **Size of club today:** Twenty-four active members and fourteen associate members.
4. **How often they meet and where:** Alternate Mondays, September through May, at members' homes.
5. **Examples of yearly themes or study papers they present:** This group covers a wide-ranging variety of subjects. The 2013 theme was "Heroes." All members, except for the

officers, write and present a program (and then host the following meeting) each season.

6. **Of note:**

- Gratia Coultas, the club's longest-active member and the longest-active member of any group I encountered while working on this book, is ninety-three years old.[7] She has been in the club for sixty-nine years, having joined in 1946. You can see her in the 2013 photo of the club I've included. She's sitting in the middle of the front row and wearing a hat and jacket. She recently presented a program and spoke for forty-five minutes without using any notes. Club member Suzie Glisson, who was my source for all of this club's information, said, "Speaking without notes was expected when the club was young, though we have strayed from that rule in the last few years." This makes Gratia's feat even more amazing. Suzie also reported that Gratia is very involved and busy in the community.

- As a special note, Suzie added, "We are also proud to have enjoyed the membership of a former city mayor, now deceased."

- She also said, "Our members particularly enjoy the period in our meetings called 'roll call,' at which time we comment on the program and share any personal news, including books and travel we've enjoyed. I would not hesitate to say that membership in this organization is very dear to all of us."

Monday Conversation Club, Jacksonville, Illinois, 2013. Gratia
Coultas, the longest-active member of any historic study club
in the United States that I could find, is in the middle of the first
row, wearing a hat and jacket. Ms. Coultas joined this study
club in 1946 and still writes and delivers original papers.
Photo by Tom Burrus

Snapshot Summary of Sorosis, Jacksonville, Illinois

Sorosis of Jacksonville, Illinois, is – to the best of my knowledge - the oldest surviving women's literary society in the United States. Its motto is "147 Years of Learning and Friendship" (which is updated each year to reflect the number of years the club has been in existence).

Unless otherwise noted, all information about Sorosis comes from club member Karyl Findley in a lengthy e-mail to me on April 29, 2013.

1. **Official name of the club:** Sorosis, named after the club in New York City, which was founded by Jane Cunningham Croly on "the first Monday in March, 1868"[8] and which is credited with starting the women's club movement.

2. **Date of founding and story of its founding:** Mrs. Harvey Milligan (Josephine) somehow got word of the founding of Sorosis in New York City and decided to found her own club for women with a similar aim—"the mental, moral, and physical improvement of its members"[9]—a few months later. She and Miss Jennie L. Eggleston, Miss A. B. Osgood, Miss Belle Woods, and Mrs. George McConnel (Maria) founded the Jacksonville club Sorosis on the stormy evening of November 30, 1868.[10] It should be noted that Mrs. Milligan, an amateur botanist of some note and a contributor of articles on a variety of subjects to the *New York Tribune*,[11] went on to found another study club, Household Science, in 1885.

3. **Size of club today:** Sixteen active members and several associate members, who attend meetings but do not present papers.

4. **How often they meet and where:** They meet every Wednesday from October to mid-November, then from January to May, with the exact number of meetings depending on the number of current active members. The meetings are held in members' homes. Members present an original paper each year and entertain the group as a hostess the week after.

5. **Types of yearly study themes:** To quote Karyl Findley from her April 29, 2013, e-mail to me: "A program committee of three members is selected in January for the next year's program. That committee is responsible for selecting a theme (usually very broad) and a selection of individual topics ranging from literary, history, science, arts, and current events." Four recent yearly themes have been 'The Backstory,' 'A Potpourri of Pertinent Publications,' 'And the Winner Is....' and 'This Could Be the Start of Something Big.'"

6. **Of note:**
   - When the club was first founded, members would slip through backyards on their way to meetings because they hoped to remain unobserved, as newspapers had published negative articles mocking "bluestocking" groups such as the first Sorosis.[12]
   - In the club's earliest days, Bronson Alcott, transcendentalist, abolitionist, advocate for women's rights, and father of Louisa May Alcott, twice visited Sorosis at their invitation, traveling from his home in Massachusetts to do so. When he visited on January 23, 1871, he commended the women for their organization and told them how important these literary societies were to the women's cause.[13]
   - At the time this chapter was written (2013), Honorary member Alice Wright (see also Household Science for her membership there) was ninety-six and the oldest member of Sorosis. She stopped giving programs in 2012 at the age of ninety-five. Alice is at one end of the age spectrum of Sorosis, and newer members in their thirties are at the other. As far as length of membership is concerned, the group has three members who have been in Sorosis for over fifty years—Alice Wright, Doris Hopper (also a member of Household Science), and Gertrude Hohmann.
   - Karyl Findley wrote that the group enthusiastically celebrates anniversaries every five years and celebrated their 145th in 2013. Approximately twenty years ago, they revived the custom of having a May

outing at the conclusion of the program year. Several years ago, they also began having a Christmas party, with husbands and honorary members invited. Many of the husbands belong to The Club or to the Literary Union, the two oldest men's literary societies in Jacksonville."[14] Yes, there are historic men's literary societies in Jacksonville and historic literary societies at one of the local colleges, Illinois College, which has seven literary societies instead of sororities and fraternities.[15]

- As a group, Sorosis donated money to help build the base of the Statue of Liberty. As individuals, they donated money for its recent renovations.
- In her e-mail to me, Karyl wrote, "We are extremely proud of our group and its historical significance to Jacksonville." The author of a piece about the founding of Sorosis, Phebe Bassett, wrote in 1925 that the charter members founded the group to "bring a fuller intellectual life to its members … a woman should be a force for good without as well as within her home … she should be equipped by study and education to share with man both the responsibilities and the problems of everyday life."[16]

Snapshot Summary of The Wednesday Class, Jacksonville, Illinois

I owe a great debt to Siri Baker, who works in development at the Columbia University Graduate School of Journalism in New York City. She met me—an alumna—for lunch in Los Angeles in December 2012. When she heard what my book was about, she offered her grandmother as a contact. Her grandmother is Louise Bone, who is a longtime member of Wednesday Class, one of the many Jacksonville, Illinois, historic study groups.

1. **Official name of the club:** The Wednesday Class.
2. **Date founded:** 1887[17]—"for mutual study and improvement."[18]

3. **Size of club today:** Twenty active members and two associate members, the latter of whom do not give papers.[19]

4. **How often they meet and where:** They meet in members' homes at 3:00 p.m., every week from mid-September to the week before Thanksgiving. Then, they have a winter break and resume in late January or early February. They do not meet on Ash Wednesday or during Easter week. They end their year in late April or early May. They have as many meetings as there are active members to present a paper,[20] but new members do not have to give a paper or entertain during their first year.[21]

5. **What kind of yearly themes or papers they present:** The theme in 2013 was "Children's Literature." Past themes have included "Voices of the South," "Banned, Burned, and Challenged," "Voices of the West," and "The Year of the Museum."[22] Papers are typically forty-five minutes long.[23]

6. **Of note:**
   - Each member presents a paper and entertains every year.
   - The officers, president, and secretary are rotated alphabetically twice a year.[24]
   - Fifty-plus-year member Louise Bone reports that the tea, which follows the presentation of the paper, is a "full English tea with all of the 'trimmings."[25] Member Cathy Green says that this includes sweets, savories, sandwiches, hot and cold items, and beverages, all served on silver pieces—not just desserts, as other groups offer.[26]
   - Cathy Green has been a member since 1972—forty-three years—and her mother, Carolyn Hart Crawford, was a member from the 1930s until her death in 2006, possibly as long as seventy years. In her later years, Carolyn was not able to participate as an active member or present papers because she had failing eyesight.[27]
   - Since the spring of 2011, all six women's Jacksonville literary societies have participated in a group luncheon,[28] during the course of which a member

from each study club explains her group's theme of study for the year. The clubs - Wednesday Class (founded in 1887), Monday Conversation Club (1888), Sorosis (1868), College Hill (1888), History Class (1896), and Household Science (1885)[29] - hope to make this event an annual tradition.[30]

- Jacksonville seems to be a very club-minded town, as it is also the home of a group claiming to be the oldest women's organization in the United States in continuous existence: the Ladies' Education Society, which was begun in 1833 by a small group of women who wanted to provide education for young women who would become teachers in their little town on the prairie. Louise Bone and Cathy Green are members of this group as well as of Wednesday Class. Each year, these two groups provide scholarship money and loans to young women.[31]

Sanpshot Summary of The Woman's Reading Club of Mattoon, Illinois

1. **Official name of the club:** The Woman's Reading Club of Mattoon, Illinois.
2. **Date founded:** The club is said to have been founded in 1877 by women who wanted to educate themselves and have access to books, as there was no library in town.[32]
3. **Size of club today:** Seven active members and one lifetime member.[33]
4. **How often they meet, from what month to what month, and where:** They meet in a church parlor, in the afternoon, once a month, from March through October.[34] This pattern is the opposite of that of 99 percent of the groups I found.
5. **Type of yearly themes or assignments:** Books are no longer assigned. Currently, each member chooses a nonfiction book to read and review. Book reviews are followed by a group discussion of the subject.[35]

6. **Of note:**
    - The club's archives are stored at the Booth Library at Eastern Illinois University, Charleston, Illinois.[36]
    - Like most historic literary clubs, the Woman's Reading Club in its earliest days had a critic or editor who told the member who had just presented a paper what errors she had made.[37]
    - Many of the club's members over the years have been librarians or teachers.[38]
    - In 2013, I was assisted in pulling together the information in this summary by the then twenty-year member Ardeth Finley, who said that her mother, Martha Clawson, was a member for sixty-one years. Ardeth said that many of the "life members" had died in recent years and were not being replaced by younger members, perhaps because the group meets in the afternoon, when many younger women are working or driving school-age children.[39]

Snapshot Summary of Anti-Rust, Springfield, Illinois

All of this information comes from several e-mails written to me by member Mary Beaumont in January 2013.

1. **Official name of the club:** Anti-Rust, taken from Robert Browning's verse novel *The Ring and the Book,* chapter 8, lines 54 and 55: "Just so much work as keeps the brain from rust, / Just so much play as lets the heart expand."
2. **Date founded:** February 1894, in Springfield, Illinois.
3. **Size of club today:** The membership always stays at twenty-five, and members do not look for a new member until a vacancy opens up.
4. **How often they meet and where:** They hold twenty-six meetings a year, meeting on virtually every Thursday, except holidays, from October to April. They meet from 10 a.m. to 12:00 noon at a downtown eating club, the Sangamo Club,

which offers them a buffet lunch in the meeting room. The following is from member Mary Beaumont:

> The 26th [meeting] is Gala Day, usually at the home of the President where, until last year, every member answered roll call with an original poem about their paper's subject. Activities at Gala Day include skits written by members, games about the topic and/or information presented during the year or field trips to pertinent places. For the first time last year [as our] topic [was] "Art in America," members could bring a piece of American art from their home and briefly talk about it, instead of a poem, if they wished.

5. **What kind of study papers the group presents (the overall topics):** The topics vary widely, such as "Walls and Bridges," for which Ms. Beaumont's paper was on "Mangroves: Bridging Sea and Shore." Another paper covered "Turkey, Bridge between East and West."

6. **Of note:** The group observes *two* roll calls. Roll call is a once-common tradition where each member delivers a required assignment after her name is called in alphabetical order. In Anti-Rust, one roll call comes before the paper. In the discussion, everyone participates by giving a quotation or a bit of information about the upcoming paper. In the roll call after the paper and discussion, in which only a few members participate, members present an explanation of a current event. At each meeting, the second, or current-event, roll call advances down the alphabet, with a few more members heard each time. Each member has about three minutes to present her current event.

Snapshot Summary of The Sunnyside Literary Circle of Springfield, Illinois

The following information is courtesy of 2012–13 President Carolyn Houston, taken virtually verbatim from her January 16, 2013, e-mailed answers to my questions.

1. **Official name of the club:** The Sunnyside Literary Circle of Springfield, Illinois.
2. **Date founded:** November 10, 1887.
3. **Founded by:** Fifteen original members, with others added shortly thereafter. A partial list includes Mrs. H. S. Dickerman, Mrs. Fred Smith, Mrs. N. D. Munson, Ms. Minnie Munson, Mrs. R. O. Post, Mrs. J. P. Lindley, Mrs. M. J. Skadden, Ms. J. Skadden, Mrs. J. Barrel, Ms. Hanney, and Mrs. J. H. Matheny.
4. **Size of club as stated in bylaws (size limit):** Twenty-five.
5. **Size of club today:** Nineteen active members, one nonresident member, and ten honorary members, the last being inactive members who do not give papers.
6. **Meeting schedule:** Once a month in September, December, and May, and twice a month from October to April, excluding December.
7. **Where they meet:** In members' homes.
8. **Election of new members:** No more than two new candidates are invited at one time. These are selected from members' nominations. Prior to election, a candidate's name is withdrawn if an active member registers concern with the president in confidence. *Relatives of current members are precluded from membership.* (Author's Note: This is unusual but not unprecedented. Most groups are proud of their family or legacy connections.)
9. **Object of the club as stated in its bylaws or constitution:** Home study and self-improvement, encouraging women to develop their minds at the same time as they pursue other careers.
10. **Dues:** $1 per year.

11. **Club motto, club flower, and club colors:** No motto or colors, but the club flower is the pink carnation.

12. **Paper or program assignment schedule and hostessing rotation schedule:** A topic related to the general theme voted on for the following year is selected on Gala Day in May. Resident active members research and present their papers in alphabetical order during the next club year. Members volunteer for hostess duties in no particular order.

13. **Length of papers or programs:** Paper presentations generally last thirty to forty-five minutes.

14. **Location of the club's yearbooks, minutes, scrapbooks, and archives:** These are passed on and reside with each year's officers.

15. **Civic achievement of the group or its members:** President Carolyn Houston reports, "All members are very involved in the community, having held leadership positions, elected offices, and civic appointments."

16. **Special events:** The president hosts a tea for the first meeting in September and a luncheon for Gala Day (the annual meeting) in May.

17. **Refreshment highlights:** Chocolate almond bark is served at every meeting. New members and active members who move to a new home serve a traditional tea the first time they hostess there.

18. **Special traditions:** On December 1, seasonal flowers are delivered to homebound or honorary members. A book is donated to the local library in memory of a deceased member.

19. **Example of a yearly theme or topic:** Topics have covered subjects in the arts, the sciences, history, and religion. The current theme is "Theater."

20. **One topic selected and presented:** "Gershwin Brothers' Role in American Musical Theater."

21. **Particularly colorful or interesting member, present or past:** The current active membership includes a physician, a former mayor, a retired state legislator, a retired university chancellor, former school board and other elected officials, government administrators, and a former school principal.

22. **Legacy members and longest-active members:** Georgina Northrup, deceased in 2012, was an active resident member since 1961, and Jean Sherrick has been an active member since 1971. When I was writing this section, Lois Brotherson was an honorary member and had attended meetings regularly since 1962. She died in 2015. No legacy members exist, probably because relatives of current members are excluded from being considered as members.

CHAPTER 10

Kansas

Six Kansas Groups

Including one, Friends in Council of Lawrence, Kansas, that seems to be the oldest women's literary society west of the Mississippi

I have no miraculous tales of dinner conversation or chatter in a store that led me to connect with the six groups in Kansas that fit the parameters of my book. It was old-fashioned research and telephone interviews that led me to each of these and got me up to speed on their history and their present condition. I found three historic women's study clubs clustered in two towns close to Kansas City, in the northeastern part of the state—Olathe's Ladies' Reading Circle, Lawrence's Kanwaka Literary Club, and Lawrence's Friends in Council, the last possibly being the oldest such group west of the Mississippi. Lawrence is the home of the University of Kansas and has a population of 87,600.[1]

I also found three historic women's groups closer to the middle of the state, in Newton, which is in Harvey County: Newton's Sorosis, Newton's Ladies' Reading Circle, and Newton's Junior Reading Circle. I was told that the Junior Reading Circle has some members in their twenties and thirties and in all of the decades beyond, so it is rather unique among virtually all of the clubs I found that are focused on—but not always successful at—attracting younger members once their longtime members age and die. Another fairly unique characteristic of one of the Kansas clubs is the meeting schedule of the Ladies' Reading Circle of Olathe. Rather than meeting from the fall through the spring as most groups do, the club members gather once a month, from March to November, with a break during the worst of the winter months. The ninety-three historic study clubs I found in the United States were so similar—although they had little knowledge of similar groups and no umbrella organization—that I was always a bit surprised when something exceptional popped up in my research.

As with all of my research, what I found in Kansas came mixed in with local history, such as the part played by Lawrence, Kansas, in the Bleeding Kansas (or Bloody Kansas) border and slavery wars, which involved abolitionist John Brown and which led up to the Civil War. I also got a bit of Harvey County history, thanks to two helpful and knowledgeable women in the historical society who are also members of two different study clubs. These women are Lana Myers and Jane Jones, whom I was able to interview by telephone and Internet. Another contact, artist Sue Langseth, who is a member of the Ladies' Reading Circle of Olathe, told me that during the town's 150th anniversary in 2007, she decorated a six-foot-tall fiberglass cowboy boot, now housed in the public library, with images of books her group had read and studied together. The boot is a reminder of the town's claim that the cowboy boot was first designed and produced by the Olathe Boot Company in 1873.

Once again, in Kansas, I found study club members who were immersed in local history and in the history of their own group.

Snapshot Summary of Friends in Council, Lawrence, Kansas

Possibly the oldest all-women literary society west of the Mississippi

1. **Official name of club:** Friends in Council
2. **Date founded:** 1871.[2]
3. **Founded by:** Elizabeth Perkins Leonard, a New Englander who was hired as Kansas University's first full-time woman professor in 1869. Ms. Leonard came to Lawrence from Quincy, Illinois, where the first Friends in Council group had begun[3] in 1869.[4]
4. **Size of club today:** Twenty-four members, which is also the limit.[5] Longtime member and unofficial historian of the group Betty Laird says that "there has been a sudden resurgence of interest in the group in the last four or five years … women coming back after their careers."[6]
5. **When they meet:** They meet every week on Tuesdays, except for the third Tuesday of the month. This tradition began in the club's early days because a university chancellor's wife had a standing appointment on that Tuesday and could not attend Friends in Council. Not ones to break with tradition, club members have continued to shun the third Tuesday ever since.
6. **Refreshments:** Tea is served once a month only.[7]
7. **Topics and papers:**
   - Members vote to choose a topic each year.[8] Whoever proposes the winning overall topic then must come up with the subjects of the individual papers for the coming year.[9] One recent topic was China, and an individual paper based on that topic was "The Chinese Scholar and His Garden."[10]
   - There is no rotation schedule for paper assignments. Members simply sign up for papers they might be interested in.[11]
   - As long as a member chooses to present papers, she is considered an active. Once she chooses not to present papers, she is inactive. It is her choice.[12]

8. **About the group:**
   - Members of this club believe that theirs may be the oldest women's literary society west of the Mississippi River.[13] In my research, I didn't locate an older one in that part of the country.
   - Several of the club's current officers have been professors at Kansas University (KU). The club's unofficial historian and longtime member Betty Laird, who once taught freshman English at KU, is quoted in a newspaper article as saying, "A lot of us have some connection to the university."[14]
   - Betty Laird told me that she is also a playwright and actor. She said that she is currently working on a play about Sarah Brown, the first secretary of the Lawrence Friends in Council. Sarah was the daughter of John Stillman Brown, the first Unitarian minister in Lawrence,[15] who had been a member of the utopian community Brook Farm in West Roxbury, Massachusetts.[16] Sarah was a teacher in Lawrence's pioneer-era schools and was also involved in the women's suffrage movement.[17]

Snapshot Summary of Kanwaka Literary Club, Lawrence, Kansas

Kanwaka is a township west of Lawrence, Kansas, and was the home of the founders of this group. Today, most of the club's members live in Lawrence.

1. **Official name of club**: Kanwaka Literary Club
2. **Date founded:** 1899, although proper constitution and bylaws were not drawn up until 1920. According to the new by-laws, prospective members had to be proposed and voted on. The only exception to this new membership requirement was that daughters of members were automatically considered and approved for membership, although this was strictly a tradition and not a rule.[18]

3. **Founders:** Mrs. J. R. Topping, Miss May Etta Richardson, and Miss Leonora Ricker of Kanwaka. These women put an ad in nearby Lawrence's *Jeffersonian Gazette* in April 1899, asking women interested in founding a club for the purposes of fulfilling their "social and intellectual needs" to meet with them "for mutual improvement."[19]

4. **How many members today:** Member Marilyn Orr, who said in 2013 that she is a relative newcomer, having then been a member for only ten years, counted the names in a current roster for me and found twenty-eight members, with approximately fourteen of them being active. All are dues-paying.[20]

5. **Programs:** Typically, members speak on subjects of interest to them. However, once a year, during their April meeting or founders' day, they have an outside speaker. Marilyn Orr says that older, longtime members remember the days when papers delivered needed to be researched and annotated, with outside sources, but she says that this is difficult for older members. Therefore, today's programs are more relaxed and informal.[21]

6. **Location of club archives:** The club's archives, from 1908 to 2005, have been transferred to four microfilm rolls and are located at the Kansas Historical Foundation in Topeka.[22]

Snapshot Summary of Junior Reading Circle of Newton, Kansas

1. **Official name of club:** Junior Reading Circle
2. **Date founded:** 1894.[23]
3. **Founders:** Linda Krehbiel Haury, Edith Steinkirchner Boyd, and Joanna Jackson Graybill.[24]
4. **Number of members:** Thirty-five active members, some of whom are as young as their late twenties or early thirties. Once a woman has served as president, she may become an associate member. The club has eighteen associate members.[25]

5. **When and where they meet:** They meet twice a month at 1:00 p.m. on the first and third Thursday of the month, October through April.[26]

6. **Refreshments:** New members must serve a tea at their first meeting. Other than that, the hostess for each regular meeting may offer whatever refreshments she chooses.[27]

7. **Types of papers/topics:** Junior Reading Circle topics are similar to Sorosis and Ladies' Reading Circle topics.[28]

8. **Of note:**
   - The club is said to have "more social events than Sorosis."[29]
   - Members refer to the club as JRC.[30]
   - Member Susan Koehn, who answered several of my questions in a telephone interview, said that her grandmother Terrie Kinney Krehbiel was also a member, having joined the new club in 1895, one year after its founding.

Snapshot Summary of Ladies' Reading Circle, Newton, Kansas

The archivist of the Harvey County, Kansas, Historical Museum and Archives, Jane Jones, is a member of Ladies' Reading Circle. She was my source for all of the information below. It was through her feature story on women's study clubs in the museum's blog, *Voices of Harvey County,* that I found the three historic and independent Newton literary societies that are still active today. She also very kindly gave me contacts for the two groups of which she is not a member.

1. **Official name of the club:** Ladies' Reading Circle.
2. **Date founded:** 1880.
3. **Founders' names:** Theodora Dean, Louise Bunker, and a Miss Chapman, whose first name has been lost to time. The three women were neighbors. Dean and Chapman traveled "back East," where women's study clubs were very popular,

and returned to Newton determined to start their own. The first meeting was in Louise Bunker's home.

4. **Size of membership:** Twenty-one active members, nine corresponding members (who have moved away), and five associate members who have been members for at least ten years and have asked not to be bound by membership duties.

5. **When they meet:** Once a month between October and May.

6. **Where they meet:** Mostly in members' homes, but also in local venues for special events.

7. **Refreshments:**
   - The club recently reverted to an old tradition: passing chocolates. Hostesses have always provided coffee and tea. Now, they also provide these chocolates.
   - Interestingly, new members must provide a "new-member tea"—a bountiful tea table, which they prepare.
   - Aside from these two types of refreshments, food is also featured at special events, such as the president's luncheon at the beginning of the club year, the Christmas party, and a party the members call the midwinter party.

8. **Topics:** Jane Jones modestly concluded that the current kinds of topics the group covers are "not up to the standards of the original members," who would have been studying more serious subjects. And she said that they do have outside speakers on occasion, more so than in the past. She added that in 2013, the president had picked the topic of "Getting to Know You," for which each member was asked to answer predetermined questions about herself—a sort of personal presentation. Jane said that previous topics revolved around gardening, for one, and the fine arts organizations of Newton, for another.

9. **Of note:**
   - Dr. Lucena Axtell (1865 – 1951), LRC member and mother of four, was one of Kansas' first women physicians. She and her physician husband, John Axtell, founded the Axtell Clinic and Hospital in

Newton in 1887. She also founded and ran the Axtell School of Nursing – Kansas' first school for registered nurses – and was said to have a particularly loving approach to the care of the sick. She is remembered on the National Library of Medicine's website as a Local Legend.[31]

- Currently, Ada Mae Haury, a retired speech and debate teacher, is also a local legend and Honorary member of the Ladies Reading Circle. In the 1940's, she taught at Russell, KS High School, and one of her debate squad members was Arlen Specter, who became a U.S Senator from Pennsylvania.

Snapshot Summary of Sorosis Club, Newton, Kansas

Every bit of the following information comes from Sorosis member Lana Myers, who presented a history of the women's club movement and the history of her own club at a Sorosis meeting on October 6, 2011. She shared the histories with me, along with other details, in e-mails written on July 9 and 10, 2013. Lana had been a member of Sorosis for thirty-one years in 2013 and was its president when it celebrated its hundredth birthday. She is the office manager of the Harvey County Historical Society and is the author of two books, *Prairie Rhythms: The Life and Poetry of May Williams Ward* and *Newton Medical Center: Merging the Past with the Future.*

1. **Official name of the club:** Sorosis, in honor of the first women's study club, founded in NYC in 1868 by Jane Cunningham Croly and bearing the same name.
2. **Date founded:** February 23, 1911. At the invitation of Mrs. Alma Becker of Newton, Kansas, ten women met to discuss forming a literary organization. Mrs. Becker was the club's first president. Other charter club members, including those who did not attend the first meeting, were Dora Becker, Mrs. Phil Anderson, Laura Cheney, Lucile Chandler, Mrs. P. F. Grogger, Rose Lander, Cordelia Lawton, Frances Miller, Nelly Prather, Josephine Rhoades, and Gertrude Welsh.

3. **Size of club:** There was originally a limit of sixteen active members. This was raised to twenty in 1918, and it is twenty-four active members today, to keep the size small enough for all members to fit into a living room. In addition, there are currently seven honorary members, including the newly minted honorary member and my contributor to this summary, Lana Myers. A member becomes honorary after thirty years of membership and may choose at that time to stop giving papers, although several honorary members still participate actively. The club's longest-active member in 2013 was Barbara McCall, who was an honorary who still participates. Kathleen Karlowski had been an inactive honorary member for ten years as of 2013, when she was living in. Wichita. Both women had been members for fifty-seven years as of 2013.

4. **How often they meet and where:** They meet once a month, October through April, on the first Thursday of the month at 1:00 p.m., except in January, when there is a luncheon on the third Thursday. They usually meet in members' homes, although they may meet in other locations having to do with the day's program.

5. **Dues:** $20 annually for active members; $10 for honorary members. There may be additional charges for a luncheon or special occasion.

6. **Refreshments:** Typically, a dessert plus coffee and tea is served. Often, the dessert relates to the holiday closest to the meeting, such as Valentine's Day for the February meeting. There is a hostess and a cohostess for every meeting except the one in January. The January luncheon has a January luncheon committee.

7. **Example of topics, papers, and roll call:** This group lists roll call subjects in the roster of upcoming programs in their annual yearbook, along with the topic of the program for the day. This way, members know what subject they will be expected to speak about briefly when their name is called for attendance. For 2013–14, the roll call on October 3 was "How You Exercise," and the program dealt with exercise. On November 7, the roll call was "The Last Book I Read,"

and the program was a book highlight. I found the roll call tradition in several of the groups I studied. It was a more common tradition in the earlier groups, which emphasized getting previously housebound women comfortable with public speaking and even debate.

8. **Club colors and flower:** The club colors are green and white. The club flower, chosen in 1928, was the rosebud, although in the group's earlier days, the flower was the daisy and then the carnation.

9. **Where club archives are held:** The Harvey County Historical Society, which is where I found the women who helped me with the three historic Newton women's study clubs: Sorosis, Ladies' Reading Circle, and Junior Reading Circle.

10. **Of note:**
    - Gifts are exchanged during the group's December/ Christmas meeting.
    - When new officers are installed in the spring, they read an original poem they've composed. This tradition was begun in 1960.
    - The club has donated funds to charities or local causes, especially in its earliest years, and even joined the local Needlework Guild in Newton to help sew clothes for the poor.
    - As with many clubs, Sorosis' meetings and social events in the early part of the 1900s were avidly covered by the local newspapers in great and worshipful detail.
    - In 1998, the club overhauled its constitution and bylaws to reflect the demands of modern life.

Snapshot Summary of Ladies' Reading Circle, Olathe, Kansas

I was able to make contact with one member of the Ladies' Reading Circle after tracking her down via the Internet. I was also able to find out a good deal about the group from a very fine article written for *The Best Times,* a publication of the Johnson County, Kansas, Department of Human Services in 2013, and from another fine article written for KansasTravel.org.

1. **Official name of club**: Ladies' Reading Circle
2. **Date founded:** 1883.[32]
3. **Founder(s):** One of the founders of this group is often said to be Mrs. John St. John (Susan),[33] wife of a former governor of Kansas who also ran for president of the United States on the Prohibition Party ticket.[34] However, presumably more accurate historic reference materials eliminate her as a founder and, instead, name her sister-in-law Emma Parker, along with Celestin Stevenson and Celona Pickering,[35] as the group's three founders.
4. **Size of group today:** Thirty-five members, although the group was originally limited to thirty.[36] Like virtually every other group of this type, membership is by invitation.[37]
5. **When they meet:** This club meets once a month[38] from March to November, taking a break over the hardest winter months. Sue Langseth, who has been a member for thirty-two years—since 1983—wrote me that until "about five years ago, they met September through May,"[39] like most of the other literary societies I uncovered for this book.
6. **Where they meet:** In the homes of hostesses. The jobs of hostess and cohostess are rotated.
7. **Topics studied:** Topics are diverse. In 2010, the group heard a paper on the art of Thomas Hart Benton, whose Kansas City home and studio they visited in 2010, on one of their yearly road trips.[40] The first vice president is responsible for setting up the monthly programs, which can focus on a variety of subjects and might also be a book discussion with the entire group participating.[41]
8. **Of note:**
   - Like members of many other historic all-female literary societies, the women of the Ladies' Reading Circle worked to start the Olathe Public Library beginning in 1889. Aside from helping to organize a groundswell that led to the founding and funding of the library by

the city council and by Andrew Carnegie, in 1899, they spent $2 to secure the loan of fifty books—the first library books for the town—from the Kansas State Library for six months. The Ladies' Reading Circle's support for the public library continues today.[42] To commemorate this, artist and longtime club member Sue Langseth and her artist husband, Chris Langseth, were chosen to decorate a six-foot-tall fiberglass cowboy boot with reminders of the Ladies' Reading Circle and some of the books they've read and studied together. The boot is on permanent display in the Olathe Public Library.[43] It was one of twelve huge boots placed in different locations around town (like the cows in Chicago and the angels in L.A.) to celebrate the town's 150th anniversary in 2007 and to commemorate the invention and introduction of the cowboy boot, purportedly by Olathe Boot Company in 1873.[44] The title of the Langseth's boot sculpture is "Read Any Good Boots Lately?"[45]

- In 2013, one woman had belonged to the group for 51 years, and another member died at almost 101 years of age in 2009.[46]

CHAPTER 11

Wooster, Ohio

A Cluster of Three Historic Women's Study Clubs

In a casual conversation on the back porch of friends' lake house in Camden, Maine, during the summer of 2013, I discussed my book with Wooster, Ohio, resident Judy Seaman. Judy turned out to be a member of her town's historic Travelers Club, a women's study club founded in 1891. She led me via e-mail to member Sally Bernhardt, who had prepared the club's program on its 100th and 110th anniversaries, and Sally led me to contacts in the town's Monday Club and Thursday Club. Ruth MacKenzie agreed to help me with the history of Monday Club; Dorothy Iams, with Thursday Club.

These groups' makeup, operation, and need to find new members who might be able to do the work and fit in would be familiar to members of the other historic study clubs I found in all parts of the country. Two of the Wooster groups seem to thrive. One has very few members but still continues to meet.

Snapshot Summary of The Monday Club, Wooster, Ohio

All of the following information comes from my telephone interview of the then ninety-four-year-old Ruth MacKenzie, who told me, when we spoke on September 11, 2013, that she had been a member "since the 1960s"—fifty-some years.

1. **Official name of the club:** The Monday Club.
2. **Date founded:** 1903.
3. **Founders' names:** Mrs. MacKenzie was unsure of the names of the founders, so I wrote to the Wayne County Historical Society, the keeper of the club's archives, on September 11, 2013, asking for the information and a more exact founding date. However, I never did receive a reply.
4. **Size of club:** Monday Club traditionally had about thirty members. Recently, their numbers were closer to twenty-five. With two recent deaths, they are now at twenty-three members. Of the twenty-three, three are honorary members and two are associate members.
5. **How often, when, and where they meet:** Monday Club meets on the second Monday of the month at 1:30 p.m., from September to May, excluding January. They meet for dessert, which is served at the beginning of the meeting, usually with members seated, perhaps with plates in their laps. They move on to the business portion of the meeting, and the delivery of that month's paper comes after that. They usually meet in members' homes, but they may also meet in a Presbyterian or Methodist church or in the local library's meeting room.
6. **Examples of yearly themes:** "Cradle of Civilization," which was an overview of many beginnings; "A Series of Brushes," which was the study of various painters; "The College of Wooster," which was an overview of the various departments in the college; "Amazing Melting Pot," which was the story of various minority women; and "Secrets of Ohio Success." The papers are usually about forty-five minutes long. Members,

who range in age from their fifties to their nineties, stand to deliver their papers.

7. **Of note:** The club's archives are preserved by the Wayne County Historical Society.

Snapshot Summary of The Thursday Club, Wooster, Ohio

All of the following information comes from a September 12, 2013, telephone interview of member Dorothy Iams, who joined the club in the 1990s.

1. **Official name of the club:** The Thursday Club.
2. **Date of founding:** 1887.
3. **Names of founders:** Mrs. Coover, Nellie Coover (the former's daughter), Miriam Phillips Kauke (after whom a dorm at the College of Wooster is named), Gertrude Leonard, Martha E. McClellan, Sarah Phillips (Mrs. Kauke's sister), and Miss Sonnedecker.
4. **Size of club:** The members are meeting rather informally now. The club has no elected officers, and there are currently only eight members. Mrs. Iams said that they are not actively recruiting new members, but they still keep to a schedule and still have members deliver original programs.
5. **When and where they meet:** The club meets once a month for a 12:30 lunch at a local restaurant in September, October, November, December, March, April, and May. After lunch, they hear one of their members deliver her paper or program.
6. **Examples of yearly themes and/or papers:** Each of the papers or programs is about forty-five minutes long. Two of the more recent yearly themes were "Place of Origin," with each speaker discussing her own town or city of origin, and "Guest Speaker," in which each speaker did a biography of a famous person, with the members having to guess who it was. Mrs. Iams chose C. S. Lewis and said that no one could guess who he was once she finished delivering her paper. Other yearly themes have been "Ohio Philanthropists,"

"Countries," and "This Is My Life," the last of which was an autobiographical project.

7. **Of note:**
    - Early meetings were conducted with great social correctness, with the members dressed in hats, gloves, and their best attire.
    - Thursday Club has always had a close association with the College of Wooster, with many of the early members being faculty or faculty wives. Several dorms are named after former members.
    - There have been several legacy chains throughout the years.

Snapshot Summary of the Travelers Club, Wooster, Ohio

1. **Official name of club:** Travelers Club
2. **Date founded:** 1891.[1]
3. **Founders:** Travelers Club was founded by a group of middle-aged Wooster women reported to be of some social standing. They wanted "to expand their horizons by studying the countries of the world."[2]
4. **Number of members today:** A total of thirty-three active, associate, and honorary members.[3]
5. **When and where they meet:** The club holds nine monthly meetings from September to May, in members' homes. Occasionally, they use public meeting rooms. The May meeting is a luncheon with an outside speaker. Otherwise, the hostess and assistant hostess serve refreshments at regular meetings.[4]
6. **Types of topics and papers:** Members choose their own topic when asked to deliver a paper. The club's original intent to study foreign countries and travel has morphed into a wider range of subjects,[5] although member Sally Bernhardt reports that members may "use their own travel destinations for program topics."[6] One example of a nontravel-related topic was a recent paper presented by a woman who was

born in China and who traced the story of a special watch her mother had received as a gift.[7]

7. **Of note:** My contact, member Sally Bernhardt, wrote me and said that she found the following story especially on-target when discussing the intangible value of a woman's club such as Travelers:

> During the late 1940s, a former club president was interviewed on a local radio show, and she was recorded as saying, "This business of meeting week after week with a group of women that gradually become as comfortable as one's own family, listening to each other's papers, when you could probably find better material at the library—all this could be a little prosaic, even a little stuffy. It could be, but as a matter of fact, it isn't, because, at bottom, at heart, it is based upon something important—the need, the delight of human beings in each other. There is so much division, so much separation in our world, that any excuse, flimsy or wise, that brings people together for the sheer joy of togetherness is good."[8]

CHAPTER 12

Durham, North Carolina

The Old Girls' Network Helps
Me Find Four Historic Clubs

Laura Micham, director of the Sallie Bingham Center for Women's History and Culture, and curator of gender and sexuality history for Duke University's David M. Rubinstein Rare Book and Manuscript Library, was a great help to me in early 2014. She answered my questions about a one hundred-year-old women's study club in Durham called Halcyon, which I had seen mentioned in the Duke library's online archives. Laura wrote me that the club was still meeting in Durham, and she said that she would approach her contact in Halcyon to see if she and her club would cooperate with me on my book. Her contact was the helpful and efficient Lucy Grant, who had written a history of her club on its hundredth birthday and had also taken her club's archives for storage to both Duke's Rubinstein Library and the Durham County Library, where the archives became part of the latter's North Carolina Collection.

After Laura had gotten in touch with her, Lucy soon contacted me. She was happy to help, ably answering my questions and then doing something much harder: finding contacts who would answer my questions in three other Durham women's study groups, which were equally as old and which fit the parameters of my book. I had thought that Halcyon was the only women's literary society in Durham that had survived to today, but Lucy proved me wrong.

Lucy was able to find women in two of the three other clubs who would give me information about their club or find me another contact who would. I ended up with Margaret Walther, who quickly answered my questions about Tourist Club, and Lisa Powell, who was equally as quick with information about Up-to-Date Club, the oldest in Durham. However, I was stuck at an impasse with the Canterbury Club, whose first contact finally felt she could not help me. She put me in touch with another member, who was also unable to help me. One month, and then two months, went by. Then, suddenly, in April 2014, a minor miracle happened. Actually, it is an example of the old girls' network in action.

Sally Miller, now Sally Bugg, was in my dorm at Duke back in the 1960s, but it took a combination of coincidences to reconnect us after forty-some years and to get me the information I needed on Canterbury Club. First, unbeknownst to me, Lucy Grant had already asked Sally to help me without telling her my name. Sally declined, and so Lucy gave me two other possible Halcyon contacts, neither of whom worked out. I was in limbo with Canterbury, although I'd gotten quick responses from the three other historic women's study clubs in Durham. Then, coincidentally, Sally and her husband traveled to Birmingham, Alabama, where the latter was scheduled for back surgery. While in Birmingham, Sally had lunch with my friend Lucie Bynum (who was the inspiration for this book and who had also lived in the same dorm at Duke), and Lucie told her about my book. Sally immediately realized that I had been the author whom Lucy Grant had tried to get her to talk to. Sally and I finally connected, after which time we wrote and talked at length.

It is quite wonderful to find a cluster of four historic groups in one town with a population of 288,000.[1] The four groups are very similar to the other 90-some groups I've found around the country in virtually all respects, although, as I've repeated many times, there is no connection or communication between clubs. The four Durham groups are strong and have a certain social cachet, which helps them survive. Also, being in Durham, with Chapel Hill just a few miles away, these clubs have many members involved in the universities in both towns, women whose lives, or the lives of their husbands, revolve around learning, tradition, and history—the basis of these literary societies. I suspect that their university involvement gives the club members an added strength. Of course, these four Durham groups are similar to the others mentioned in this book in that they find that their membership is aging a bit and members need to work hard at finding younger members.

A summary of all four groups follows this introduction.

Snapshot Summary of Canterbury Club, Durham, North Carolina

All of the following information comes from one e-mail from Canterbury Club member, Sally Bugg, dated April 25, 2014.

1. **Official name of the club:** Canterbury Club. However, the club's original name for its first nine years was Eclectic Club.
2. **Date founded and founders' names:** In the summer of 1910, eight young women met to organize a literary club for single women. Their names were Lila Wright, Jean Venable, Roberta Henshaw, Lottie Sharp, Rosa and Eleanor Green, Annie Louise and Lida Carr Vaughan. Because they were out of town for this organizational session, Anna Branson and Mrs. W. F. Carr (maiden name unknown) may not be considered true founders, although they did attend the first actual meeting in October, possibly bringing the number of founders to ten. After being a singles-only club for nine years, the club, by way of a vote, began to accept married members in 1919.
3. **Size of club today:** According to Sally Bugg, the bylaws limit the number of active members to thirty-five, and that has always been the actual number of members. The club may have any number of honorary members, a status that may be asked for and then granted by the executive committee when members reach the age of eighty, if they want a less active role (no papers, no entertaining).
4. **When and where the club meets:** Canterbury meets on the second Thursday of the month in October and November, and January through May. The location, time, and description is described by Sally in this passage from her e-mail:

   > For each meeting, there are two hostesses and one program-giver. Generally, the meeting is held at the home of one of the hostesses and follows the general format: business meeting and program … then lunch. But occasionally, the hostesses might choose to have it at a club or other location … occasionally, it is a

morning coffee. The time and place is whatever is agreed upon by the program-giver. For our March meeting this year, our hostesses invited us for High Tea at the Washington Duke Hotel ... very elegant! For a number of years now, the May meeting has been a cocktail/dinner party to which husbands are invited. It is given by the Executive Committee (officers and Program Committee) and usually held at the home of the President.

5. **Types of topics covered, and examples of yearly themes:** In the earliest years, topics were subject-oriented. Examples are "Egypt, the Cradle of Civilization" and "Modern Drama." In later years, themes picked by the program committee were more book-oriented. Examples of this approach are "Current Books by North Carolina Authors" and "Eighteenth-Century Women of Influence." Papers can be anywhere from twenty to forty-five minutes long. There is no set requirement there.

6. **Of note:**
    - Sally told me that legacies are very important to and very prevalent in Canterbury. She herself came to Duke from her hometown of Buffalo, New York, but her husband, whom she met at Duke, was from a Durham family who had several members active in Canterbury. Sally was asked to join in 1974, five years after graduating from Duke, marrying, and settling in Durham. Her husband's grandmother, mother, and two aunts, and Sally's sister-in-law, were or are members of Canterbury. A Durham family with the last name Carr has always had at least one member in the club as long as Sally has been a member. She named several women with deep family connections to Duke, including Brenda Brodie, whose husband was the president of the university for ten years.
    - The most engaging answers I received while researching this book were in response to my often-asked question, "Can you tell me about any interesting

members, and who is your oldest or longest active members?" Sally described an honorary member, Margaret "Peaches" McPherson, who was active until "a couple [of] years ago." Peaches joined Canterbury in 1949, which means that she was active for an estimated sixty years. In addition, her "best friend growing up in Baltimore was Scottie Fitzgerald, daughter of F. Scott Fitzgerald."

- A particularly talented and enthusiastic club member named Penny Bridgers, who is now living in London, served as recording secretary for seven consecutive years starting in 1996. She loved the job and was said to be spectacular at it. Sally reported to me that Penny turned the minutes into brilliant compositions. When she finished reading them during the business segment of each meeting, the membership would burst into applause. Penny was a tough act for the next recording secretary to follow.
- In the club's early years, the minutes were written in verse.
- In the club's earliest years, members met every two weeks. Now, there are just six meetings a year with programs, and the seventh meeting is the annual party in May, to which husbands are invited.
- The club's archives are held privately by club members and have not yet been donated to a library or historical society.

Snapshot Summary of Halcyon Club, Durham, North Carolina

Most of the following information was sent to me in several e-mails during January 2014 by the club's historian, Lucy Grant. As previously mentioned, Lucy had worked on a history of the club for its hundredth anniversary and had also helped securely store the club's archives and history in two locations—Duke University's Rubenstein Library and the Durham County Library—"in hopes that someone would find the information relevant to the role of women and their organizations in our country's history."[2] Lucy helped me establish the existence of three other very strong and historic women's study clubs in Durham and also found me contacts in all of them: Up-to-Date (the oldest in Durham), Canterbury, and Tourist Club.

1. **Official name of the club:** Halcyon Club.[3]
2. **Date founded and founder's name:** In the spring of 1910, twelve women who all lived in the Durham area[4] decided to form the third literary club in their town. The group met at the home of Mrs. Paul Taylor on East Main Street. Mrs. Taylor and three friends had come up with the idea of the club while playing the newfangled game of bridge whist. They realized that their friends who did not play bridge could not socialize with them at the parties where the game was played.[5] One of the twelve founding members is identified as Mrs. William Boyd. Her daughter, Mary Elizabeth Hamilton, and granddaughter, Elizabeth Cavett French, also became club members over the years.[6]
3. **Size of club today:** The size is limited to thirty members, and the club has thirty active members today. There are also two honorary members.[7]
4. **When and where the club meets:** Halcyon meets once a month, October through May, on the third Thursday of the month, typically in a member's home. The traditional May luncheon is held at the Hope Valley Country Club.[8]
5. **Types of topics studied and examples of yearly themes covered in members' papers:** According to club historian Lucy Grant, themes for the last three years have been "Durham, a Place to Be" (2011–12), "Reader's Choice: A Potpourri" (2012–13), and "Journeys: Literal or Literary" (2013–14).[9] Lucy explained that each member giving a program is free to pick her own angle on the topic.[10]
6. **Of note:**
   - Founding members and earliest members were wives of men who were "Duke faculty members, bankers, lawyers, and tobacco magnates."[11] The names of the earliest members resonate for me, as the Duke

campus, where I spent four years of my young life, has buildings, quadrangles, and other facilities named after the Halcyon Club's founders' husbands.

- There are four multigenerational legacy chains in Halcyon, as well as "many daughters, daughters-in-law, and their mothers."

- Halcyon's secretary's minutes are often amusing and highly original. They are always full of accurate observations and details, often of the domestic setting of the meeting, so they serve as wonderful historic documents.[12]

- A special tradition is the club's "very spiked eggnog" served at their Christmas meeting. It is a tradition started by Mrs. William Wannamaker, so it is called the "Wannamaker eggnog."[13]

- The longest-active Halcyon member ever was Estelle Flowers Spears, who was a member from 1929 to 1990—sixty-one years. She was the first woman to sit on Duke University's board of trustees, where she served from 1952 to 1968.[14]

- Member Annie Kizer Bost was North Carolina's commissioner for charities and public welfare from 1930 to 1944. The University of North Carolina awards the Annie Kizer Bost Prize each year to "a graduating student who shows the greatest potential for service to the public welfare system of North Carolina."[15]

- The club historian, Lucy Grant, organized and compiled a notebook summary of the club's history for its hundredth anniversary and placed copies of this history, along with the club's archives, in both a Duke University library and the Durham Public Library, hoping that someone like me would find it.

- The club has always had a close and supportive relationship with the Durham Public Library.[16]

- Frances Gray Patton, who wrote the best-selling novel *Good Morning, Miss Dove,* was a member of Halcyon from 1954 until her death in 2000 at the age of ninety-four.[17] She became an honorary member of Halcyon in 1978.[18] Her husband, Dr. Lewis Patton, was a professor of English at Duke from 1926 to 1972.[19] He was an august presence in the English department when I was a student there, majoring in English.

Snapshot Summary of The Tourist Club, Durham, North Carolina

All of this information comes from two e-mails from Club President Margaret Walther on March 10 and 11, 2014.

1. **Official name of the club:** The Tourist Club.
2. **Date founded and founders' names:** The club was founded in 1900 by Mrs. Victor Bryant, Mrs. Louis Carr, Mrs. W. D. Carmichael, Mrs. W. A. Erwin, Mrs. Howard Foushee, Mrs. R. B. Fuller, Mrs. William Graham, Mrs. Isham F. Hill, Mrs. John S. Hill, Mrs. Meritt H. Jones, Mrs. Bessie S. Leak, Mrs. Abbott E. Lloyd, Mrs. George L. Lyon, Mrs. Edward K. Powe, Mrs. James E. Stagg, Mrs. R. L. Thompson, Mrs. John F. Wily, and Mrs. Robert W. Winston. Club President Margaret Walther wrote that her mother, grandmother, great-grandmother, and great-great-grandmother (founder Mrs. Victor Bryant) have been members, making Margaret the only fifth generation legacy member of a literary society I identified while researching and writing this book.
3. **Size of club today:** Forty members.
4. **When and where the club meets:** The group meets on the second Thursday of every month from October to May, usually in members' homes.
5. **Yearly topics and individual paper examples:** The club "was originally founded to present members' reports of their trips to other countries. This was halted briefly during the world wars when travel was difficult. Current programs also feature travel, but are not limited to that." An occasional guest speaker might be an author speaking about his or her book.

6. **Of note:** The club's archives have long been kept in the Duke University Libraries, and Margaret reports that they are often used in the women's studies curriculum at Duke, adding that the club's concentration on travel and international politics means that their minutes and presentations show "important changes in women's views over the last century."

Snapshot Summary of the Up-to-Date Club, Durham, North Carolina

Unless otherwise noted, all of the information in this summary comes from a series of e-mails written by members of Up-to-Date in mid-February 2014. My contacts in the club were Lisa Powell, Shirley Few, and Mary John Caldwell, who worked together to complete the summary via these e-mails.

1. **Official name of the club:** Up-to-Date Club.
2. **Date founded and founders' names:** Up-to-Date Club was founded in 1896 and is the oldest women's literary society in Durham County. The six charter members each asked one other woman to join, bringing the original club size to twelve. The club records list these founders as Mrs. Thomas D. Jones, who invited Mrs. E. J. Parrish; Mrs. Leo D. Heartt, who invited Mrs. Ed Heartt; Mrs. Brodie L. Duke, who invited Mrs. William A. Erwin; Mrs. W. L. Wall, who invited Mrs. John M. Manning; Mrs. R. C. Stanard, who invited Mrs. Julian S. Carr; and Mrs. Eugene Morehead, who invited Mrs. Samuel Finley Tomlinson.
3. **Size of club today:** Thirty-nine active members and twenty-four honorary members. The bylaws limit the group's active membership to forty women.
4. **When and where the club meets:** Up-to-Date meets for lunch on the second Thursday of the month from October to May. In December, there is usually a Christmas party with a gift exchange. There is also a social each May, alternating between a luncheon one year and a dinner with spouses the next. The March meeting is a business meeting and book

swap. Meetings are usually in members' homes, but other venues used have been an art gallery, a sophisticated bed-and-breakfast, the campus of American Tobacco, "private clubs, historic buildings, and the Duke University Library Rare Book Room."

5. **Examples of yearly topics covered and examples of members' papers on the topic:** A different member is in charge of the program each month. Members may present a paper on a topic of their choice, such as the history of hemp and its uses or the program on "The First Lady of Duke University—Mrs. William Preston Few." Members' travels are also often the subject of programs. One year, Up-to-Date dedicated each meeting to a different and notable woman in each of the decades of the twentieth century. In addition, local authors might be asked to speak to the group about a book they have written.

6. **Of note:**
   - The club has a number of longtime members and a number of legacies. For instance, Mrs. Herschel A. Caldwell (Anita), whose husband served Duke University as an assistant football coach and held other coaching positions at Duke for 41 years,[20] was an active member from 1944 until 2010 (she was 102 years old in 2010, and she died the following year.)[21] Her daughter-in-law, Mrs. Herschel A. Caldwell Jr. (Mary John), has been active since 1971.
   - Mrs. William Preston Few (Mary), wife of the first president of Duke University,[22] was a club member from 1912 to 1945. Her daughter-in-law, Mrs. Randolph R. Few (Shirley), has been an active member since 1958. Shirley's two daughters are active members of the club.
   - In 2014, Mrs. Edwin S. Yarbrough Jr. (Doreen) was said to be an active member at the age of ninety-eight and has been a member since 1950. Two of Doreen's daughters were also active members.
   - Mrs. Albert G. Carr (Katherine) was a member of Up-to-Date for sixty-five years, from 1947 to her death

in 2012. Two of her daughters are active members today.

- The club's archives are kept in the Durham County Library's North Carolina Room.

CHAPTER 13

A Directory of Single Clubs (Not Part of a Geographical Cluster)

Snapshot Summary of Saturday Morning Club, Boston, Massachusetts

1. **Official name of the club:** Saturday Morning Club.
2. **Date founded:** November 2, 1871.[1]
3. **Founder(s):** Julia Ward Howe is usually credited with founding this club for her youngest daughter, Maud, who was sixteen at the time, and for Maud's friends,[2] but a book written about the club by club members to commemorate the group's sixtieth anniversary says that Mrs. Howe was assisted by Mrs. Robert E. Apthorp in founding the Saturday Morning Club (SMC).[3] Mrs. Apthorp was a member of Boston's social elite, "The 400."[4] Julia Ward Howe is today best known for having written the lyrics to "The Battle Hymn of the Republic," but in the late 1800s she was one of this country's most prominent spokeswomen for women's rights, including the right to vote; for women's need to self-educate and to educate more broadly; for the abolition of slavery; for world peace; and for the establishment of Mother's Day. She was a founder of many groups focused on advancing women[5] to what she saw to be their rightful place in the world. In addition, she was the founder of women's clubs and of other clubs or federations that organized and advanced women's clubs. She was also the mother of seven (one child died in infancy), an author, a poet, and a public speaker. Her husband, Samuel Gridley Howe, a reformer and physician, forbade her to work outside the home. He also controlled her inheritance, with rather disastrous results.[6] After Samuel's death in 1876, Julia had forty years of independence, during which time she happily made her living to support herself.[7] She died in 1910 at the age of ninety-one.[8] Two of her daughters, including Maud, for whom Julia had formed Saturday Morning Club, helped write their mother's biography, which won the Pulitzer Prize in 1917.[9]
4. **How often they meet and where:** The club meets on alternate Saturdays at 11:00 a.m., October through March or April, at the Harvard Club, first hearing two original papers delivered by members and then adjourning for lunch.[10]

5. **Size of club today:** "About 30 Active members, with 24 giving papers"[11] during a club year. Longtime member Marion Kilson wrote me that the club members range in age from their early forties to their nineties and are mostly professional women, artists, and academics.[12]

6. **Examples of yearly themes they study and examples of individual topics for their papers:**

    • Marion Kilson feels that members' papers have improved in quality in the nearly thirty years she's been a member.

    • Susan Hackley, who was president in 2013, when I was researching this section, wrote me the following description of the group's themes and paper topics:

    > In recent years, at least, we have not had a theme for the year. Rather, members submit topic ideas (typically a word, sometimes a phrase) and the list is narrowed down to the correct number. Two members write papers on that topic and give them on a Saturday. This year's topics will include: Mentor, Expectation, Provincial, Crescendo, and Cities. Members can range far and wide in their papers and often do. Many papers are quite personal while others are more scholarly.[13]

7. **Of note:**

    • The club's archives are stored in the Schlesinger Library on the History of Women in America, Radcliffe Institute for Advanced Study, Harvard University.

    • In 2013, the club's current president, Susan Hackley, was described in a Harvard web site as having a background in journalism, policy analysis, communications, and Internet philanthropy and entrepreneurship. She is the managing director of Harvard Law School's Program on Negotiation.[14]

Snapshot Summary of Nondescript Club, Bronxville, New York

Nondescript Club chose not to participate in my book research, citing their tradition never to mention the club outside the club circle. Their wish for privacy is so great that club members ask family members not to mention Nondescript when writing their obituaries. However, I was told that the club is still meeting to hear original papers, usually in members' homes, and that this is usually followed by tea. Given that, and the few basic facts mentioned below, I can only surmise that Nondescript Club is similar to the other historic women's literary societies still active in this country today.

1. **Official name of the club:** Nondescript Club.
2. **Date founded:** 1895, in a home parlor in the Lawrence Park section of Bronxville, New York. Bronxville is a New York City suburb in southern Westchester County.[15]
3. **Of note:** Meetings are usually held at 2:30 on the third Tuesday of the month, October through May. Tea is served after the presentation of an original paper or papers. However, for the first meeting in October, the group divides up and has lunch at several homes before the meeting.

Snapshot Summary of The Monday Club, Camden, Maine

Except where noted, the information for this summary comes from a meeting over lunch with three club members, Becky Flanagan, Ann Montgomery, and Sally Enggass, on August 13, 2012.

1. **Official name of the club:** The Monday Club.
2. **Date founded:** 1885.
3. **Name of founders:** Mrs. Henry L. Alden (Annie), in her home in Camden, Maine, which was the meeting place for the group for many years. There were ten charter members: Sarah Adams, Ella Adams, Annie Alden, Louise Bean,

Julia Burgess, Charlotte Glover, Emma Hosmer, Myra Montgomery, Ellen Norwood, and Elizabeth Stetson.[16]

4. **Size of club as stated in bylaws (size limit):** Thirty.

5. **Size of club today, including active members, honorary members, and any other category of member:** Thirty active members and eight honorary members (2012).

6. **Meeting schedule:** They meet on Mondays at 2:00 p.m., from the first Monday in November to the first Monday in April. There are typically nineteen to twenty-one meetings per year.

7. **Where they meet:** Members' homes.

8. **How new members are elected:** When there is an opening, a letter of recommendation (or two or three) is read, after which the prospective members are voted on. Only one may be selected.

9. **Object of the club as stated in bylaws or constitution:** "The object or mission of this Club shall be the mutual intellectual improvement of the members, through the study of literature, art, science, history, and the vital interests of the day, as well as the provision of occasional lectures and entertainments."[17]

10. **Dues:** $15 per year.

11. **Club colors, flower, and motto, if any:** None.

12. **Paper or program assignment schedule and hostessing schedule:** To quote member Essie Sexton, "Assignments for hostessing are done alphabetically, although it doesn't look this way from looking at the roster. Assignment of hostesses is similar to assignment of papers."[18]

13. **Location of the club's yearbooks, minutes, and archives:** The secretary holds these.

14. **Civic achievements of the group or of its individual members:** As with many of the groups I studied, Monday Club members wrote to Andrew Carnegie to secure help in starting a public library in Camden, Maine. They were also instrumental in getting the public library building fund committee started.

15. **Special events of the year:** There is a holiday "open" meeting, to which each member may invite one male or

female guest, and an end-of-year luncheon in May, for which every member brings an assigned dish. The May luncheon is also the business meeting, at which the next year's topic is chosen.

16. **Refreshment highlights:** Tea, coffee, baked goods, and sandwiches are served after each meeting.[19] Certain recipes whose original cooks have died have been saved. The dishes are still prepared and brought to the opening meeting, the December open meeting, and the April luncheon and business meeting.[20] Ann Montgomery, the longest-active member (she joined in 1954), always brings a tomato aspic.

17. **Special traditions:** The group claims to have no special traditions, but the bringing of certain food items to certain meetings certainly qualifies as a tradition, as do the club's special events.

18. **Example of overall yearly theme or topic:** "Follow the Money."[21]

19. **Example of an individual paper or assignment based on that topic:** "Russian Oligarchs: Communism to Capitalism."[22]

20. **Longest-active member in today's club:** Ann Montgomery, who joined in 1954 and was still attending meetings as an honorary member when I had lunch with her in 2012. Ann was one of the club members who took me to lunch so we could discuss the Monday Club.

21. **Particularly colorful or interesting member, present or past:** See below for information about Annie Alden. See above and below for information about Ann Montgomery.

22. **Legacy members:** Ann Alden, daughter of the founder and charter member Annie Alden, was still alive and living in a Camden nursing home in 1985, during the club's centennial. She was over a hundred years old and had been a member of the club for many years. Another family, descended from charter member Myra Montgomery, produced five Monday Club members in three generations, with one member, Ann Montgomery, still living and active in the club and lending her home on High Street in Camden for meetings.

Snapshot Summary of The Ramblers, East Hampton, New York

1. **Official name of the club:** This club's name, The Ramblers, was chosen because the club's original intent was to study travel-related literature and foreign countries, to mentally ramble through various countries by studying them, "in search of knowledge and amusement."[23] The group no longer limits itself to the study of travel and foreign countries.
2. **Date founded:** January 22, 1901, in East Hampton, New York.[24]
3. **Founder's name:** Mrs. Florence Osborne.[25]
4. **Size of group today:** Forty members is the limit.[26] Currently, there are thirty-seven active members, three honorary members, and two associate members.[27] Members must live in the township of East Hampton, New York.[28]
5. **When and where the group meets:** They meet on the second Tuesday of the month from October to June at 7:30 p.m. in the Session House of the First Presbyterian Church of East Hampton.[29]
6. **Examples of yearly themes and paper topics:** Papers or programs are done by a committee, with three to five women in a committee contributing their portion of a program. Therefore, there is a committee and a chairwoman for each meeting, and these women are also in charge of refreshments for that evening. In 2005–06, the overall topic seems to have been literature. For the opening meeting in October, four members spoke on poetry, with one woman acting as chair of the group. Other months' programs covered mystery books, children's books, biographies, dramatic works, and so on.[30] Members are reminded to deliver their portion of the program "in as much of their 'voice' as possible"[31] and not to merely copy the information from the Internet or other sources. Programs last for thirty to forty-five minutes.[32]
7. **Of note:**
    *   Helen Rattray, who lives in East Hampton and is the publisher of the town newspaper, *The Star,* brought

the Ramblers to my attention when we were chatting at my future granddaughter's baby shower in Brooklyn, New York, on September 15, 2013. Helen is not a member of the club, but she knew other women who were. Some of her family members had belonged. Two days after the baby shower, Helen sent me a detailed e-mail with additional information about the group, some of which she had gotten from the current president, Elizabeth Sarfati. Helen's former mother-in-law, Jeanette Edwards Rattray (who died in 1974), was the publisher of *The Star* at one time. Jeanette and her mother, Florence Huntting Edwards, were members of the Ramblers. The newspaper's files still hold a few original papers written by these women for presentation to the club. Helen mentioned one paper written by her mother-in-law's mother. Delivered in 1956, it is called "The Evolution of the Best Seller." This paper includes notes about the appearance of a member who was dressed in a costume reflecting the style of the time period in which author Samuel Richardson's works *Clarissa* and *The Vicar of Wakefield* are set. The meeting at which the paper was read included readings by this costumed member and a musical finale.[33]

- A story in *The Star* in 1985 quotes the oldest living member of the club reminiscing about the club in earlier days, presumably when the group studied countries and travel: "Whole winters were devoted to the history, people, literature, and physical conditions of any country you might name. Everyone was required to write a paper on an assigned subject, materials for which, if not available locally, were obtained … from that awesome, far-away entity, the State Library."[34]
- There is an opening dinner, possibly a potluck, in October, and a final dinner in June.
- Members try to abide by "The Unspoken Rules of Ramblers" as described in an open letter written by

317

Jane Talmage in February 2002. Mostly, these rules include guidelines for good manners, such as dressing with care for meetings and letting the chairwoman for the evening know when one cannot attend a meeting or would like to bring a houseguest. Members are also reminded not to discuss politics and not to try to sell tickets to charity events. Members may possibly make announcements of charity events, but only after discussing the matter with the president.[35]

Sanpshot Summary of Fredonia Shakespeare Club, Fredonia, New York

This group studies subjects other than Shakespeare, using Shakespeare as their inspiration. I was able to interview a longtime club member, Florence McClelland, by telephone about this still-active club. Also, I found two recent articles about the group that appeared in a local newspaper's blog.

1. **Date founded:** 1885.[36]
2. **Founders:**
   • Notable among the twenty founding members—a group that contains both well-to-do and well-educated wives of prominent men plus less affluent but well-educated schoolteachers and librarians—was Annie Moffet Webster, Mark Twain's niece.[37] Her husband, Charles Webster, was Mark Twain's business manager and publisher, and her daughter, Jean Webster, was the beloved author of the classic best seller *Daddy Long-Legs*,[38] along with other novels and a play based on *Daddy Long-Legs*.[39]
   • Ella Lapham, who graduated from Vassar and helped to support her family by giving lecture classes on Elizabethan literature, helped Helen Shaw Jennings with her plan of organizing the Fredonia Shakespeare Club. Ms. Lapham, who was too busy with her lectures to join, is listed as only an honorary member in the

club's rolls, while Mrs. Jennings (then Ms. Shaw) is acknowledged to be the founder. The first meeting was held at the latter's house on Main Street.[40]

- Two charter members from the 1885 founding, Mrs. George M. Newton and Mrs. Herbert Miner, survived for the next fifty years and were able to celebrate their fifty-year anniversaries with the club in 1935.[41]

3. **Size of club as stated in bylaws:** There is a limit of twenty members.[42]

4. **Size of club today:** Ms. McClelland said that there are about seventeen active members and five honorary members.[43]

5. **Meeting schedule:** The club meets for a maximum of twenty times a year, from October to March,[44] with an additional April luncheon and a June picnic.[45] They meet every Thursday afternoon at 2:30 during the club year, with "as many meetings as there are members,"[46] as each member hosts once a year and presents one paper every year.[47] I was told that, in 2013, if the membership number held to seventeen, there should be seventeen regular meetings.

6. **Where they meet:** In members' homes, unless there is a special occasion, like the mid-April birthday luncheon for Shakespeare, which might be held at an upscale restaurant.[48]

7. **Election of new members:** Membership is by invitation only. The membership votes on prospective new members.[49] Prospective members usually are invited to the opening event, the October tea, which is held on the second Thursday of the month.[50]

8. **Paper and program assignment schedule:** Members must hostess once a year and give a paper once a year.[51]

9. **Location of archives:** The Darwin L. Barker Library in Fredonia (a public library).[52]

10. **Special events:** A fall tea with an elaborate tea table; Shakespeare's birthday luncheon, usually in mid-April; and a June picnic at the home of the president-elect.[53]

11. **Example of a yearly theme and individual topics:** In 2002–03, the overall topic was "The Mediterranean World." Several papers given that year were "The Spanish Armada," "The Crusades," and "Seafaring Homeric Heroes."[54]

12. **Special traditions:**

- There is an elaborate tea table presented at the end of every meeting, with a silver tea service and an array of teatime goodies. At Christmas, longtime member and oft-time president Constance Van Scoter traditionally holds the meeting at her house and prepares a plum pudding for the group.[55]
- Members should always say yes when asked to occupy any office for which they are nominated. They should come to every regular meeting unless they are sick or out of town. They should give a paper and act as hostess once a year. And they should notify the president and provide a substitute if they cannot present the paper assigned to them.[56] I found these to be the written or unwritten rules of virtually every group I visited.
- Members may bring a guest to the opening tea held on the second Thursday in October, at which there is always a guest speaker who speaks on a topic related to the year's topic. The actual meetings and papers begin the following week.[57]
- At the mid-April Shakespeare luncheon, there is a cake and a toast to the Bard. At the end of the meal, it is traditional for the group to play a word game of some kind, one based on the year's theme or study topic. There are prizes for the winners. Even former members may attend this event.[58]
- The topic for the coming year is chosen in March.[59]
- At the June picnic, members choose the title for the paper they will do for the coming year.[60]
- Members address each other by "Mrs." or "Miss" during the meeting,[61] but they revert to using first names over tea at the end of each meeting.[62] This is a very common practice among historic literary societies.

Sanpshot Summary of The Quarante Club, New Orleans, Louisiana

1. **Official name of the club:** The Quarante Club. The name is said to come from the number of members of the French Academy,[63] forty members, or *quarante immortels* which translates as "forty immortals," which is how the members of the academy are known.[64] There may have also been a connection to the maximum number of members allowed in the club,[65] as a New Orleans newspaper article from January 1886 reports that Mrs. Thomas Hunton had just returned from a visit to New York City and was determined to organize a club of about forty women to meet once a week.[66] Her club was originally called the Shakespeare Class for about two weeks, before being named Quarante Club in late February of 1886. However, the study of Shakespeare continued for about two years, with the day's lecture often delivered by an outsider, possibly a male.[67] By 1891, after abolishing the practice of having a paid discussion leader, the members had taken over the hard work of choosing topics, doing the research, and delivering the papers.[68] At that point, the women were on their own—and there was tremendous talent within the club to draw from.

2. **About the club's founding:**
   - The club was founded in early February 1886 by Ella McGehee Hunton[69] (Mrs. Thomas Hunton),[70] the wife of a prosperous local lawyer who attended West Point with General Sherman and then found himself on the opposite side of his old friend when the South seceded from the Union in 1860.[71] Mrs. Hunton was inspired, perhaps, by a visit to New York City, where she may have seen such a women's group, or by the New England activist Julia Ward Howe, who was living in New Orleans for a brief time. Wherever she traveled, Ms. Howe urged women to start self-education groups. In fact, she revived a book club in New Orleans while she was living there to run the

women's department of the World's Industrial and Cotton Centennial Exposition in 1884–85.[72] The club she may have inspired, the Quarante Club, contained an impressive list of founding members who were writers. Among these was the celebrated author Ruth McEnery Stuart (after whom another New Orleans literary society, founded in 1915, was named, which is now a hundred years old and still going strong—the Ruth McEnery Stuart Clan). Other women writers in Quarante's founders' circle were Grace King and Mollie Moore Davis, the latter holding literary salons that made her a "vital force"[73] in the city's unique Creole/American/Anglo/European cultural life. Another giant of Southern literature who helped found Quarante was Mary Ashley Townsend, a celebrated writer and poet much admired in the 1870s and 1880s for her regional works.[74] In 1884, Julia Ward Howe asked Ms. Townsend, who later served as the president of Quarante from 1888 to 1890, to write and present a poem for the opening ceremony of the Cotton Centennial.[75]

- The Quarante Club, in turn, inspired the founding of Cadmean Circle in Birmingham, Alabama, in 1888, after a founding member, Mrs. William Hardie, was impressed by her mother-in-law's club (Quarante) in New Orleans.[76] Cadmean Circle is covered in this book and was the first club I discovered and visited. (See chapter 1.)

3. **Size of club today:** Today, the club is an association of forty women who, according to member Carolyn Kolb, "by their joint study of topics and individual presentation of papers before the group, contribute to their mutual education."[77] Active members must write and present twelve papers before becoming what the group calls "senior members." Senior members are not required to write papers.[78] As noted below, members research and deliver an original paper every two years, so it is logical to assume that the retiring members would each have been active for at least twenty-four years.

4. **How often they meet and where:** The club meets in members' homes on Friday afternoons, from October to May, to hear papers presented by members on a topic chosen by way of a group vote. Every one of the club's forty members can expect to present a paper every other year.[79] With twenty papers a year (half of the membership) and a final meeting with no assignment (see below), this adds up to twenty-one meetings in seven months. However, I am guessing about this, as the club did not give me this piece of information, perhaps because of their tradition of secrecy.[80] There may be additional meetings or social events.

5. **Examples of yearly topics:** Again, this was not something Quarante shared with me, other than mentioning the fact that members vote on each year's theme.[81] However, I got some clues from two sources. There are a few very old papers archived in the general Tulane University library system, which I was able to find online. Two examples are "Nuremberg" by Mrs. J. T. Halsey, an eighteen-page, typewritten, bound paper delivered to the Quarante Club on March 4, 1932,[82] before WWII or the Nuremberg trials after WWII, and "Audubon" by Mary Bradford, an eighty-two-page booklet with illustrations that was read before the Quarante Club in 1897.[83] See "Of note," below, for a further explanation of the club's archives and possible access to other research papers. An online encyclopedia of Louisiana history reports that the club has, at some point, studied such subjects as "Victorian poets, Shakespeare's history plays, and eighteenth-century French, German, and English writers."[84]

My second clue to the types of topics the group covered came when, a year after my original research on the group was finished, I heard from a librarian at Tulane who had additional information. She sent me two papers presented by club members in 2012 and 2013. This gave me a far more accurate picture of the kinds of subjects the club is covering today. One of the papers, by author and member Patricia Brady, is titled "Picturing Martha Washington" and has to do with Patricia's search for a youthful portrait of our very first First Lady for the cover of her recently published book *Martha Washington.* Another paper, by member Sandra Freeman, is titled "Transportation in la Belle Epoque," which is a thirteen-page research paper on the subject.

6. **Of note:**

- The presentation of a paper is followed at each meeting by a tea.[85]
- The final meeting of the club year is called "The Easy Chair," and it features members' creative writing.
- The club representative, Carolyn Kolb, wrote that Quarante stores its archives in Tulane University's library system. Initially, I could not find any confirmation of this claim online, but I was eventually told by a general librarian at Tulane to contact Sean Benjamin, librarian for the Louisiana Research Collection, part of the Howard-Tilton Memorial Library at Tulane and the resting place of Quarante's archives. Mr. Benjamin reported back to me that none of the Quarante Club's material has finding aids in the online format. He said that the library is working toward this goal. The club's materials stored there were in seventeen boxes, dating from 1891 to 2003[86]—nothing more recent at that time, although, as I explained in item 5, I did later learn about newer papers stored in the archives. Although Mr. Benjamin said that the Howard-Tilton Memorial Library has Quarante's membership lists, constitution, bylaws, minutes, and papers presented by members, I was not able to access any recent papers online to find out what their most recent topics might have been. However, Quarante's archives are accessible to visitors to the Louisiana Research Collection's reading room, who are advised to visit the website to get started: http://larc.tulane.edu/patron/use.[87]
- Quarante Club annually funds prizes for writing at the New Orleans Center for Creative Arts and the University of New Orleans.

Causeries du Lundi, New York City

Without anyone to corroborate my claim, I assume that this group is still active. Despite making several attempts, I was never able to reach a member of this group. However, I had at my disposal an excellent feature article on Causeries du Lundi written by Dinitia Smith that appeared in the *New York Times* on June 12, 2005, proving that the group was alive and well that year. I was also able to spend a day reading through the group's archives at the New York Historical Society on Central Park West in New York City in December 2011.

1. **Official name of the club:** Causeries du Lundi, meaning "Monday Chatterings." The name is said to have been taken from the title of a literary column by the French critic Charles Augustin Sainte-Beuve, whose articles appeared in a mid-nineteenth-century Parisian newspaper.[88]
2. **Date founded:** April 12, 1880.[89]
3. **Name of founder:** Elizabeth Hamilton Cullum, Alexander Hamilton's forty-nine-year-old granddaughter, who invited fifty of her friends to have lunch with her in her Fifth Avenue home. Her purpose for this meeting was to form a club to develop the women's talents, which would lead them to be seen as more than mere society figures. Mrs. Cullum was the wife of well-to-do former Civil War general and philanthropist George Cullum.[90]
4. **Size of club today:** The club had twenty-three active members when the *New York Times* article was published in 2005. At that time, dues were $25 a year.[91]
5. **When and where they meet:** They meet in members' homes on the first Monday of the month, from November to May.[92]
6. **Topics of papers:** Members take turns reading essays on "topics that interest them."[93] There may be two essays at a meeting, as there were when the *New York Times* journalist visited the club in 2005. According to the resulting newspaper article, popular subjects for the club to study seem to be travel, art, historical figures, personal recollections, and family histories.[94] One fascinating and relatively recent

paper remarked on in the *New York Times* article was "Les Grandes Horizontales," about the courtesans of France in the 1880s and 1890s.[95]

During the club's earlier days, members were allowed to have another member read their paper for them, and papers were limited to thirty minutes in length.[96]

I was unable to find in the group's archives any papers written after 1996. As interesting as the earlier topics seem, they might not be representative of the group's current offerings. However, I was impressed by the intelligence found in seven papers written by a former club president named Dorothea C. Williams (Mrs. Roderick) in the years from 1978 to 1995. Those papers are stored in the last of the eighteen boxes of archives I examined at the historical society—boxes that I had to request and then wait for in the society's reading room.

Mrs. Williams also read a paper at the meeting attended by the *New York Times* reporter in 2005, when she was ninety-one years old, the oldest member of the group and, perhaps, the longest-active member, at thirty years of membership.[97] Her paper that day was a recollection of her father's world and her growing up in her grandfather's home, "a colonnaded mansion on Riverside Drive"[98]—a remnant of old New York.

Among Mrs. Williams' other papers stored in the clubs archives are "The Enchanted Realm of Fairy Tales," "The Phoenix Rises" (about Greek and Roman influences in our world), "Devas and Magic" (about the spiritually based, nature-communicating Findhorn Foundation in Scotland), and "Lost Worlds and Imaginary Kingdoms" (about Atlantis-type legends[99]), the last being a paper that comes complete with a scholarly bibliography. Clearly, this extraordinary member had an interest and perhaps training in myth and legends, but, beyond that, I can find out very little about her, except that she and her husband lived in New Canaan in 2005.[100] Without having met Mrs. Williams, I feel she represents the kind of extraordinary women I've found in these surviving literary societies—women who leave no great mark on the world but who vastly improve it through their intelligence and dedication. That Mrs. Williams was still giving papers and traveling into New York City from the far suburbs in her nineties is further proof that these groups are good for the body and the mind.

7. **Membership requirements:** To quote the *New York Times* article: "There's no such thing as 'blackballing.' ... A candidate must be introduced by a member. 'You go to three meetings, and then you're approved or you're not.'"[101] A "Rules of Government" booklet for the group, last amended in 1970, showed that the group used to ask its newest members to be "substitute members" for one year before attaining full membership.[102] That may no longer be the case (if the above quotation from a member in 2005 is accurate).

8. **Club archives:** In 1983, Causeries du Lundi donated its archives to the New York Historical Society on Central Park West in New York City. I was able to view them there.

9. **Of note:**
   - In its "Guide to the Records" of the group's archives, the New York Historical Society repeats the club's claim that the Causeries du Lundi is the "second oldest women's literary society in the U.S. still active today."[103] However, while doing four years of research on historic women's study clubs, I found that this is not true, as the founding dates of several groups in this book will attest. The oldest clubs I could find (and this does not rule out there still being more of these "oldest" surviving literary societies, as they are deeply private and often difficult to locate) were Sorosis of Jacksonville, Illinois, founded in 1868; Friends in Council of Lawrence, Kansas, founded in 1871; Portfolio Club of Syracuse, New York, founded in 1875; and Social Art Club of Syracuse, New York, also founded in 1875. That makes Causeries du Lundi, perhaps, the fifth oldest women's literary society in the United States still active today.
   - The early members were often figures from the social register, were historic figures themselves, or

were from families whose names now appear as the names of streets, parks, buildings, or neighborhoods throughout New York City. To quote Causeries du Lundi's archival "Scope and Content" entry at the New York Historical Society,

> The Causeries du Lundi records contain many essays by women of prominent New York backgrounds with last names such as Lefferts, Peabody, Roosevelt, Delano, Erving, Pierrepont, and Parsons. ... One paper of historical interest was submitted by Mrs. Edward Curtis, whose husband performed Abraham Lincoln's autopsy. She included an article written by her husband in 1926 about the event.[104]

In reading through the club's archives, I spotted additional members whose names are vital parts of New York City's history and geography: Tweed, Van Cortland, Delafield, Schieffelin, Astor, Frick, Beekman, Van Rensselaer, and even Emma Lazarus!
• As reported in the club's anniversary booklet dated 1955, the group has an unwritten rule "barring controversy from meetings [so that the meetings are] a refuge from turmoil."[105]

CHAPTER 14

Additional Historic All-Women Clubs

Including a Look at What Happened to Two of the Earliest Study Clubs

Historic African-American Women's Clubs

Semper Fidelis Club, Birmingham, Alabama

In the process of trying to find historic African-American literary societies still meeting today, I stumbled on the Semper Fidelis Club, founded in Birmingham, Alabama, in 1900, but I soon learned that it is a civic club with a strong charitable component and not a study club at all. I felt it was still worthy of note, as it very closely resembles the clubs I studied. But Semper Fidelis existed in a parallel universe, one with a segregated world, as it was founded in the early part of the twentieth century. I felt that the club's founders were, by necessity, helping the community they lived in rather than using their leisure time to study college-level courses or the plays of Shakespeare.

On February 23, 2011, I had the great pleasure of interviewing Dr. Danetta K. Thornton Owens, who had at that point been a member of Semper Fidelis for forty-three years. Her mother and one of her paternal aunts were also club members. The club is old enough to be considered for this book, but in addition to being a civic organization with a strong charitable component, the group has only guest speakers and is a member of several umbrella organizations. The groups I cover in this book are independent study clubs that do their own programming or papers and are at least a hundred years old. However, Semper Fidelis, which is not independent, seems to be an impressive group and one I think worthy of note.

The club's archives are held at the Birmingham Public Library, which is where I interviewed Dr. Owens. To quote a story about the group that was published on its hundredth anniversary, "The Semper Fidelis Club counted as members the wife of A. H. Parker, who founded Birmingham's first black high school; Pauline Bray Fletcher, the state's first black nurse and founder of Camp Fletcher; and Mildred Johnson, whose daughter, Alma, went on to marry General Colin Powell."[1] In the club's archives is a photo of club members dressed in hats, gloves, and beautiful dresses. They are clustered around the speaker of the day, Jesse Owens. Other speakers over the years were Booker T. Washington and Thurgood Marshall. In 1980, it was said that 92 percent of Semper Fidelis' members had been teachers at one time.[2] Dr. Owens told me that she sees the club's ranks dwindling, as African American women are able to climb ladders previously denied them and, therefore, find themselves with less time to devote to club life. The number of members is limited to twenty-six,[3] and there are just fourteen active members today.

Dr. Owens, who holds both a PhD and a JD, is on the advisory board of the Birmingham Museum of Art. She told me that she is a member of a club called the Cottages, which is similar to Semper Fidelis, and she attends those meetings while vacationing in Martha's Vineyard, where she has a second home in the village of Oak Bluffs. She said that Cottages is philanthropic and literary. One must be a homeowner to join.

The Indianapolis Fortnightly Literary Club, Indianapolis, Indiana

This fortnightly club is still active. It was founded in Indianapolis in 1923,[4] making it a bit too young, at the age of ninety-two, for a more detailed look in this book, in which all of the clubs discussed are at least a hundred years old. However, I think it is important to mention this club and two other groups of African-American women that fall just slightly outside the parameters of *Smart Women* by virtue of the clubs' civic involvement (rather than being strictly study clubs) or comparative youth.

In forming these types of clubs, friends asked friends to join them. This way, women from the same background, same church, etc., banded together, making the clubs all-white or all-black in the days when people of different races did not mix easily.

Members of the Indianapolis Fortnightly Literary Club are said to have been "teachers, librarians, social workers, and businesswomen."[5] Today, the members "review books and discuss timely topics" when they meet during the school year.[6] The club's archives are held at the Indiana Historical Society. Confusingly, there is also a large group, also in Indianapolis, called the Fortnightly Literary Club, which is listed in chapter 7. That club was founded in 1885. It was all-white when founded, although I was told that this fortnightly and the Woman's Club – another Indianapolis Club detailed in chapter 7 - have since made an attempt to integrate and bring diversity to their groups.

Utopian Literary Club, Atlanta, Georgia

Founded in 1916, the Utopian Literary Club is a bit too new to be given a longer look in this book, but I felt it was worth a mention since it is another example of an African-American literary or study group very similar to those I cover in these pages. I have no contact at Utopian, but the Emory University Library's website says that the library holds part of the Utopian archives and that these are dated up to 2003.[7] Here is a direct quote from the Emory Library's web site:

> The Utopian Literary Club was founded in 1916 by a group of African American women in Atlanta, Georgia. Meeting for the simple purpose of "The mental advancement of its members," the Utopian Literary Club is primarily a social club that assembles regularly to discuss literature, listen to lectures and music, and debate current events. The organization also hosts an annual Christmas party and "Party for Friends," a social event opened to non-club members.[8]

There is also a very large Utopian archive at the Auburn Avenue Research Library on African-American Culture and History. In May 1996, some club records dating from 1919 to 1996 were officially donated to the library as a part of the library's inaugural Annie L. McPheeters Lecture Series. Mrs. McPheeters, the first African-American professional librarian in the Atlanta-Fulton Public Library System, was a lifelong member of the Utopian Literary Club.[9]

It seems highly likely, given that papers in one of the club's archives are dated as recently as 2003, that this group is still active.

The Detroit Study Club, Detroit, Michigan

This group of socially prominent activist African American women was founded in 1898 as a Browning club but soon widened its scope to include Shakespeare, as well as other authors, and social issues.[10] As of 2014, members were still meeting and contributing their records to the Detroit Public Library's Burton Historical Collection. Members were also the subject of a 2008 newspaper article about the club's history and continued success, with the headline, "Club's Name

Is Its Goal for 110 Years."[11] Various articles state that the club still limits membership to forty-five and that several generations of one family can be found on the membership rolls, but I have not been able to verify any of this information by way of a personal interview. The group is said to meet monthly now and to be composed largely of professional women.[12] I have not included this strong and vibrant group in the main body of this book because it appears that they are meeting to debate and affect social change as well as discuss literature and history.[13] The Detroit Study Club may also be a member of a larger organization, the Detroit Federation of Women's Clubs and/or the Association of Black Women's Clubs, but I am unable to verify this. On the website of the Detroit African American History Project, the group is described as "a literature and poetry reading group, which later evolves into a leading social reform agency fostering oral and racial up-lift ... the first African-American women's club to join the Detroit Federation of Women's Clubs."[14]

Additional Shakespeare Clubs for Women

What follows is a list of Shakespeare clubs that are all-female, independent of any parent group, *probably* still active, still assigning research papers or original programs to members, and following much the same format—of meeting during the school year for study and socializing—as 90 percent of the historic women's study clubs discussed in this book. I found all but the last of these groups listed on a blog by a coed Shakespeare club in Warren, Pennsylvania. The blog is called *Warren Shakespeare Club: Other Shakespeare Clubs,* and it seems to have appeared online in 2004 or thereabouts, with content supplied by the individual clubs. I have been unable to reach any of these clubs, including the Warren club. I would have liked to ask the Warren club about its research methods and for the names of its contacts. I am assuming, without personal corroboration, that the information is accurate and that these groups are still active today.

The Woodland Shakespeare Club, Woodland, California

This is a club for which I have a second source, aside from the Warren blog, to support my theory that it is still active. I had no contact with anyone in Woodland Shakespeare Club, which is based in the town of Woodland, California (population: fifty-five thousand), near Sacramento. I do have what appears to be a fairly recent entry about the club, probably written by a club member, for the *Warren Shakespeare Club*'s online listing of "Other Shakespeare Clubs," and I have an even more recent (May 16, 2013) newspaper article about the club's April birthday party for Shakespeare and the group's long history in Yolo County. The photo from that luncheon shows long tables full of women, at least fifty members, if not more.

The club was founded in 1886[15] and has studied Shakespeare's plays for most of its 129 years.[16] However, the latest newspaper story says that the club is now branching out from the study of Shakespeare and would be studying California's history and the idea of "California Dreamin'"—what it means to be a Californian—in 2014.[17] Books to be discussed included Jack London's *The Valley of the Moon,* Frederick Kohner's *Gidget,* and John Muir's *My First Summer in the Sierras.*[18]

The group's entry in the *Warren Shakespeare Club* blog says that the club has fifty active members, twenty inactive members, and seven meetings per year.[19]

Regular meetings feature a simple tea break at intermission, between program and discussion groups, but more substantial fare is offered at the January tea – a guest day - and at the Shakespeare birthday luncheon in April, where members bring potluck dishes and a birthday cake for the Bard. The cake is traditionally cut by a person whom the president chooses to honor.[20]

The group claims to have members of a wide range of ages[21] and members who have mothers or grandmothers in the group.[22] Furthermore, members say that not only does the club have a full waiting list, but it also has a waiting list *for* the waiting list.[23]

* * *

The following are the all-women Shakespeare study clubs for which I have only an entry in the Warren Shakespeare Club blog or another publication as proof of their existence. This is not particularly sound journalism, but it is likely that these clubs are still active and going about their club business in precisely the same way as the other groups in this book. Unfortunately, the Warren Shakespeare Club did not respond to my requests for more information and personal contacts.

The Greenville Shakespeare Club, Greenville, Illinois

This club was founded in 1888; had twenty members when a club representative responded to the Warren club's blog request; meets eighteen times per season on alternate Fridays at 2:00 p.m.; and still requires its members to present original papers.[24]

The Shakespeare Study Club of McMinnville, Oregon

Founded in 1902, this club had twenty-six members when the Warren Shakespeare Club posted its blog on "Other Shakespeare Clubs", probably in 2004. In that year, this club had six meetings a year, meeting once a month from October to April, with topics for papers leaning toward the theater and the arts—apparently not always strictly Shakespearean subjects. However, when roll is called, members must respond with a quotation from Shakespeare—a tradition that I heard about in many of the clubs I studied. A description of the club says that members still don gloves and hats when attending the April luncheon.[25]

Grove City, Pennsylvania, Shakespeare Club

Although I had no personal connection within this group, which was founded in 1884, it does appear to remain active, according to Kathleen Scheil, who uses the group as a reference point in her new book, *She Hath Been Reading: Women and Shakespeare Clubs in America,* which was published after I'd finished the first draft of my manuscript. When she was researching her book, Ms. Scheil was in touch with the daughter of a current member.[26] Several mentions of the club in recent obituaries I found online point to its being alive and well as an independent literary society, still doing original papers or programs.

Other Clubs

Following are the women's groups for which I have only an online listing of their archives, or a newspaper article, or a suggestion by a nonmember or former member that they are probably still active.

Clover Club of Beaufort, South Carolina, was founded in 1891 by Mary Elizabeth Waterhouse.[27] After the town's library books were carted away by the Union Army and then were burned in a Smithsonian fire before they could be returned, thirty members of the Clover Club founded a circulating library in 1902 and raised money for a permanent library. When the building was completed seven years later, Clover Club members donated their two thousand books to the new library.[28] According to the article, which was my primary source for this information, the club's "members are still active supporters of the county library."[29] I learned about this historic club from a former member of Clover Club who is also a longtime member of the Syracuse Portfolio Club, Mary Ten Eyck.

Peripatetics Club, Minneapolis, Minnesota, was founded on March 12, 1890. The club's archives show that members met—and probably still meet—every other week on Mondays, with members taking turns delivering papers on topics chosen for the year.[30] Mrs. A. E. Wells was the club's founding president.[31] The archives contain an elaborate set of programs from the club and a report on the club's history that was presented by members during the club's centennial year, 1989–90.[32] I was referred to this group by a member's sister in another city, but I never got a response to my e-mails to the Peripatetic member. The records of the group, up to 1997, are held by the Minnesota Historical Society's Manuscript Collection, and even more of their records are held by the Hennepin County Library, up to the year 2000. I cannot be certain that the group is still active. In this case, I have only a mention of this group by a family member, who alerted me to its continuing existence.

Pine Hills Fortnightly Club, Pine Hills, New York, was founded in 1898 and had an average membership of twenty members in the years leading up to 2003, the last year of the club's archival records in the M. E. Grenander Department of Special Collections and Archives, University Libraries, State University of New York at Albany. In 2003, the focus of the club's meetings was the presentation of papers researched and written by members on a wide range of topics, decided by a program committee.[33]

The Fortnightly, Jamestown, NY was founded in 1894 and was still active in 2011.[34]

The Fortnightly Club, Rockville Centre, New York, was founded in 1898 and was still active in 2011.[35]

The Fortnightly Club, Honeoye Falls, New York, was founded in 1895 and was still active in 2011.[36]

The Fortnightly Club, Stillwater, New York, was founded in 1898 and was still active in 2011.[37]

The Fortnightly Club, Columbia, Missouri, was founded in 1892 for wives of faculty at the University of Missouri. Today, the club has four hundred members, all of whom must hold or be retired from a university position, or have a husband who is still employed at such a university job or retired from one. The club offers a wide variety of small interest groups, or study groups.[38] They do not have a clubhouse and are independent of a larger organization, so they fit squarely into this book, although the overall group is huge. It's more like a collection of small study clubs. Their archives are held at the State Historical Society of Missouri.[39] I was able to access their winter 2012 newsletter online. With four hundred members in 2012, the group, I would assume, is still active.

The Fortnightly Club, Pullman, Washington, was founded in 1893 and was still active in 2013, when its members were listed as giving a donation to the Neill Public Library in Pullman.[40] A summary of the club's archives at the Washington State University Libraries in Pullman reports that the club meets from September to April and that members still present papers on works of "poetry, drama, and fiction."[41]

A Cluster of Four (Almost Five) Historic, Hundred-Year-Old, All-Women Study Clubs in Waco, Texas

After completing my work on this book, or so I thought, I stumbled on a blog with a news article about four—very nearly five—historic all-women literary societies in Waco, Texas, which I assume are still meeting today, as the article is dated November 2009. I am also assuming that these clubs are independent of any larger affiliation and, therefore, are appropriate for this book. The blog *Waco Today* is affiliated with the *Waco Tribune* newspaper. The possible fifth literary society mentioned in the article, the Thursday Study Club, was founded in 1920, so it is not old enough for this book, but the others were founded in 1891 (Waco Literary Club), 1892 (the Woman's Club of Waco), 1899 (Current Event Club), and perhaps 1900 (the Contemporary Current Event Club). All five groups are said to have about thirty members who must research, write, and deliver original papers, these days using Internet research and PowerPoint presentations. Social events are said to be integral to all of these clubs. The now-retired journalist who wrote the piece, whom I was unable to reach despite several efforts, wrote that "the tea table is still a sensory highlight of each meeting, but it is often brought to a more contemporary level of food and drink."[42] These four/five historic groups make a remarkable cluster. I'm hoping to hear from a member of one of these groups after this book is published, as I would like to find out more about the clubs. Any additions and corrections can go into a second edition of *Smart Women*.

* * *

What Has Happened to Two of the Earliest Clubs?

Sorosis, New York City

Sorosis was founded in 1868 in New York City by journalist Jane Cunningham Croly, after she was refused admittance to a press dinner for Charles Dickens. This group is always cited as the mother of all literary societies and the mother of many of the women's clubs formed during the women's club movement. Brian Coburn, manager of the Women's History and Resource Center of the General Federation of Women's Clubs, told me in a telephone interview in July 2013 that a representative of the General Federation, which Sorosis helped to found and of which it is still a member, had recently attended the celebration of Sorosis' 145th anniversary. Because of this, I knew that this group was alive and well. Brian Coburn then gave me a contact in Sorosis, which led me eventually to the current president, Margarita Bloch. She replied to my questions, saying that Sorosis is a 501(c)(4) social welfare organization with membership under a hundred. The club does have guest speakers, and the members do no original research.[43] Combined with the fact that Sorosis is still a part of the General Federation of Women's Clubs, a parent organization, it is clear that it is not part of my target for this book. But because of Sorosis' historical significance to the women's club movement, as the mother of all study clubs, I hated to leave them out. Also, I was just plain curious about what had happened to them. Their archives up to 1972 are held in the Sophia Smith Collection, Smith College.

The New England Women's Club, Boston, Massachusetts

Julia Ward Howe, who founded Saturday Morning Club, was also one of the founders of the New England Women's Club, in 1868, just after the founding of Sorosis, the first club in the women's club movement. Today, the New England Women's Club has disbanded, but the remaining members recently used the club's endowment to fund a Bostonian Society scholarship in their disbanded club's name.[44]

EPILOGUE

Still Learning Together After All These Years

As I finish my work on this book, I remain amazed by the fact that so many historic all-women study clubs that are at least a hundred years old have survived and often thrived in America today, when many demands are put on a woman's time and when many special interest groups and activities vie for women's attention and participation. Equally surprising is the fact that once women were allowed to apply to virtually every college and university in the country, they were still interested in self-education within this kind of structured group, long after their academic careers were finished.

I believe that I've taken the measure of the strong and intelligent women in these groups, and I feel certain that a good number of their historic study clubs will long survive, perhaps for another 100 years or more. Some that were faltering when I interviewed one or more of their members will almost certainly die, as they have been unable to keep up with the need for new, younger members as their current membership ages.

The groups that will survive will almost certainly include those that are located in college towns, where learning and tradition are sacred, and in towns where membership in such clubs carries a certain social cachet.

The study clubs of the future will probably remain the provenance of women between the ages of fifty and ninety, with a few notable exceptions. The clubs' bylaws, constitutions, traditions, and meetings will remain surprisingly similar, despite the fact that there is no connection between clubs and, until this book was published, virtually no knowledge of one club by any of the others. I suspect that these highly private groups, which one must be asked to join, will continue to be private and will continue to be independent of any larger organization, although most were members of a local, state, or national federation of women's clubs in their earliest days.

Family legacies will continue to the limited extent that they now occur, with some groups emphasizing outreach to family members more than others.

For most – but not all - groups, subject matter to be studied will remain less challenging than it was in the clubs' earlier days, and club schedules will often consist of once-a-month meetings during the club year, not the once-a-week schedule that many of these groups originally kept. But members will still be required to present a paper or original program on a rotating basis and also share the duties of hostessing and club leadership on a rotating basis.

The history of the all-women literary societies, study clubs, Shakespeare clubs, and fortnightlies shows the earliest members doing civic good deeds, finding the strength to organize for the first time in order to implement the building of the town's first library or to help found the first kindergarten. And then history shows the movement of some members into groups fighting for women's right to vote or for Prohibition. Today's book clubs are also a direct outgrowth of these early groups.

Despite ridicule and trivialization by outsiders and members' husbands alike, the groups have survived, against all odds, as small, private, independent clubs. The women in the groups work quietly inside a social framework, which is the essence of civilization. They do not look for publicity, and they no longer work as a group toward civic goals as their founding mothers once did. They meet to study, learn, and socialize. The members are strong, smart, and efficient, and most are veterans of a wide range of community jobs and boards.

While learning, socializing, and creating human bonds together, members of these clubs seem to add years to their lives—useful years of learning and friendship. I found many women in their nineties still participating, not the least of these being the woman whom I believe to be the longest-active member in any of today's clubs, Gratia Coultas of Jacksonville, Illinois, who was born in 1921 and who joined the Monday Conversation Club in 1946. She is still delivering her original papers at club meetings for forty-five minutes without the aid of notes.

In short, I feel that these groups are the essence of civilization and a part of the framework of a healthy lifestyle in a rather uncivilized and dumbed-down world. *Smart Women* is dedicated to the wonderful women of these groups, with the hope that this book helps them understand the miracle of their groups' survival and the glorious role they have played in our country's history. I'd like them to see that they are not alone and that their clubs are all facing the same problems, all moving forward into the twenty-first century while using an infallible road map from the nineteenth century.

Author's note: I invite any additional all-women literary societies, which are at least 100 years old, independent of a larger organization, without a clubhouse, and still having members deliver original programs or papers, to contact me through my author's web site. I hope to add your group to a future edition of *Smart Women.*

COMPLETE LIST OF HISTORIC, ALL-WOMEN STUDY CLUBS FOUND WHILE RESEARCHING "SMART WOMEN"

To have been covered in detail in this book, clubs must be at least 100 years old, must be independent of any other group, must require members to take turns delivering original papers or programs, and – most important – must be all-women. Furthermore, these groups should not own a clubhouse and should not be a civic action club or an all-purpose "woman's club."

Alabama

Cadmean Circle, Birmingham
Cosmos Club, Birmingham
The Highland Book Club, Birmingham (now a speakers' series)
New Era, Birmingham (not 100 years old)
Nineteenth Century Club, Birmingham
Semper Fidelis Club, Birmingham (a civic organization)

Arkansas

Aesthetic Club, Little Rock
The Edelweiss, Little Rock

California

F.R.F.G. Study Club, Gilroy
Friday Shakespeare Club, Santa Cruz
Woodland Shakespeare, Woodland

Colorado

Boulder Fortnightly, Boulder
Denver Fortnightly, Denver
Denver Monday Literary Club, Denver
Golden Fortnightly, Golden

Georgia

Utopian Literary Club, Atlanta (not 100 years old)

Illinois

Anti-Rust, Springfield
Charleston Reading Circle, Charleston
College Hill Club, Jacksonville
Greenville Shakespeare Club, Greenville
Household Science, Jacksonville
Monday Conversation Club, Jacksonville
Sorosis, Jacksonville
Sunnyside Literary Circle, Springfield
The History Class, Jacksonville
The History Club, Bloomington
The Wednesday Class, Jacksonville
The Woman's Reading Club, Mattoon

Indiana

Fortnightly Literary Club, Indianapolis
Indianapolis Fortnightly Literary Club (too new to be covered in
    detail in this book, having been founded in 1923)
Indianapolis Woman's Club, Indianapolis

Progress Club, Elkhart
Riverside Club, Elkhart
Thursday Club, Elkhart

Kansas

Friends in Council, Lawrence
Junior Reading Circle, Newton
Kanwaka Literary Club, Lawrence
Ladies Reading Circle, Newton
Ladies Reading Circle, Olathe
Sorosis, Newton

Louisiana

Philistoria Study Club, Baton Rouge
Quarante Club, New Orleans
Ruth McEnery Stuart Clan, New Orleans
The Study Club, Baton Rouge

Maine

The Monday Club, Camden

Massachusetts

New England Women's Club, Boston (recently disbanded)
Saturday Morning Club, Boston

Michigan

Detroit Study Club, Detroit (said to be more of a social reform club)

Minnesota

Peripatetics Club, Minneapolis

Missouri

The Fortnightly Club, Columbia

New York

Alpha Study Club, Ogdensburg (not verified)
Causeries du Lundi, New York City
Fortnightly of Auburn, Auburn
Fredonia Shakespeare Club, Fredonia
Hamilton Fortnightly, Hamilton
Leisure Hour Club, Skaneateles
Leisure Hour Literary Club, Union Springs
Monday Evening Club, Manlius
Monday Evening Club, Skaneateles
Nondescript Club, Bronxville
Oneida's two historic clubs (names unknown at this point)
Outlook Club, Sandy Creek (not verified)
Philomath, Fayetteville
Pine Hills Fortnightly Club, Pine Hills
Portfolio Club, Syracuse
Roundabout Club, Auburn
Social Art Club, Syracuse
Sorosis, New York City (mother of all literary clubs for women but now 501C4 social welfare organization)
The Coterie, Fayetteville
The Fortnightly, Jamestown
The Fortnightly Club, Honeoye Falls
The Fortnightly Club, Rockville Centre
The Fortnightly Club, Stillwater
The Ramblers, East Hampton
Thursday Club, Aurora
Wednesday Morning Club, Utica (not verified)

North Carolina

Canterbury Club, Durham
Halcyon Club, Durham

The Tourist Club, Durham
Up-To-Date Club, Durham

Ohio

Monday Club, Wooster
Thursday Club, Wooster
Travelers Club, Wooster

Oregon

Fortnightly Club of Eugene, Eugene
Monday Book Club of Eugene, Eugene
The Shakespeare Club of Eugene, Eugene
The Shakespeare Study Club, McMinnville

Pennsylvania

Grove City Shakespeare Club

South Carolina

Clover Club, Beaufort

Texas

Contemporary Current Event Club, Waco
Current Event Club, Waco
Dallas Shakespeare Club, Dallas
The Pierian Club, Dallas
The Standard Club, Dallas
The Thursday Study Club, Waco (not 100 years old)
The Woman's Club of Waco, Waco
Waco Literary Club, Waco

Washington

The Fortnightly Club, Pullman

About the Author

Ann Dodds Costello earned a BA in English at Duke University, and twenty-eight years later, she earned a master's degree at Columbia University's Graduate School of Journalism. She has worked in the fields of magazine and book publishing, among other careers, and has contributed feature articles to newspapers as a freelance journalist. Her first book, *Bookmarks,* is available from Blurb.com. Ms. Costello grew up in Dallas, Texas, and then lived for many years in the New York City area. She and her husband now live in Los Angeles and Maine. She is fascinated by lifelong learning and is a member of three book groups.

Notes

Introduction: A Hidden World

1 "Club movement," *Encyclopædia Britannica*, www.britanica.com/ EBchecked/topic/122525/club-movement.

2 Evangeline Holland, "Lifting As We Climb: The Women's Club Movement," *Edwardian Promenade,* last modified February 1, 2010, accessed May 4, 2015, http://edwardian promenade.com/ African-american/lifting-as-we-climb/.

3 "Women's club, United States," *Wikipedia*, http://en.wikipedia.org/wiki/ Women's_club.

4 Ibid.

5 "Club movement," http://www.nwhm.org/online-exhibits/progressiveera/ africanamericanreform.html.

6 George Eliot (Mary Anne Evans), *Middlemarch* (Oxford: Oxford University Press, 1998 and 2008), 785.

7 "Literary society," *Wikipedia*, http://en.wikipedia.org/wiki/ Literary_society.

8 Dr. Karen Blair, "The History of Women's Clubs" (paper presented at the Washington State History Museum, Tacoma, Washington, March 29, 2007).

9 Ibid.

Chapter 1: Birmingham, Alabama

1 Dr. Wayne Flynt, interview by Ann Costello, October 21, 2011.

2 Ibid.

3 Oral History, "Sue Bigler [member of Highland Study Club from 1907 to 2003] interview with Dr. Wayne Flynt," March 1990.

4 "Birmingham, Alabama," *Wikipedia*, http://en.wikipedia.org/wiki/ Birmingham,_Alabama.

5   "Vulcan statue," *Wikipedia,* http://en.wikipedia.org/wiki/Vulcan_statue.

6   "Club Women Organize," *Birmingham News,* December 19, 1971, C-90.

7   Ibid.

8   Cadmean Circle Yearbook, 2010–11, 12.

9   Margaret Livingston, "A Cadmean Memoir" (paper delivered to Cadmean Club, November, 2004), 1.

10 Cadmean Circle Yearbook, 1987–88, 5.

11 Ibid., title page, 6, 7.

12 Cadmean Circle Yearbook, 1895 and 2010–11.

13 Cadmean Circle archives.

14 Tim L. Pennycuff, "Hillman Hospital," *Encyclopedia of Alabama,* last modified October 31, 2012, encyclopediaofalabama.org /article/h-1592.

15 "Virginia Foster Durr," *Wikipedia,* http://en.wikipedia.org/wiki/ Virginia_Foster_Durr.

16 Ibid.

17 "Moving Up through New South Society," Oral History interview with Virginia Foster Durr, March 13, 14, 15, 1975, G-0023-1, Southern Oral History Program Collection (#4007), Oral Histories of the American South, http://docsouth.unc.edu/sohp/G-0023-1/excerpts/ excerpt_2968.html.

18 Leah Rawls Atkins, *Nineteenth Century Club: Celebrating 100 Years of "Mutual Mental Improvement" (1895–1995), Birmingham, Alabama* (Birmingham: The Nineteenth Century Club, 1995), 9.

19 Ibid., 21

20 Ibid., 22.

21 Ibid.

22 Ibid.

23 Helen London, "The Young Bluestocking"(paper presented to the Nineteenth Century Club, October 5, 1994), Nineteenth Century Club Archives, Birmingham Public Library.

24 Atkins, 31.

25 "Constitution and Bylaws," Cadmean Circle Yearbook, 2010–11.

26 "Club Women Organize," *Birmingham News,* December 19, 1971, C-90.

27 Carey Hinds, e-mail message to author, May 7, 2013.

28 Cadmean Circle Yearbook, 2013–14, 5.

29 Hinds, May 7, 2013.

30 "History," Cadmean Circle Yearbook, 2010–11, 18.

31 Quarante Club member Carolyn Kolb, email message to author, May 7, 2013.

32 "Cadmean Circle: Club women organize," *Birmingham News,* Dec. 19, 1971.

33 Ibid.

34 "Constitution and Bylaws," Cadmean Circle Yearbook, 2010–11, 19.

35 Lucie Bynum, e-mail message to author, May 7, 2013.

36 Cadmean Circle Yearbook, 2010–11, 22–25.

37 "Club Women Organize."

38 Cadmean Circle Yearbook, 2010-11., 4–17.

39 Bynum, May 7, 2013.

40 Ibid., 20.

41 "Constitution and Bylaws," Cadmean Circle Yearbook.

42 Ibid.

43 Cadmean Circle Yearbook, 2010–11, constitution, article XII, 20.

44 Margaret Livingston, interview by Ann Costello, February 22, 2011.

45 "Club Women Organize."

46 Livingston interview.

47 Carey Hinds, e-mail message to author, May 7, 2013; and information originally found in a member's centennial-year paper and in the University of Alabama at Birmingham archives.

48 Bynum, May 7, 2013.

49 Lucie Bynum, e-mail message to author, January 14, 2013.

50 Ibid.

51 Livingston interview.

52 Bynum, May 7, 2013.

53 Ibid.

54 Cadmean Yearbook.

55 Ibid.

56 "The Cadmean Circle 1888: A Look at Its Founding and Founders," Cadmean Circle archives, n.p.

57 Ibid.

58 Ibid.

59 Livingston interview.

60 Ibid.

61 Cosmos Club roster, 2011–12.

62 Ibid.

63 Lillian Naumann, ed., "Cosmos Club 1908–2008, Memories of a Hundred Years," including an original club history by Mrs. S. L. Morrow, former club historian, 3.

64 Ibid.

65 Roster.

66 Ibid.

67 Results of author's attending Cosmos Club luncheon and meeting in March 2012.

68 Roster.

69 "Ensley (Birmingham)," *Wikipedia,* http://en.wikipedia.org/wiki/ Ensley_(Birmingham).

70 Cosmos Club history, 15.

71 "Arlington Antebellum Home & Gardens," *Wikipedia,* http://en.wikipedia. org/wiki/Arlington_Antebellum_Home_%26_Gardens.

72 Cosmos Club history, 15.

73 Karen Blatter, e-mail message to author, January 18, 2012.

74 Roster, bylaws, 13.

75 Karen Blatter, e-mail message to author, July 16, 2012.

76 Roster, 3.

77 "Objectives," Roster, 6.

78 Karen Blatter, e-mail messages to author, 2012.

79 Blatter, January 18, 2012.

80 Ibid.

81 "Devoted Life: Creek Indians to Honor City Woman for Aid," *Birmingham News,* October 12, 1980.

82 Cosmos Club history, 3.

83 Interviews and observational results from meeting attended by the author, March 2012.

84 Ibid.

85 Ibid.

86 Ibid.

87 Ibid.

88 Annotated Roster, 2011–12, 7.

89 Lillian Willson Naumann obituary, *Birmingham News,* May 1, 2011.

90 Georgene Gainey obituary, *Birmingham News,* February 2011.

91 Flodia Powell obituary, *Birmingham News,* October 2011.

92 http://www.concentric.net/~pvb/GEN/jwb.html.

93 "Devoted Life."

94 Cosmos Club history, 17.

95 Cosmos Club history, 13.

96 Atkins, 7–12.

97 Elberta Reid, e-mail message to author, March 28, 2013.

98 Nineteenth Century Club roster, 2011–12.

99 Atkins, 22.

100 Anecdotal research; Nineteenth Century Club roster; and Elberta Reid, e-mail message to author, November 21, 2011.

101 Ibid.

102 Ibid.

103 Ibid.

104 Atkins, flyleaf (quotation from 1895 Nineteenth Century Club constitution).

105 Anecdotal research from author's attending a Nineteenth Century Club meeting, March 14, 2012.

106 Archival paper discussed in October 3, 1990, minutes re: Mrs. McGriff's paper on the history of the Nineteenth Century Club.

107 Anecdotal research from author's attending of a Nineteenth Century Club meeting in March 2012.

108 Reid, March 28, 2013.

109 Research, both anecdotal and archival.

110 Jane McGriff, e-mail message to author, April 3, 2013.

111 Ibid.

112 Personal observations, anecdotal information, and research.

113 Ibid.

114 Nineteenth Century Club roster, 2011–12.

115 Ibid.

116 Reid, March 28, 2013.

117 Conversation at tea table after meeting of Nineteenth Century Club, March 14, 2012.

118 Hannah Elliott obituary, *Birmingham News,* October 6, 1956.

119 Ibid.

120 "Sewanee: The University of the South," *Wikipedia,* http://en.wikipedia.org/wiki/Sewanee:_The_University_of_the_South.

121 Ibid.

122 http://about.sewanee.edu/university-history.

123 Atkins, 22.

124 Reid, March 28, 2013.

125 Ibid.

Chapter 2: Dallas, Texas

1   Dallas Shakespeare Club Yearbook, 2011–12, constitution, article V, section 3.

2   Willie Newbury Lewis, "Part 1, 1886–96," in *History of the Dallas Shakespeare Club* (Dallas: Dallas Shakespeare Club, 1986), 5.

3   Dallas Shakespeare Club Yearbook, 2011–12, constitution, article I, section 2.

4   http://thefullcalatrava.wordpress.com/2013/09/20/3-bridges-project-dallas-usa/.

5   Dallas Shakespeare Club Yearbook, 2011–12, constitution, article IV, sections 1–6.

6   Mrs. A. Earl Cullum, Jr.,"The Waning of the Century," in *History of the Dallas Shakespeare Club*, pages not numbered.

7   Lewis, "Part 1," in *History of the Dallas Shakespeare Club*, 4.

8   Ibid.

9   Ibid.

10   Dallas Shakespeare Club Yearbook, 2011–12, constitution, article I, section 2.

11   Joan Jenkins Perez, "Exall, May Dickson," *The Handbook of Texas, Texas State Historical Association*, www.tshaonline.org/handbook/online/articles/fex02.

12   Ibid.

13   Nell DeLoache Davidson, "Part VI, 1954–70," in *History of the Dallas Shakespeare Club*, 60.

14   Dallas Shakespeare Club Yearbook, 2011–12, constitution, article I, section 2.

15   Dallas Shakespeare Club Yearbook, 1942–43, Dallas Shakespeare Club Archives, Dallas Historical Society.

16   Davidson, "Part VI," *History of the Dallas Shakespeare Club*, 59.

17   Mary C. Swain, "1911–25," in *History of the Dallas Shakespeare Club*.

18   Linda Alchin, "Lawrence Fletcher," www.bardstage.org, June, 2015.

19   Swain, *History of the Dallas Shakespeare Club*, 32.

20   Ibid., 33.

21   Ibid., 33–34.

22   Ibid., 34.

23   Dallas Shakespeare Club Yearbook, 2011–12, March 9 of yearly calendar, n.p.

24   Bess Walcott Jones, "1925–39," in *History of the Dallas Shakespeare Club*, 36.

25   Lawson Taitte, "Dallas Actors Return Home for Theater Roles," *The Dallas Morning News*, Sept. 10, 2010, updated Sept. 20, 2010, http://www.dallasnews.com/entertainment/columnists/lawson-taitte/20100919-Dallas-actors-return-home-for-theater-2342.ece.

26   Jerome Weeks, "Review: Henry IV at the Dallas Theater Center," *Art Seek*, Sept. 29,2010, http://artandseek.net/2010/09/29/review-henry-iv-at-the-dallas-theater-center/

27   Jessie Lee Rembert Willis, "Introduction," in *History of the Dallas Shakespeare Club*, ii.

28 "Our Pierian Heritage," in Pierian Club Yearbook, 2011–12; Mrs. Thompson Laird and Mrs. Frank Brimm, "The Pierian Family 1888–1968," Pierian Club Archives, Dallas Historical Society; and Pierian Club Yearbook, 2011–12.

29 "Pierian Spring," *Wikipedia, https://en.wikipedia.org/wiki/Pierian_Spring.*

30 "Our Pierian Heritage," 4.

31 Ibid., 3.

32 http://www.findagrave.com/cgi-bin/fg.cgi?page=gr&GRid=51479180.

33 Laird and Brimm, "The Pierian Family 1888–1968," 2.

34 Ibid.

35 Pierian Club Yearbook, 2011–12, frontispiece.

36 Walt Whitman, "Now Finale to the Shore," *The Walt Whitman Archive, Published Works, Books by Whitman, Songs of Parting,* http://www.whitmanarchive.org/published/LG/figures/ppp.00270.503.jpg.

37 Kate Nkansa, "Time for Africans to Explore Africa," *Feint and Margin,* Oct. 1, 2010, http://feintandmargin.com/time-for-africans-to-explore-africa/.

38 Pierian Club Yearbook 2011–12 (found on *Feint and Margin* website, October 2010), 15.

39 Ledee Sachs, interview by Ann Costello, October 25, 2010.

40 "Dallas Civic Leader Dies In Hospital," *Rootsweb, Obituaries 1931-1935,* http://freepages.history.rootsweb.ancestry.com/~jwheat/obits/obits3135.html.

41 "Part 1," *History of the Dallas Shakespeare Club,* 5.

42 Dallas Shakespeare Club Yearbook, 2011–12, frontispiece.

43 Ibid., constitution, article IV, section 1.

44 Ibid., article IV, sections 3–4.

45 Ibid., article I, section 2.

46 Ibid., article IV, section 2.

47 Ibid., bylaws, 4.

48 "Part II, 1897–1911," in *History of the Dallas Shakespeare Club,* 18.

49 Ibid., 16.

50 Ibid., 19.

51 Michael V. Hazel, "Dallas Women's Clubs: Vehicles for Change," *Heritage News* (Dallas County Heritage Society) (Spring 1986), 18.

52 Ibid., 19.

53 "Customs of the Dallas Shakespeare Club," item 4, Dallas Shakespeare Club Yearbook, 2011–12.

54 Marion Exall, e-mail message to author, August 30, 2012.

55 "Our Pierian Heritage"; and Pierian Club roster, 2011–12, 3.

56 Brimm and Laird, "The Pierian Family," 2.

57 "Constitution of the Pierian Club," 2011–12 roster, 29.

58 Marie Chiles, e-mail message to author, October 9, 2012.

59 "Constitution," Pierian Club of Dallas Yearbook, 2011–12, 29.

60 Chiles, October 9, 2012.

61 Pierian Club roster, 2011–12.

62 Marie Chiles, telephone interview by Ann Costello, October 17, 2011.

63 Ibid.

64 Ledee Sachs interview by Ann Costello, October 25, 2011.

65 Ibid.

66 Marie Chiles, e-mail message to author, October 9, 2012.

67 Pierian Club roster, 2011-12, frontispiece.

68 Pierian Club roster, 2011–12, 1.

69 Chiles, October 9, 2012.

70 Ibid.

71 "Our Pierian Heritage," 3.

72 Pierian Club roster, 2011–12.

73 Chiles, October 9, 2012.

74 "Our Pierian Heritage."

75 Pierian Club roster, 2011–12.

76 Ibid., 17

77 Chiles, October 9, 2012.

78 Pierian Club roster, 3.

79 "Allen House Details & History," *First London Securities, 2013,* www. firstlondon.com/about-us/the-allen-house.

80 Brimm and Laird, "The Pierian Family."

81 Chiles, October 9, 2012.

82 Margot Gill and Jackie McElhaney, "From the Beginning: The Standard Club," first page of "History of Standard Club" section (n.p.).

83 Ibid.

84 Ibid.

85 The Standard Club bylaws, article III: Membership, Standard Club Yearbook, 2011–12, 23–24.

86 The Standard Club Yearbook, 2011–12, membership list, 12–15.

87 Gill and McElhaney, "From the Beginning."

88 The Standard Club Yearbook, 5–11.

89 Ibid., article III: Membership, 23–24.

90 The Standard Club bylaws, article II: Object, 23.

91 Ibid., article VII, section 1, 28.

92 Gill and McElhaney, "Sketches of a Few Interesting Members," in "From the Beginning," n.p.

93 Ibid.

94 Standard Club members, interview by Ann Costello, November 2, 2011.

95 Columbus Marion "Dad" Joiner obituary *Find A Grave*, http://www. findagrave.com/cgi-bin/fg.cgi?page=gr&GRid=5952

96 Gill and McElhaney, "From the Beginning."

97 Author's notes from Standard Club meeting, February 28, 2012.

98 The Standard Club Yearbook, 2011–12, membership list.

99 Gill and McElhaney, "From the Beginning," 10.

Chapter 3: Denver, Boulder, and Golden, Colorado

1 http://www.preservationnation.org/information-center/law-and-policy/legal-resources/preservation-law-101/resources/Viewshed-Protection.pdf.

2 Silvia Pettem, *Separate Lives: The Story of Mary Rippon* (Longmont: Book Lode, 1999), 59.

3 A footnote in Silvia Pettem's *Separate Lives* refers to the article "An Interesting History of the Fortnightly Club," *Boulder Daily Camera,* May 27, 1930.

4 Pettem, *Separate Lives,* 59.

5 Susan Boucher, "History of Boulder Fortnightly" (paper presented at Boulder Fortnightly's Guest Day meeting), April 21, 2011.

6 Kathy Raybin, e-mail message to Nancy Sievers, forwarded to author, April 17, 2013.

7 Peggy Archibald, conversation with author, April 21, 2011.

8 Raybin, April 17, 2013.

9 Kathy Raybin, conversation with author, April 21, 2011.

10 Raybin, April 17, 2013.

11 Ibid.

12 Ibid.

13 Boulder Fortnightly Club Archives, Norlin Library, University of Colorado at Boulder. This taken from the introduction to the archives, and a club history written by a Fortnightly member c. 1981.

14 Raybin, April 17, 2013.

15 "Welcome to Boulder History Museum," *Boulder History Museum,* http://boulderhistory.org/rippon.asp.

16 Rosemary Trigg, "One of Boulder's Cultural Heritages," Box 8–3, Boulder Fortnightly Club Collection, University of Colorado Library.

17 Nancy Sievers, conversation with author, April 21, 2011.

18 Boulder Fortnightly Club Yearbook, 1999–2000, frontispiece.

19 Raybin, April 17, 2013.

20 Boulder Fortnightly Club calendar.

21 Pettem, *Separate Lives,* introduction; and http://www.rootsweb. ancestry.com/~nwa/rippon.html.

22 "Welcome to Boulder History Museum."

23 Ibid.

24 Pettem, *Separate Lives,* 59, 223.

25 Information gathered during the meeting the author attended, April 21, 2011.

26 Raybin, April 17, 2013.

27 Denver Fortnightly Club President Mollie Eaton, e-mail message to author, February 7, 2013.

28 "Brief History of Fortnightly," Denver Fortnightly Club Yearbook, 2011– 12, n.p.

29 Original ledger of club minutes, 1881, Box 1, Denver Fortnightly Club Archives, Denver Public Library (main branch).

30 Eaton, February 7, 2013.

31 Ibid.

32 Ibid.

33 Mollie Eaton, e-mail message to author, February 2, 2013.

34 Eaton, February 7, 2013.

35 Ibid.

36 Denver Fortnightly Club bylaws, revised 2012, 5.

37 Notes on Denver Fortnightly Club by visiting Boulder Fortnightly member Barbara Corsen, October 10, 2010.

38 Denver Fortnightly Club bylaws.

39 From the 2012 Denver Fortnightly Club revised bylaws, as conveyed by Mollie Eaton in an e-mail message to author, February 7, 2013.

40 Eaton, February 7, 2013.

41 "Falkenberg Memorial Paper," Denver Fortnightly Club Archives, Denver Public Library (main branch).

42 Ibid.

43 Mollie Eaton, "Everything's Coming Up Roses" (paper presented at Denver Fortnightly Club meeting, October 16, 2007).

44 Multiple archival mentions, in old dinner programs, etc.

45 Eaton, February 7, 2013.

46 Ibid.

47 "Historical Notes, October 5, 1993," Denver Fortnightly Club Archives, Denver Public Library.

48 Denver Fortnightly Club centennial paper, April 1981, Denver Fortnightly Club Archives, Denver Public Library.

49 Eaton, February 7, 2013.

50 Mollie Eaton, e-mail message to author, June 28, 2012.

51 Ibid.

52 Eaton, February 2, 2013.

53 "Brief History."

54 Ibid.

55 Ibid.

56 Denver Fortnightly Club centennial paper.

57 Notes on Denver Fortnightly Club by visiting Boulder Fortnightly member.

58 Eaton, February 7, 2013.

59 Ibid.

60 Mollie Eaton, e-mail message to author, February 24, 2013.

61 Louisa Ward Arps (1901–1986), obituary, *Rocky Mountain News*, January 13, 1986.

62 Taken from display cards at the 2014 exhibition of Ms. Chain's artworks at the Denver Public Library's main branch, Western History Art Gallery.

63 Ibid.

64 Tom Noel, "Noel: Helen Henderson Chain, a pioneer in Denver's art history," *The Denver Post,* June 21, 2014, http://www.denverpost.com/opinion/ci_26002859/helen-henderson-chain-pioneer-denvers-art-history.

65 Ibid. All information in this paragraph about Helen Henderson Chain, except for the one quotation from the *Denver Post,* was taken from display cards from the Denver Public Library's exhibition of the artist's work in 2014.

66 Eaton, February 24, 2013.

67 Gretchen Bering, e-mail message to author via Mollie Eaton, February 26, 2013.

68 "Penny Chenery," *Wikipedia,* http://en.wikipedia.org/wiki/Penny_Chenery.

69 Eaton, February 24, 2013.

70 Monday Literary Club members, "A History of Monday Literary Club, 1881–93," 1893.

71 Helen Christy, assembler, written answers to "Snapshot Summary" questions, October 27, 2012.

72 Ibid.

73 Ibid.

74 Ibid.

75 Ibid.

76 Ibid.

77 Ibid.

78 Ibid.
79 Ibid.
80 Ibid.
81 Ibid.
82 "Index to Politicians," *Political Graveyard,* Politicalgraveyard.com/archibold-armstead.
83 "The Rescue of Denver's Mayan Theater," *Catch Carri*, http://catchcarri.com/mayan-theatre-history-denver/
84 Helen Christy, interview by Ann Costello, March 18, 2012.
85 Christy interview.
86 Christy, written answers.
87 "Martha Hughes Canon," *Utah History to Go,* http://historytogo.utah.gov/people/marthahughescannon.html.
88 "Helen Ring Robnishon: Colorado Senator and Suffragist (Timberline Books), *Amazon,* http://www.amazon.com/Helen-Ring-Robinson-Suffragist-Timberline/dp/1607321467.
89 Christy, written answers.
90 Christy interview.
91 Ibid.
92 Ibid.
93 Ibid.
94 www.Inloveandwarbook.com; www.familytree.genpro.com; "Familia Hepp"; and interview with Helen Christy, March 18, 2012.
95 Christy interview.
96 Carol V. Dickinson, address given at a luncheon to celebrate the centennial of Golden Fortnightly, October 14, 1986, Golden Fortnightly Archives, History Colorado, Denver.
97 "Bylaws," Yearbook of Golden Fortnightly Club, 2011–12, 14.
98 Ibid., 15.
99 Ibid., frontispiece.
100 Notes by author while attending March 21, 2012 meeting. Additional information from Frani Bickart, e-mail message to author, September 25, 2012.
101 Dickinson, address.
102 "Program Committee," Golden Fortnightly Yearbook, 20.
103 Dickinson, address.
104 Ibid.
105 "Bylaws," Golden Fortnightly Club roster, 2011–12, 14.
106 Dickinson, address.

107 "Thomas Babington Macaulay, 1st Baron Macaulay," *Wikipedia,* http://en.wikipedia.org/wiki/Thomas_Babington_ Macaulay,_1st_Baron_Macaulay.

108 Dickinson address; and newspaper (name unknown) clipping, c. 1896, Golden Fortnightly Archives, History Colorado, Denver.

109 "Bylaws," Golden Fortnightly.

110 Golden Fortnightly President Frani Bickart, e-mail message to author, September 16, 2012.

111 Ibid.

112 Ibid.

113 Ibid.

114 Ibid.

115 Donald Dickinson obituary, http://obits.dignitymemorial.com/dignity-memorial/obituary.aspx?n=Donald-Dickinson&lc=2156&pid=1627821 98&mid=5406728.

116 Golden Fortnightly, minutes, September 23, 1930, Golden Fortnightly Archives, History Colorado, Denver.

117 Frani Bickart, e-mail message to author, September 25, 2012.

118 Golden Fortnightly, roster, 2011–12.

119 Frani Bickart, e-mail message to author, September 24, 2012.

120 Ibid.

121 Golden Fortnightly, roster.

122 Several members of Golden Fortnightly, conversation with author, March 21, 2012.

Chapter 4: Eugene, Oregon

1   "History," Fortnightly Club of Eugene Yearbook, 2011–12, 4.

2   "Customs and Traditions," constitution and bylaws, Fortnightly Club of Eugene Yearbook, May 2011, 6.

3   "Customs and Traditions."

4   "Program," Fortnightly Club of Eugene Yearbook, 10–11.

5   Ibid.

6   Nancy Kibbey, e-mail message to author, September 19, 2012.

7   Ibid.

8   Fortnightly Club of Eugene Yearbook.

9   Ibid.

10 Fortnightly Club of Eugene, constitution and bylaws, 7.

11 Nancy E. Kibbey, *The History of the Fortnightly Club of Eugene* (Eugene: History Fortnightly Club of Eugene: 2010), 7.

12 Kibbey, September 19, 2012.

13 Ibid.

14 "Pledge," Fortnightly Club of Eugene Yearbook, 3.

15 Fortnightly Club of Eugene, constitution and bylaws, 18.

16 Kibbey, September 19, 2012.

17 Ibid., 17.

18 Irene Williams, handwritten history, delivered on December 13, 1928, Fortnightly Club of Eugene Archives, Knight Library, University of Oregon.

19 "A Rich History," Eugene Public Library Foundation, eplfoundtion.org/history.

20 Williams, handwritten history.

21 "George W. Lilly" (husband of Adelaide), *Wikipedia,* http://en.wikipedia.org/wiki/George_W._Lilley.

22 "A Rich History," Eugene Public Library Foundation, http://eplfoundation.org/about/history/.

23 Fortnightly Club of Eugene, constitution and bylaws, 18.

24 Ibid.

25 Ibid.

26 Ibid., 16.

27 Ibid., 17–18.

28 Ibid., 17.

29 Nancy Kibbey, conversation with author, April 5, 2012.

30 Notes from author's visit with Boulder Fortnightly member Barbara Corson, January 28, 2011.

31 Elma Havemann, welcome speech to new members, 1926–27, Boulder Fortnightly Archives, Knight Library, University of Oregon.

32 Kibbey, *The History of the Fortnightly Club of Eugene,* 5.

33 Havemann, welcome speech.

34 Kibbey, *The History of the Fortnightly Club of Eugene,* 5.

35 Kibbey, September 19, 2012.

36 Jan, "Idaho J. Cogswell Campbell," http://www.findagrave.com/cgi-bin/fg.cgi?page=gr&GRid=29810727, last modified Sept. 18, 2008, accessed May 30, 2012.

37 Kibbey, September 19, 2012.

38 Monday Book Club of Eugene, summary of minutes, 1911–20.

39 Ibid.

40 Monday Book Club of Eugene constitution, article III: Membership, 1.

41 Monday Book Club of Eugene, constitution.

42 Monday Book Club of Eugene, bylaws, article II: Purpose, 1.

43 Monday Book Club of Eugene, constitution, article II.

44 Monday Book Club of Eugene, summary of minutes, 1970s, club archives.

45 Barbara Lienallen, Mondy Book Club of Eugene history, club archives.

46 Anne Carter, e-mail message to author, received January 7, 2013.

47 Overview of Monday Book Club of Eugene minutes, 1980s, club archives.

48 Carter, January 7, 2013.

49 Ibid.

50 Ibid.

51 Ibid.

52 Marian Wilson obituary, *Salt Lake Tribune,* May 4, 2011.

53 Sue Mallott, "Memories of Marian Wilson," Monday Book Club of Eugene archives.

54 Marian Wilson obituary.

55 Monday Book Club of Eugene, summary of minutes, October, 1959–May, 1969, Monday Book Club of Eugene archives.

56 Eugene Shakespeare Club, constitution and bylaws, 2004.

57 Ledger dated May 13, 1912–April 20, 1914, Eugene Shakespeare Club Archives, Knight Library, University of Oregon.

58 Rosemarie Ostler, Eugene Shakespeare Club historical sketch, Oregon Collection, Knight Library, University of Oregon, May 2005, 2.

59 Ostler, historical sketch, 1.

60 Eugene newspaper (unknown name) article (unknown title), April 25, 1909.

61 Letter from Mabelle Gilstrap to an unknown party, probably written in 1929, Eugene Shakespeare Club archives.

62 Letter from Mrs. Hammond to an unknown party, sent to the archives of Eugene Shakespeare Club by Mrs. M. B. Potts, November 28, 1927.

63 Ibid.

64 Emme R. Knapp, "A History of the Eugene Shakespeare Club," 1957.

65 Eugene Shakespeare Club, constitution and bylaws.

66 Eugene Shakespeare Club, membership list, 2011–12

67 Eugene Shakespeare Club, calendar, 2011–12.

68 Historical sketch, 1.

69 Esther Enford, e-mail message to author, March 10, 2013.

70 Constitution and bylaws, 2.

71 Constitution and bylaws, preamble.

72 Dina Wills, e-mail message to author, March 10, 2013.

73 Ibid.

74 Lydia Lord, e-mail message to author, March 8, 2013.

75 Enford, March 10, 2013.

76   Ibid.

77   Newspaper (name unknown) account of *Twelfth Night,* December 28, 1931.

78   Historical sketch, 1.

79   Wills, March 10, 2013.

80   "Val R. Lorwin," *Wikipedia,* last modified June 1, 2015, accessed June 16, 2015, http://en.wikipedia.org/wiki/Val_R._Lorwin.

81   Ibid.

82   "The Valley News," Eugene Shakespeare Club archives, November 30, 1976.

83   Ancestry.com message board, *Search the Boards – Madge Lorwin,* http://boards.ancestry.com/surnames.grassman/13.1/mb.ashx.

84   Amazon.com, "Dining with William Shakespeare" by Madge Lorwin, http://www.amazon.com/Dining-William-Shakespeare-Madge-Lorwin/dp/0689107315/ref=sr_1_1?ie=UTF8&qid=1434472952&sr=8-1&keywords=dining+with+william+shakespeare%2C+Madge+Lorwin

85   "The Valley News."

86   Newsletter, Center for the Study of Women in Society, 2010, http://csws.uoregon.edu/?p=5841.

87   Lord, March 8, 2013.

Chapter 5: Northern California

1   "California State Route 17," *Wikipedia*, http://en.wikipedia.org/wiki/California_State_Route_17.

2   Official club history, 2003.

3   Ibid.

4   *Pioneers of Santa Clara County 2011 Essay Contest Winners,* Honorable Mention: Elizabeth Barratt, http://www.californiapioneers.com/essay_contests/june_2011/Elizabeth%20Barratt/FRFG%20Essay-modified.pdf.

5   Ibid.

6   Ibid.

7   The Friday Shakespeare Club, bylaws, roster, 2010–11.

8   The Friday Shakespeare Club, roster, 2010–11.

9   Friday Shakespeare Club, bylaws.

10   Barbara Lewis, e-mail message to author, March 26, 2013.

11   Bylaws.

12   Bylaws.

13   Lewis, March 26, 2013.

14 Official club history.

15 Ibid.

16 Gail Olson, e-mail message to author, March 27, 2013.

17 Gail Olson, e-mail message to author, March 25, 2013.

18 Roster.

19 Club memorial scrapbook, 1903–2003.

20 Elizabeth Barratt, "The F.R.F.G. Women's Study Club of Gilroy, California" (an essay entered in the Pioneer Californians of Santa Clara County 2011 Essay Contest).

21 Ibid., 8.

22 Ibid., 3.

23 Ibid., 3.

24 Ibid., 3.

25 Ibid., 4.

26 Ibid., 12.

27 Ibid., 14.

28 Ibid., 13.

29 Ibid., 11.

30 Ibid., 14.

31 Elizabeth Barratt, FRFG topics over the years, supplied in 2011.

32 Ibid., 12.

33 Ibid., 13.

34 Ibid., 4.

35 Ibid.

36 Ibid., 4–5.

37 Ibid., 7–8.

38 Ibid., 13.

Chapter 6: Upstate New York and the Greater Syracuse Area

1   O.W.H. Mitchell, "The First Fifty Years," in Betty Maltby and Preston Mitchell, *Portfolio Club: A Goodly Heritage* (Syracuse: Hall and McChesney, 1975).

2   Ibid.

3   Nancy Bond, e-mail message to author, February 5, 2013.

4   Jean Messinger, "A Short History of the Fortnightly" (paper delivered to the club in December 1967).

5   The Fortnightly of Auburn, constitution, revised and adopted on October 21, 2010.

6   The Hamilton Fortnightly program (roster), 2011–12.

7   Notes from author's meeting with six Auburn Fortnightly members, October 10, 2012.

8   Ibid.

9   Fortnightly of Auburn Yearbooks, 2010–11 and 2011–12.

10 "Procedures for New Member," Fortnightly of Auburn papers, given to author by Auburn Fortnightly members.

11 Author's notes from meeting, October 10, 2012.

12 Ibid.

13 Historian Barbara Clary, e-mail message to author, September 1, 2012.

14 Author's notes from meeting, October 10, 2012.

15 Ibid.

16 "A Short History of the Fortnightly."

17 Individual summaries of careers and civic achievements sent from Auburn Fortnightly members to the author, fall 2012.

18 Ibid.

19 Author's notes from meeting, October 10, 2012.

20 Ibid.

21 Ibid.

22 Ibid.

23 Ibid.

24 Author's notes from meeting, October 10, 2012.

25 Ibid.

26 Hamilton Fortnightly, roster, 2010–11 and 2011–12.

27 Barbara Clary, e-mail message to author, December 3, 2012.

28 "John Foster Dulles," Encyclopædia Britannica, http://www.britannica.com/EBchecked/topic/173368/John-Foster-Dulles.

29 Author's notes from meeting, October 10, 2012; and notes from the author's visit to Seward House, Auburn, New York.

30 Author's notes on Fortnightly archives, October 10, 2012.

31 Bourke's entry is taken from an e-mail message sent from Bourke to the author, November 28, 2012, and from the author's meeting with Fortnightly Club members, October 10, 2012.

32 http://www.sports-reference.com/olympics/athletes/sh/gillian-sheen-1.html.

33 Auburn Fortnightly program roster, membership list, 2011–12.

34 Author's notes from meeting, October 10, 2012.

35 Ibid.

36 All information in this outline comes from an e-mail message from member Jackie Alexander to the author, December 3, 2012.

37 Ibid.

38 Ibid.

39 Ibid.

40 Ibid.

41 Ibid.

42 Ibid.

43 Author's notes taken during a Thursday Club meeting on October 11, 2012.

44 Ibid.

45 http://www.fultonhistory.com/Fulton.html.

46 The Thursday Club, constitution and bylaws, updated and approved on March 16, 2006.

47 Thursday Club members, e-mail message to author, February 13, 2013.

48 Thursday Club President Mary Ellen Ormiston, written answers to author's questions, October 2012.

49 Author's notes from meeting, October 11, 2012.

50 Ormiston's answers to author's list of questions.

51 Ibid.

52 The Thursday Club, constitution.

53 Ibid.

54 Author's notes from meeting, October 11, 2012.

55 The Thursday Club, constitution.

56 Club members, February 13, 2013.

57 Ibid.

58 Ormiston, answers to questions.

59 Author's notes from meeting; and "Aurora Village—Wells College Historic District," *Wikipedia,* http://en.wikipedia.org/wiki/Aurora_Village%E2%80%93Wells_College_Historic_District.

60 Author's notes from meeting.

61 Ibid.

62 Club members, February 13, 2013.

63 Ibid.

64 Ibid.

65 Ibid.

66 Ibid.

67 Ibid.

68 http://aurorany.org/WhatNext.html.

69 Ann Burch, e-mail messages to Mary Ellen Ormiston and the author, March 24 and 25, 2013.

70 Author's notes from meeting.

71 Club members, February 13, 2013.

72 Ibid.

73 *Merriam-Webster.com,* s.v. "coterie," http://www.merriam-webster. com/dictionary/coterie.

74 Coterie members, interview by Ann Costello, October 8, 2012.

75 Nancy Wilson, Ann Moore, and Roberta Hampson, typed answers to twenty-two questions, reviewed during interview, October 8, 2012.

76 Ibid.

77 Ibid.

78 Nancy Wilson, e-mail message to author, December 10, 2014.

79 Ibid.

80 Coterie members' interview.

81 Wilson, Moore, and Hampson, typed answers.

82 Coterie bylaws, updated April 10, 2012.

83 Written answers to twenty-two standardized questions submitted by Ann Moore, Marian Loosman, Nancy Wilson on October 8, 2012.

84 Club constitution, shared with author at a meeting with three members, October 8, 2012.

85 Ann Moore, e-mail message to author, November 19, 2012.

86 Nancy Wilson, e-mail message to author, November 16, 2012.

87 Wilson, Moore, and Hampson, typed answers.

88 Ibid.

89 Coterie bylaws.

90 Wilson, Moore, and Hampson, typed answers.

91 Wilson, November 16, 2012.

92 Ibid.

93 Ibid.

94 Wilson, Moore, and Hampson, typed answers.

95 Ibid.

96 Coterie members' interview.

97 Ibid.

98 Written answers.

99 Ibid.

100 Ibid.

101 ibid.

102 Ibid.

103 Coterie members' interview.

104 Betsy Knapp obituary, *Syracuse Herald-Journal,* March 18, 1993.

105 Betsy Knapp obituary, *DeWitt Times,* March 10, 1993.

106 *Appendix B – Green Lakes State Park Trails Plan,* http://nysparks.com/ inside-our-agency/documents/MasterPlans/GreenLakesStatePark/ GreenLakesStateParkAppendixB.pdf.

107 Ibid.

108 Betsy Knapp obituary, *Syracuse Herald-Journal.*

109 Ibid.

110 Ibid.

111 Ibid.

112 Ibid.

113 Coterie members' interview.

114 Combined Knapp obituaries.

115 Wilson, November 16, 2012.

116 "Hilda Wright Broad," *Syracuse.com,* http://obits.syracuse.com/obituaries/syracuse/obituary.aspx?pid=163930277#fbLoggedOut.

117 Coterie members' interview.

118 Carlyle M. Ashley obituary, *Syracuse Herald-Tribune,* April 15, 1993.

119 "Philomath," *Wikipedia,* http://en.wikipedia.org/wiki/Philomath.

120 Philomath's original secretary's book from the first meetings.

121 Nancy Bond, e-mail message to author, February 5, 2013; additional information from Fayetteville librarian Maija McLaughlin, November 10, 2014.

122 Nancy Bond, answers to "Snapshot Summary" questions, October 8, 2012.

123 Bond, February 5, 2013.

124 Nancy Bond, interview by Ann Costello, October 8, 2012.

125 Ibid.

126 Philomath, constitution, 1884.

127 Philomath, minutes of first meeting, April 11, 1884.

128 Philomath, roster, 2012.

129 Bond, answers.

130 Ibid.

131 Ibid.

132 Bond interview.

133 Bond, answers.

134 Bond interview.

135 Bond, answers.

136 Ibid.

137 Bond interview.

138 Agnes Cook obituary, *Syracuse Post-Standard,* July 30, 2003.

139 Mary R. Holbrow, "The Hamilton Fortnightly Club: One Hundred and Ten Years Old, 1894–2004" (club document), 2.

140 Ibid., 2–3.

141 Hamilton Fortnightly Club members, written answers to "Snapshot Summary" questions, October 2012.

142 Holbrow, "The Hamilton Fortnightly Club," 3–4.

143 Ibid.

144 Ibid.

145 Ibid.

146 Hamilton Fortnightly Club members, written answers.

147 Holbrow, 16.

148 Hamilton Fortnightly Club members, written answers.

149 Comments from informal meeting with members, October 9, 2012.

150 Hamilton Fortnightly Club members, written answers.

151 Meika Loe, "The Women's Academy Down the Hill," *The Colgate Scene,* May 2007.

152 Joanne Geyer, e-mail message to author, October 11, 2012; and "Elected Officials: Village of Hamilton," http://hamilton-ny.gov/village-of-hamilton/elected-officials, copyright 2014.

153 Comments from meeting.

154 Ibid.

155 Ibid.

156 Hamilton Fortnightly Club members, written answers.

157 Nellie Edmonston, e-mail message to Joanne Geyer, November 9, 2012.

158 Comments from meeting.

159 Edmonston, November 9, 2012.

160 Ibid.

161 Joanne Geyer, e-mail message to author, November 9, 2012.

162 Ibid.

163 Meika Loe, interview of Hamilton Fortnightly Club member Ruth Hartshorne, *The Colgate Scene,* May 2007, http://offices.colgate.edu/communications/video/2007/05/051407fortnightly.html.

164 Geyer, October 11, 2012.

165 Hamilton Fortnightly Club members, written answers.

166 Hamilton Fortnightly Club members, informal conversation with author; and Meika Loe, "The Women's Academy Down the Hill," *The Colgate Scene,*" http://www4.colgate.edu/scene/may2007/womens.html, last modified May, 2007, accessed November, 2012.

167 Ibid.

168 Debbie Kliman, e-mail message to Joanne Geyer, November 8, 2012.

169 Hamilton Fortnightly Club members, written answers.

170 Monday Evening Club President Kelly Garwood, telephone interview by Ann Costello, October 11, 2012 (unless otherwise noted).

171 Monday Evening Club President Kelly Garwood, e-mail message to author, February 10, 2013.

172 Ibid.

173 Ibid.

174 *Girl Scouts – Our History,* http://www.girlscouts.org/who_we_are/history/.

175 Phyllis Clark, e-mail message to author, November 2, 2012.

176 Phyllis Clark, e-mail message to author, November 11, 2012.

177 Phyllis Clark, telephone interview by Ann Costello, October 28, 2012.

178 Ibid.

179 Ibid.

180 Ibid.

181 Clark, November 2, 2012.

182 Clark, November 11, 2012.

183 Ibid.

184 "Shotwell Memorial Park," *Skaeateles.com,* http://www.skaneateles.com/visit/events-a-attractions/shotwell-memorial-park.

185 "Louisa Shotwell's Wild Ride," *Skaneatele*s, "http://kihm6.wordpress.com/2010/07/25/louisa-shotwells-wild-ride/.

186 Phyllis Clark, e-mail message to author, February 6, 2013.

187 Clark interview.

188 Ibid.

189 Clark, November 11, 2012.

190 Ibid.

191 Ibid.

192 Phyllis Clark, e-mail message to author, March 13, 2013.

193 Clark, November 2, 2012.

194 Skaneateles Festival, http://www.skanfest.org

195 "Katherine by the Window," KIHM, April 12, 2012, http://kihm6.wordpress.com/2012/04/12/katherine-by-the-window/.

196 Clark, November 2, 2012.

197 "Constitution," Portfolio Club Yearbook, 2012–13.

198 Mrs. George H. Bond, letter to Miss Mary Hurst, October 25, 1933.

199 Portfolio Club history, as cited by Mary Beth Hinton in an e-mail to the author, September 14, 2012.

200 Bond, letter.

201 Ibid.

202 "The Biography of Mary (Dana) Hicks Prang," www.history50states.com/NY-Onondaga-Syracuse.

203 O.W.H. Mitchell, "The First Fifty Years," in O.W.H. Mitchell and C. H. Maltby, eds., Portfolio Club: A Goodly Heritage (Syracuse: Hall and McChesney, 1975).

204 The Portfolio Club: Our Fifty Years, *1875–1925 (Syracuse: Portfolio Club, 1966).*

205 Mary Beth Hinton, e-mail message to author, September 13, 2012.

206 Portfolio Club, roster, 2012–13, flyleaf.

207 Hinton, September 13, 2012.

208 "New Members," Portfolio Club, roster, 2012–13.

209 Bond, letter, 133.

210 Hinton, September 13, 2012.

211 Portfolio Club, constitution, 27.

212 Hinton, September 13, 2012.

213 Mary Beth Hinton, e-mail message to author, fall 2012.

214 Constance Carroll, "The Portfolio Club: A Refuge of Friendship and Learning," *Syracuse University Library Associates Courier* (Fall 1991), 37.

215 Hinton, September 13, 2012.

216 Portfolio Club, "Some Practices of Officers and Committees," roster, 2012–13.

217 Hinton, September 13, 2012.

218 Ibid.

219 Mary Beth Hinton, e-mail message to author, September 15, 2012.

220 "Portfolio Club," Syracuse University Library, 1999, exhibit label.

221 Mary Beth Hinton and Michelle Combs, Syracuse University Library, 2012, "Portfolio Club" exhibit label.

222 Portfolio Club, "Some Practices of Officers and Committees," roster, 2012–13.

223 Portfolio Club, roster, 2012–13, 27.

224 Harriet Pond Davis, "Portfolian Footsteps" (poem about club by a member), date unknown, but probably between 1950 - 2000.

225 Author's notes from informal meeting with six Portfolio Club members, October 9, 2012.

226 Ibid.

227 Ibid.

228 Author's notes from meeting, October 9, 2012.

229 Hinton, September 13, 2012.

230 Ibid.

231 Mary Beth Hinton, e-mail message to author, January 11, 2015.

232 "In Memorium," *The Nottingham Connection, Spring 2011,* Ann "Bette" Walker Maltby, http://www.nottingham-connection.org/connection%20 2011.pdf.

233 Dick Case, "Club Opens Worlds to Women for 134 Years," *Syracuse Post-Standard,* April 28, 2009.

234 http://library.syr.edu/about/people/phonelist.php.

235 Historian Michele Combs, e-mail message to author, September 17, 2012.

236 "Book Club Corner," *Beaufort County Library,* http://www.beaufortcountylibrary.org/htdocs-sirsi/club3.htm.

237 "Portfolio Club" exhibit label, Syracuse University Library.

238 Ibid.

239 Lucia Whisenand, e-mail message to Jeanette Mattson, April 11, 2013, forwarded to author on April 12, 2013 by Jeanette Mattson.

240 Yearbook of Social Art Club, 2012–13, constitution and bylaws, 18–19.

241 Ibid., 10–16.

242 Ibid., 4–9, 23–24.

243 Ibid., 2.

244 Ibid., 18.

245 Ibid.

246 Jeanette Mattson, e-mail message to author, September 24, 2012.

247 Yearbook of Social Art Club, 19–20.

248 Ibid., 20.

249 Ibid.

250 Ibid., 27.

251 Ibid., 19–20.

252 Jeanette Mattson, e-mail message to author, April 10, 2013.

253 Ibid.

254 Mattson, September 24, 2012.

255 Ibid.

256 Ibid.

257 Ibid.

258 Yearbook of Social Art Club, 25.

259 Ibid., 26–29.

260 Cleota Reed Gabriel, "Irene Sargent: Rediscovering a Lost Legend," *The Courier* 16.2 (1979): 3–13; and "Irene Sargent Collection," *Syracuse University Archives,* http://archives.syr.edu/collections/faculty/sua_sargent_i.htm.

261 Mattson, April 10, 2013.

262 "Former Residents of Dewitt, NY Circa 1940 - 1960, *DeWitt Registry,* http://www.erhutchison.com/dewittregistry.html.

263 Lucia Whisenand, e-mail message to author, April 13, 2013.

264 "Tchaikovsky's The Nutcracker," *Syracuse.com,* http://blog.syracuse.com/video/2007/11/tchaikovskys_the_nutcracker.html.

265 "Member Awards," *Junior League of Syracuse, Inc., https://www.jlsyracuse.org/member-awards/*

266 Social Art Club, roster, 2012–13.

267 Lucia Whisenand, e-mail message to author, April 13, 2013.
268 Lucia Whisenand, e-mail message to Jeanette Mattson, April 11, 2013.
269 Lydia Hecht, "A History of Leisure Hour Literary Club" (paper delivered at the Leisure Hour Literary Club's centennial celebration, 1996).
270 Leisure Hour Literary Club, bylaws, printed in the 2011–12 club roster.
271 Ibid.
272 Hecht, "A History of Leisure Hour Literary Club."
273 "A Night at the Museum" (paper presented by member Pat Kimber at a joint meeting with the Aurora Thursday Club, November 3, 2008, at the Frontenac Historical Society and Museum); and an overview of several articles from the *Union Springs Advertiser,* 1903–05.
274 "Ameican Memory," *The Library of Congress, Women's History,* Zobedia Alleman, http://memory.loc.gov/cgi-bin/query
275 Hecht, "A History of Leisure Hour Literary Club."

Chapter 7: Indiana

1   Quoted with permission from the archives of the Indianapolis Woman's Club, 1875–2007, Manuscript Collections Department, William Henry Smith Memorial Library, Indiana Historical Society, last updated October 2, 2008.
2   "Elkhart, Indiana," *City-Data.com* http://www.city-data.com/city/Elkhart-Indiana.html.
3   Judy Kelly, e-mail message to author, January 19, 2013.
4   Ibid.
5   Ibid.
6   Ibid.
7   Cathy Gibson, e-mail message to author, August 19, 2013, quoting Jean Snoddy, *A Brief History of the Fortnightly Literary Club: 1885–1985, Indianapolis, Indiana* (October 1985).
8   Ibid.
9   Ibid.
10 Gibson, August 19, 2013.
11 Ibid.
12 Ibid.
13 Ibid.
14 Ibid.
15 "The Indianapolis Propylaeum," http://www.thepropylaeum.org/.
16 Cathy Gibson, e-mail message to author, August 30, 2013.
17 Ibid.

18 Gibson, August 19, 2013.

19 Gibson, August 30, 2013.

20 Ibid.

21 Ibid.

22 Ibid.

23 Ibid.

24 Ibid.

25 "Indianapolis Woman's Club Records, 1875–2007," *Indiana Historical Society,* http://www.indianahistory.org/our-collections/collection-guides/indianapolis-womans-club-records-1875-2007.pdf.

26 Ibid.

27 Nora Hiatt, e-mail message to author, July 16, 2013.

28 "Indianapolis Woman's Club Records."

29 Hiatt, July 16, 2013.

30 "Indianapolis Woman's Club Records."

31 Ibid.

32 Cathy Gibson, e-mail message to author, July 19, 2013.

33 Ibid.

34 Gibson, July 19, 2013.

35 Nancy Fyffe, e-mail message to author, September 16, 2013.

36 Ibid.

37 Ibid.

38 "Indianapolis Woman's Club Records."

Chapter 8: Little Rock, Arkansas, and Baton Rouge, Louisiana

1   Aesthetic Club History Committee, *Aesthetic Club: Centennial History, 1883–1983* (Little Rock: Rose Publishing Co., 1983), iv.

2   Aesthetic Club Yearbook, 2011–12, 31–33.

3   Aesthetic Club Yearbook, frontispiece.

4   Lee Moore, e-mail message to author, May 17, 2012.

5   Aesthetic Club Yearbook, 3.

6   Ibid.

7   Aesthetic Club, *Centennial History,* 131.

8   Ibid., flap copy.

9   Author unknown, e-mail message from state.archives@arkansas.gov to author, February 5, 2013.

10 Moore, May 17, 2012.

11 Moore, May 17, 2012; and "Douglas MacArthur," *Wikipedia,* http://en.wikipedia.org/wiki/Douglas_MacArthur.

12 Aesthetic Club, *Centennial History,* 95–103.

13 Aesthetic Club Yearbook, 2.

14 The Edelweiss Yearbook, 2011–12, reverse side of title page.

15 Ibid.

16 Ibid.

17 Edelweiss President Marylyn Parins, e-mail message to author, January 30, 2013.

18 Moore, May 17, 2012.

19 Parins, January 30, 2013.

20 Rhonda Stewart (of the Central Arkansas Library System), e-mail message to author, January 31, 2013.

21 The Edelweiss Yearbook, 2011–12, 4.

22 Ibid., title page.

23 Parins, January 30, 2013.

24 Ibid.

25 Ibid.

26 Ibid.

27 Carol Anne Blitzer, "Lovers of History: The Philistoria literary club marks 100 years in Baton Rouge," *The Advocate* (Baton Rouge), March 12, 2006.

28 Adele Williamson, telephone interview by Ann Costello, January 22, 2013.

29 Ibid.

30 Blitzer, "Lovers of History."

31 Williamson interview.

32 Blitzer, "Lovers of History."

33 Williamson interview.

34 Carol Anne Blitzer, "A Century of Study," *The Advocate* (Little Rock), October 10, 2008.

35 Ibid.

36 The Study Club Yearbook, 2012–13.

37 Ibid.

38 Ibid.

39 Blitzer, "A Century of Study."

40 Ibid.

41 Carol Anne Blitzer, e-mail message to author, January 14, 2013.

Chapter 9: Illinois

1   "Jacksonville, Illinois," *city-data.com,* http://www.city-data.com/city/Jacksonville-Illinois.html.
2   http://www.ic.edu/Relld/614033/Svars/default/Literary_Societies.htm.
3   History Club, original ledger book, 1880, History Club Archives, McLean County Museum of History.
4   Ibid.
5   History Club, roster, 1887–88 (and others), History Club Archives, McLean County Museum of History.
6   All information in this summary comes, sometimes verbatim, from member and club historian K-Lou Ashmore, e-mail messages to author, March 25, 2013, and April 25, 2013.
7   Gratia Coultas,*411.com.* http://www.411.com/name/Gratia-Coultas
8   Jane Cunningham Croly, *The History of the Women's Club Movement in America,* vol. 1 (New York: Henry G. Allen and Co., 1898), 15.
9   Karyl Findley, e-mail message to author, April 29, 2013.
10 Phebe D. Bassett, "The Jacksonville Sorosis Organized: Founded November 30th, 1868," *Journal of the Illinois State Historical Society (1908–1964)* 18(1), Jacksonville Centennial Number (April 1925).
11 Ibid.
12 Bassett, "The Jacksonville Sorosis Organized."
13 Ibid.
14 Findley, April 29, 2013.
15 "College literary societies," *Wikipedia,* http://en.wikipedia.org/wiki/College_literary_societies.
16 Bassett, "The Jacksonville Sorosis Organized."
17 Louise Bone, e-mail message to author, December 15, 2012.
18 Sandy Bordenkircher, e-mail message to author, March 7, 2013.
19 Ibid.
20 Cathy Green, telephone interview by Ann Costello, February 3, 2013.
21 Cathy Green, e-mail message to author, February 3, 2013.
22 Sandy Bordenkircher, e-mail message to author, March 7, 2013
23 Green interview.
24 Green, February 3, 2013.
25 Bone, December 15, 2012.
26 Green interview.
27 Ibid.
28 Sandy Bordenkircher, e-mail message to author, March 7, 2013.

29 Betty Carlson Kay and Gary Jack Barwick, *Jacksonville, Illinois, The Traditions Continue* (Charleston, Chicago, Portsmouth, and San Francisco: Arcadia Publishing, 1999).

30 Green interview.

31 Green interview; and Cathy Green, e-mail message to author, February 3, 2013.

32 Ardeth Finley, e-mail message to author, July 22, 2014.

33 Ibid.

34 Ibid.

35 Ibid.

36 R. Wise (of Coles County Historical Society, Mattoon, Illinois), e-mail message to author, November 24, 2014.

37 "Queen of Clubs," by Barbara Brotman, *Chicago Tribune,* Lifestyles section, May 30, 2001.

38 Finley, July 22, 2014.

39 Ibid.

Chapter 10: Kansas

1 "Lawrence, Kansas," *Wikipedia,* http://en.wikipedia.org/wiki/Lawrence,_Kansas.

2 Andy Hyland, "Friends in Council has deep roots, ties to KU," April 7, 2012, www2.ljworld.com/news/2012/apr/07/friends-council-has-deep-roots-ties-ku/.

3 Ibid.

4 Theodora Penny Martin, *The Sound of Our Own Voice* (Boston: Beacon Press, 1987), 57.

5 Betty Laird, telephone interview by Ann Costello, June 27, 2013.

6 Laird interview.

7 Ibid.

8 Hyland, "Friends in Council."

9 Laird interview.

10 Ibid.

11 Ibid.

12 Ibid.

13 Hyland, "Friends in Council."

14 Ibid.

15 Laird interview.

16 "Brook Farm," *Wikipedia,* http://en.wikipedia.org/wiki/Brook_Farm.

17 http://www.kshs.org/p/john-stillman-brown-family-papers-
1818-1907/13994.

18 "Kanwaka Literary Club," *Kansas Historical Foundation,* http://www.
kshs.org/p/kanwaka-literary-club/13773; and Marilynn Orr, telephone
interview by Ann Costello, July 2, 2013.

19 "Kanwaka Literary Club," http://www.kshs.org/p/kanwaka-
literary-club/13773.

20 Orr interview.

21 Orr interview.

22 "Kanwaka Literary Club," http://www.kshs.org/p/kanwaka-literary-
club/13773.

23 Junior Reading Circle of Newton Archives, Harvey County Historical
Museum and Archives, conveyed by office manager Lana Myers via
e-mail message to author, July 17, 2013.

24 Ibid.

25 Susan Koehn, telephone interview by Ann Costello, July 25, 2013.

26 Ibid.

27 Ibid.

28 Junior Reading Circle Club Archives (via Myers).

29 Ibid.

30 Ibid.

31 "Meet Local Legend: Lucena Axtell, M.D.," www.nlm.nih.gov/
locallegends/Biographies/Axtell_Lucena.html.

32 Gordon L. Davis, "Ladies' Reading Circle: A commitment to learning
& camaraderie," *The Best Times,* 2013, www.thebesttimes.org/
organizations/other/0111_ladies_reading_circle.shtml.

33 "John Pierce St. John Papers 1859–1917," *Kansas Historical Foundation,*
http://www.kshs.org/p/john-pierce-st-john-papers-1859-1917/14120.

34 United States Department of the Interior, National Park Service
registration form for National Register of Historic Places, for Martin
Van Buren Parker House, Olathe, Kansas, August 27, 1988, 8.

35 Ibid.

36 "Ladies' Reading Circle."

37 Ibid.

38 Ibid., photo caption.

39 Sue Langseth, e-mail message to author, June 28, 2013.

40 "Ladies' Reading Circle."

41 Langseth, June 28, 2013.

42 "Ladies' Reading Circle."

43 Langseth, June 28, 2013.

44 Keith Stokes, "Cowboy Boots in Olathe, Kansas – Welcome Home, Cowboy Boots!" *Kansastravel.org,* http://kansastravel.org/olathe/olathecowboyboots.htm.

45 Ibid.

46 "Ladies' Reading Circle."

Chapter 11: Wooster, Ohio

1 Sally Bernhardt, e-mail message to author, July 22, 2013.

2 Ibid.

3 Sally Bernhardt, e-mail message to author, July 24, 2013

4 Ibid.

5 Sally Bernhardt, e-mail message to author, July 25, 2013.

6 Ibid.

7 Bernhardt, July 22, 2013.

8 Ibid.

Chapter 12: Durham, North Carolina

1 "Durham County, North Carolina," *United States Census Bureau,* http://quickfacts.census.gov/qfd/states/37/37063.html.

2 Lucy Grant, e-mail message to author, January 7, 2014.

3 Lucy Grant, e-mail message to author, January 23, 2014.

4 "Halcyon Club Records," *Durham County Library,* http://dur.sdp.sirsi.net/client/en_US/default/search/detailnonmodal/ent:$002f$002fSD_ILS$002f0$002fSD_ILS:586736/one?qu=Halcyon+Club

5 "A Year Down Memory Lane: Celebrating Halcyon Club's Centennial," compiled by club historian Lucy Grant (from a 1931 account in club archives), 1.

6 Grant, January 23, 2014.

7 Grant, January 7, 2014.

8 Grant, January 23, 2014.

9 Lucy Grant, e-mail message to author, January 24, 2014.

10 Ibid.

11 Grant, January 23, 2014.

12 Ibid.

13 Ibid.

14 Ibid.

15 Ibid.

16 "Durham's Venerable Halcyon Club Celebrates Its Centennial," *The Herald-Sun*, Your Community section, October 2010.

17 "Frances Gray Patton," *Wikipedia,* http://en.wikipedia.org/wiki/Frances_Gray_Patton.

18 Lucy Grant, e-mail message to author, January 25, 2014.

19 "Lewis Patton, English Professor, 91," *New York Times,* February 23, 1994.

20 "Herschel A. Caldwell," *GoDuke.com,* http://www.goduke.com/ViewArticle.dbml?ATCLID=220690.

21 "A Fond Remembrance for Anita Caldwell, 1908-2011," *Sidney Lanier.com,* http://sidneylanier.org/the-school/faculty-and-staff/.

22 "William Preston Few," *Wikipedia,* http://search.aol.com/aol/search?s_it=webmail-searchbox&q=william%20preston%20few%2C%20duke.%2C%20%20Durham%2C%20NC%2C.

Chapter 13: A Directory of Single Clubs (Not Part of a Geographical Cluster)

1 *The Story of the Saturday Morning Club of Boston: Organized by Mrs. Julia Ward Howe and Mrs. Robert E. Apthorp, November Second Eighteen Hundred and Seventy-One: On the Occasion of Its Sixtieth Birthday* (Boston: Saturday Morning Club, 1931).

2 "Saturday Morning Club (Boston, Mass.) Additional Records, 1971 – 1996," *Harvard University Library,* http://oasis.lib.harvard.edu/oasis/deliver/~sch00891.

3 *The Story of the Saturday Morning Club.*

4 "Boston's 400 is 361," *The New York Times archives, Feb. 18, 1907,* 361, "http://timesmachine.nytimes.com/timesmachine/1907/02/18/106706376.html#106706376.html?pageNumber=9&_suid=143450310688408338625043347951

5 "Julia Ward Howe," *Wikipedia,* http://en.wikipedia.org/wiki/Julia_Ward_Howe.

6 "Julia Ward Howe: Biography," JuliaWardHowe.org, http://www.juliawardhowe.org/bio.htm.

7 Ibid.

8 Julia Ward Howe: Timeline, *JuliaWardHowe.org,* http://www.juliawardhowe.org/timeline.htm.

9 "Biography: Julia Ward Howe" by Laura E. Richards and Maude Howe Elliott, assisted by orence Howe Hill, *The Pulitze Prizes,* http://www.pulitzer.org/node/2873.

10 Marion Kilson, e-mail message to author, August 10, 2013.

11 Ibid.

12 Ibid.

13 President Susan Hackley, e-mail message to author, August 15, 2013.

14 "About Susan Hackley," *Harvard Law School, Program on Negotiation,* http://www.pon.harvard.edu/author/susanhackley/.

15 Katherine M. Canaday, "Nondescript Centennial Paper—and Ladies of the Club" (October 17, 1995), 11.

16 Ethel C. Oliver, *A History of the Monday Club, Camden, Maine, 1885–1985* (1995), 7–8.

17 Monday Club, constitution, via member Essie Sexton, e-mail message to author, August 16, 2012.

18 Sexton, August 16, 2012.

19 Ibid.

20 Ibid.

21 Monday Club of Camden, Maine, roster, 2012–13.

22 Ibid.

23 Susan Rosenbaum, "The Ramblers: The World is their Oyster," July 9, 1998, *The East Hampton Star, http://easthamptonstar.com/Archive/1/ Ramblers-World-Their-Oyster*

24 Ibid.

25 Ibid.

26 Helen Rattray (publisher of East Hampton's *The Star* newspaper), e-mail message to author, September 17, 2013.

27 President Elizabeth Sarfati, e-mail message to author, September 23, 2003.

28 The Ramblers, constitution and bylaws, adopted February 1984, revised 1998 and 2003.

29 Ibid.

30 The Ramblers, roster, 2005–06.

31 Ibid.

32 Ibid.

33 Rattray, September 17, 2013.

34 Ibid.

35 Jane P. Talmage, "The Unspoken Rules of Ramblers," February 2002.

36 "Other Shakespeare Clubs," *Warren Shakespeare Club,* http:// warrenshakes.blogspot.com/p/other-shakespeare-clubs.html.

37 Florence McClelland, telephone interview by Ann Costello, July 30, 2013.

38 McClelland interview.

39 "Jean Webster," *Wikipedia,* http://en.wikipedia.org/wiki/Jean_Webster.

40 "Darwin R. Barker Historical Museum: The Beginning of the Freedonia Shakespeare Club," *blogspot.com,* June 13, 2013, http://darwinrbarkermuseum.blogspot.com/2013/06/the-beginnings-of-fredonia-shakespeare.html.
41 ibid.
42 Rebecca Schwab, "The bard's best ladies," October 21, 2012, http://www.observertoday.com/page/content.detail/id/577349/The-bard-s-best-ladies.html?nav=5060.
43 McClelland interview.
44 "Other Shakespeare Clubs."
45 Ibid.
46 McClelland interview.
47 Ibid.
48 "Other Shakespeare Clubs."
49 Schwab, "The bard's best ladies."
50 McClelland interview.
51 "Other Shakespeare Clubs."
52 Schwab, "The bard's best ladies."
53 Ibid.; and "Other Shakespeare Clubs."
54 "Other Shakespeare Clubs."
55 McClelland interview.
56 "Other Shakespeare Clubs."
57 Schwab, "The bard's best ladies."
58 Ibid.
59 "Other Shakespeare Clubs."
60 Ibid.
61 Schwab, "The bard's best ladies."
62 McClelland interview.
63 Member Carolyn Kolb, e-mail message to author, May 7, 2013.
64 "Académie française," *Wikipedia,* http://en.wikipedia.org/wiki/Acad%C3%A9mie_fran%C3%A7aise.
65 Carey T. Hinds, "Lightseekers: The Rise of the Women's Club Movement in the 19th Century," October 2013 (a paper written for the occasion of Cadmean Club's 125th anniversary).
66 Hinds, "Lightseekers"; and Pherabe Kolb, "Broadening the Horizons of Life: The Beginnings of a Women's Literary Club in Nineteenth Century New Orleans" (master's thesis, Dartmouth College, 1994).
67 Hinds, "Lightseekers."
68 Ibid.
69 Kolb, May 7, 2013.

70 "Full Text of Philip Hunton and his descendants," from the Boston Public Library, *archive.org,* http://archive.org/stream/philiphuntonhisd00hunt/philiphuntonhisd00hunt_djvu.txt.

71 "Civil War Emancipation – Sherman Explains the New Facts of Life," *wordpress.com,* posted on Aug. 26, 2012, https://cwemancipation.wordpress.com/2012/08/26/sherman-explains-the-new-facts-of-life/

72 Hinds, "Lightseekers."

73 Ibid.

74 "Mary Ashley Townsend," *Wikipedia,* http://en.wikipedia.org/wiki/Mary_Ashley_Townsend.

75 Ibid.

76 Hinds, "Lightseekers."

77 Kolb, May 7, 2013.

78 Ibid.

79 Ibid.

80 Hinds, "Lightseekers."

81 Kolb, May 7, 2013.

82 Hinds, "Lightseekers."

83 "Quarante Club," *Tulane University Libraries – Classic Catalog,* http://voyager.tcs.tulane.edu/vwebv/search

84 www.knowla.org.

85 Kolb, May 7, 2013.

86 Sean Benjamin, e-mail message to author, May 23, 2013.

87 Ibid.

88 Dinitia Smith, "A Drawing Room of Their Own," *New York Times,* June 12, 2013.

89 Ibid.

90 Ibid.

91 Ibid.

92 Ibid.

93 Ibid.

94 Ibid.

95 Ibid.

96 "Rules of Government of Causeries du Lundi," June 1970, Causeries du Lundi Archives, New York Historical Society.

97 "A Drawing Room."

98 Ibid.

99 Causeries du Lundi of New York City Archives, Box 18, New York Historical Society.

100 Smith, "A Drawing Room."

101 Smith, "A Drawing Room."

102 "Rules of Government of Causeries du Lundi."

103 http://dlib.nyu.edu/findingaids/html/nyhs/causeries_content.html.

104 Ibid.

105 Barbara Cheney, "Anniversary Booklet," April 12, 1955, Causeries du Lundi Archives, New York Historical Society.

Chapter 14: Additional Historic All-Women Clubs, Including a Look at What Happened to Two of the Earliest Study Clubs

1   Hannah Wolfson, "Birmingham Black Women's Clubs Open Historic Doors," May 15, 2010, *blog.al.com*, http://blog.al.com/spotnews/2010/05/birmingham_black_womens_clubs.html.

2   Semper Fidelis, anniversary booklet, 1980, Semper Fidelis Archives, Birmingham Public Library.

3   Semper Fidelis, constitution and bylaws, Semper Fidelis Archives, Birmingham Public Library.

4   "Fortnightly Literary Club Collection," *Indiana Historical Society – Manuscripts and Archives,* http://www.indianahistory.org/our-collections/collection-guides/fortnightly-literary-club-collection.pdf.

5   Ibid.

6   Ibid.

7   "Utopian Literary Club (Atlanta, GA), *Emory Libraries and Information Technology,   http://findingaids.library.emory.edu/documents/utopianliterary991/*

8   Utopian Literary Club, http://findingaids.library.emory.edu/documents/utopianliterary991/.

9   "Inventory of the Utopian Literary Club Records," *Auburn Avenue Research Library*, http://dlg.galileo.usg.edu/aafa/html/aafa_aarl96-010.html.

10 Katherine West Scheil, "Case Study, The Detroit Study Club," in *She Hath Been Reading: Women and Shakespeare Clubs in America* (Cornell: Cornell University Press, 2014) (location 3035 in Kindle edition).

11 Desiree Cooper, "Club's Name Is Its Goal for 110 Years," *Detroit Free Press,* May 7, 2008.

12 Desiree Cooper, "Club's Name its Goal for 110 Years," *Detroit Free Press,* https://traditionofexcellence.wordpress.com/tag/detroit-study-club/.

13 Ibid.

14 "Detroit Historical Events," *Detroit African-American History Project*, http://www.daahp.wayne.edu/1900_1949.html.

15 Ibid.

16 Jessica Smith, "Woodland Shakespeare Club celebrates long history in county," May 16, 2013, *Daily Democrat, http://www.dailydemocrat.com/arts-and-entertainment/20130516/woodland-shakespeare-club-celebrates-long-history-in-county*

17 Ibid.

18 Ibid.

19 "Other Shakespeare Clubs," *Warren Shakespeare Club,* http://warrenshakes.blogspot.com/p/other-shakespeare-clubs.html.

20 Ibid.

21 Ibid.

22 Smith, "Woodland Shakespeare Club celebrates long history in county"

23 "Other Shakespeare Clubs."

24 Ibid.

25 Ibid.

26 Scheil, *She Hath Been Reading*, preface.

27 http://beaufortcountylibrary.org/htdocs-sirsi/club3.htm.

28 Ibid.

29 Ibid.

30 "Clubs and Organizations Annotated Index," Hennepin County Library, https://apps.hclib.org/collections/clubsandorgs.cfm.

31 "Peripatetics, An Inventory of its Records at the Minnesota Historical Society, www.mnhs.org/library/findaids/00203.xml.

32 Ibid.

33 "Pine Hills Fortnightly Club, Inc." M.E. Grenander Dept. of Special Collections and Archives, SUNY Albany, https://library.albany.edu/speccoll/findaids/apap031.htm

34 "The Fortnightly, Search on to Find History of Clubs Across United States", March 27, 2011, special to "Jamestown Press Journal" from Rockville Center, NY newspaper (unnamed and uncredited.)

35 Ibid.

36 Ibid.

37 Ibid.

38 "Fortnightly Club – University of Missouri," http://fortnightly.missouri.org/

39 Ibid.

40 "Friends of Neill Public Library," http://www.friendsofnpl.com/businesses.html.

41 "Guide to the Fortnightly Club (Pullman, Wash.)," *Washington State University Library Archives*, http://ntserver1.wsulibs.wsu.edu/masc/finders/cg108.htm

42 Mary Helen George, "Changing with the Times," *Waco Today via digital.publicationsprinters.com,* November, 2008, http://digital.publicationprinters.com/article/Changing+With+The+Times/253859/0/article.html.

43 Sorosis President Margarita Bloch, e-mail message to author, July 23, 2013.

44 "New Engand Women's Club," *The Bostonian Society,* http://www.bostonhistory.org/?s=librarymuseum&p=newc.

Index

D

E

F

G

Gage, Matilda Josyln 164
Garwood, Kelly 196, 198, 376
General Federation of Women's
  Clubs 340
Getman, Margaret Pimm 218
Gibson, Cathy 228, 380–381
Gill, Margot 81, 83–84, 362
Gilroy, CA 5, 119, 141, 143–145, 150–
  153, 348, 371
Glisson, Suzie 259–260
Golden, Colorado 85, 363
Golden Fortnightly 87–89, 107, 109–
  111, 348, 366–367
Good Morning, Miss Dove 303
Grant, Lucy 297–298, 301–303,
  386–387
Green, Cathy 265–266, 383–384
Greenville, IL 336, 348
The Greenville Shakespeare
  Club 336
Grove City, PA 336, 351

H

Hackley, Susan 312, 388
Halcyon Club, Durham, NC 301–303,
  350, 386–387
Hamilton Fortnightly 163, 165, 169,
  191–192, 194–195, 350, 371–372,
  375–376
Hamilton, NY 169
Hanna, Ione (Mrs. John Hanna) 97
Hardie, Mrs. John T. 8, 27
Hardie, Mrs. William 8, 322
Hartshorne, Ruth 192, 194, 376
Harvey County Historical
  Museum 385
Harvey County, KS 275–276, 280,
  282, 284, 385
Haury, Ada Mae 282
Hennepin County Library 337, 392
Hepp, Frances Fulenwider 106
Hiatt, Nora 227, 381
Hicks, Mary Dana 161, 163, 205, 211

Highland Book Club, Birmingham, AL
  5–7, 14, 347
Hillman Hospital, Birmingham, AL 14,
  28, 30, 356
Hinton, Mary Beth 161, 165, 207–209,
  377–378
History Colorado 87, 108, 366–367
Honeoye Falls, NY 338, 350
Hopper, Doris 258, 263
Household Science, Jacksonville, IL
  258, 262–263, 266, 348
Houston, Carolyn 252, 269–270
Howard-Tilton Memorial Library,
  Tulane 324
Howe, Julia Ward xiii, 161, 163, 205,
  311, 321–322, 340, 387
Howe, Samuel Gridley 311
Hunton, Ella McGehee 321

I

Iams, Dorothy 289, 291
Illinois College xix, 251, 256, 258, 264
Indiana Historical Society i, 227–228,
  237, 332, 380–381, 391
Indianapolis Fortnightly Literary Club
  228, 234, 332, 348
Indianapolis, IN 227–228, 332
Indianapolis Woman's Club i, 227,
  236–237, 348, 380–381

J

Jacksonville, IL xix, xx, 204, 251–252,
  256, 258–259, 261–262, 264,
  327, 344, 383–384
Jamestown, NY 338
Jarzemsky, Susan ("Suki") 44
Jones, Jane 276, 280–281
Jorstad, Mary 254
Junior Pierians, Dallas, TX 64–65, 77
Junior Reading Circle, Newton,
  KS 349

K

Kansas Historical Foundation, Topeka
  279, 385

400